AF836279

QUALITY OF LIFE IN ALCOHOL DEPENDENTS: A LONGITUDINAL STUDY

QUALITY OF LIFE IN ALCOHOL DEPENDENTS: A LONGITUDINAL STUDY

JOHN FOSTER

Nova Science Publishers, Inc.
New York

Copyright © 2007 by Nova Science Publishers, Inc.

All rights reserved. No part of this book may be reproduced, stored in a retrieval system or transmitted in any form or by any means: electronic, electrostatic, magnetic, tape, mechanical photocopying, recording or otherwise without the written permission of the Publisher.

For permission to use material from this book please contact us:
Telephone 631-231-7269; Fax 631-231-8175
Web Site: http://www.novapublishers.com

NOTICE TO THE READER

The Publisher has taken reasonable care in the preparation of this book, but makes no expressed or implied warranty of any kind and assumes no responsibility for any errors or omissions. No liability is assumed for incidental or consequential damages in connection with or arising out of information contained in this book. The Publisher shall not be liable for any special, consequential, or exemplary damages resulting, in whole or in part, from the readers' use of, or reliance upon, this material.

Independent verification should be sought for any data, advice or recommendations contained in this book. In addition, no responsibility is assumed by the publisher for any injury and/or damage to persons or property arising from any methods, products, instructions, ideas or otherwise contained in this publication.

This publication is designed to provide accurate and authoritative information with regard to the subject matter covered herein. It is sold with the clear understanding that the Publisher is not engaged in rendering legal or any other professional services. If legal or any other expert assistance is required, the services of a competent person should be sought. FROM A DECLARATION OF PARTICIPANTS JOINTLY ADOPTED BY A COMMITTEE OF THE AMERICAN BAR ASSOCIATION AND A COMMITTEE OF PUBLISHERS.

LIBRARY OF CONGRESS CATALOGING-IN-PUBLICATION DATA

Foster, John.
Quality of life in alcohol dependents : a longitudinal study / John Foster.
p. cm.
Includes index.
ISBN 1-60021-443-6
1. Alcoholics--England--London Metropolitan Area--Longitudinal studies. 2. Alcoholism--England--London Metropolitan Area--Longitudinal studies. I. Title.
HV5450.L65F67 2006
616.86'1--dc22

2006029576

Published by Nova Science Publishers, Inc. ✢ New York

Dedication

To my late Father Raymond John Foster and Bernadette and Alice

CONTENTS

PREFACE

There is a paucity of studies that have investigated the quality of life (QoL) of alcohol dependent individuals. Intuitively because there are deleterious physical and psychological health consequences resulting from alcohol consumption it is possible to put forward the hypothesis that not-relapsing to heavy drinking will result in an improved QoL and in contrast that the consequences of relapsing to heavy drinking will be a deterioration in QoL. The present study tests this hypothesis and also seeks to ascertain those variables that are predictors of outcome. In addition it examines the role played by sociodemographic and other confounding factors in the QoL of alcohol dependent individuals.

Two-hundred and forty subjects were recruited from six sociodemographically diverse study centres. At baseline sociodemographic (in particular the Jarman Index –a measure of area-based social deprivation), tobacco/alcohol use/history, family history, previous alcohol-related treatment and data concerning the use of prescription and illicit drugs were collected. In addition the following QoL/QoL-related indices were administered; Severity of Alcohol Dependence (SADQ), Alcohol Problems Questionnaire (APQ), Rotterdam Symptoms Checklist (RSCL), Life Situation Survey (LSS), General Health Questionnaire (GHQ-28), Nottingham Health Profile (NHP) and Short-Form-36 (SF-36). Participants were then followed up at three, six, and twelve month intervals when the RSCL, LSS, GHQ-28, NHP, SF-36 and tobacco/alcohol consumption data were gathered.

Overall the QoL scores were poor compared to general population norms.

The follow-up rates were, three months (n=232, 97%), six months (n=231, 96%) and twelve months (n=228, 93%) respectively. At three months one hundred and sixteen (50%) of the participants had relapsed, by six months this figure was (n=142, 61%) and at the end of the study it had reached (n=163, 71%). A relapse was defined as the consumption of at least 21 units of alcohol for males and 14 units of alcohol for females over a 7-day period at anytime during the follow-up period. In the United Kingdom one unit is the equivalent of 8-10 grams of alcohol.

A regression model was constructed using the baseline variables to assess their impact on relapse and changes in QoL scores over 12 months.

At three months the baseline predictors of outcome were Jarman scores, SF-36 bodily pain scores and prescription of vitamins. By six months Jarman and SF-36 bodily pain scores both remained significant and there was one other predictor, living alone. The 12 months predictors were Jarman scores, number of residential treatments, and units of alcohol consumed. The changes in baseline and 12 month scores of those subjects who relapsed (n=163) and did not relapse (n=65) were computed. In both cases the "within group" changes were not significant following statistical controls.

This study has demonstrated the important role played by sociodemographic and other confounding factors in QoL of alcohol dependent individuals both at baseline and in consequence of relapse and non-relapse to heavy drinking.

PART ONE: QUALITY OF LIFE

Chapter 1

INTRODUCTION

This monograph describes the quality of life (QoL) changes in a group of diverse alcohol dependent individuals (ADI) recruited from different treatment centres based in London and surrounding areas.

Shortly after the Second World War the World Health Organisation defined health as "A complete state of physical, mental, and social well being and not merely the absence of disease" (World Health Organisation 1948), thereby enshrining the quality of an individual's life as an important concept. Nowadays Quality of Life (QoL) is increasingly used as a measurement in health care research.

Until twenty years ago quality of life assessment was virtually unknown. However a Medline search conducted at the end of October 2003 using the database 1966-present returned 59,302 articles when the key-words "Quality of Life" was entered.

QoL revolves around "the subjective perception of satisfaction or happiness" (Oleson 1990). Thus there are many aspects of QoL which are only indirectly related to health such as economic resources, housing, neighbourhood safety and political conditions. Variables related to disease and treatment outcomes are generally investigated under the term "health related quality of life" (HRQoL). HRQoL has in turn been defined as "the subjective perception of the impact of health status, including disease and treatment, on physical, psychological and social functioning and well-being (Leidy et al 1999).

To be considered as an index of HRQoL the measurement *must* have at least three core domains physical, psychological and social (Shumaker and Berzon 1995) . It is unclear where HRQoL begins and ends. Leidy et al (1999) insist that it includes physical, psychological symptoms, physical functioning, social functioning and emotional well-being. Other dimensions which could be included under this heading are role function, cognitive function, sleep problems, sexuality and sexual function, vitality/energy, pain, life satisfaction, body image, and general perceptions of health. The present author believes that the QoL of ADI goes beyond the health-related issues. In the present study the impact of social deprivation or privilege is measured and assessed., thus QoL is conceptualised very widely and the term Quality of Life (QoL) is used.

Previous work from the current author indicates that the subjective views of the individual should be assessed when designing future research studies. There is a poor correlation between the physician's and patient's assessment of HrQoL in ADI (Foster et al 2002) and the tendency has been to show a greater interest in "hard endpoints" (Longabaugh et al 1994) . These include abstinence rates or improvements in biochemical parameters (Liver toxicity and function tests), that *may* coincide with a subjective perception of improved QoL but this is not guaranteed.

Measurement Approaches Used in the Current Study

One of the key decisions that the researcher has to make is what is the best method of measuring QoL? One possibility is to ask a *global question* such as "Please rank your QoL at present on a scale of 1-5". These are usually an adjunct to other items as it is doubtful whether one question can assess QoL adequately. In addition to asking a global question the researchers may have two other possible options. Firstly to use a *generic* measure or secondly a *condition-specific* index, should one exist. Generic measures can compare QoL scores across a series of disease states and populations, one inherent disadvantage; is that they *may* be less sensitive to treatment effects for a specific disease (Patrick and Deyo 1989). Condition-specific measures are sometimes referred to as disease or situation-specific and measure the QoL effects associated with a discrete disease. A condition-specific measure will have an increased level of sensitivity. However it cannot be compared across different disease conditions unless it is demonstrated that such a comparison is valid. Thus a symptom checklist may well have a cluster of symptoms which although designed for a particular disease are applicable to a number of disease states. In the current study a symptom-checklist originally designed for cancer patients, the Rotterdam Symptoms Checklist (deHaes et al 1990) was applied to ADI There is no alcohol-dependency specific questionnaire that has been subject to the peer-review process; but arguably the Alcohol Problems Questionnaire (APQ) (Drummond 1990) is a HrQoL measure as it has physical, psychological and social components. However to date only generic measures have been applied to ADI to measure HrQoL/QoL. In the current study two generic HrQoL/QoL measures were used; the Nottingham Health Profile (NHP) (Hunt et al 1986) and the Short-Form-36 (SF-36) (Ware et al 1993).

It is unlikely that either generic or condition-specific measures could provide a comprehensive coverage of the variables that contribute to HrQoL/QoL. On such occasions a *battery* can be used. This involves using multiple instruments to measure one construct. It was the methodology adopted in the present study when measurements of mood and dependency were added. When using this approach aggregation into a composite score is impossible and the results have to be presented as a profile.

Other Measurement Approaches

Before considering the issue of subject burden there are two types of HrQoL measures that should be briefly mentioned; the SEIQoL and health economic measures. The designers of the SEIQoL (The Schedule for the Evaluation of Individual Quality of Life) (McGhee et al 1991) criticise existing HrQoL/QoL measures on the grounds that "they do not represent a free choice of the individual" and are in practice imposed medical constructs. They felt that when assessing HrQoL/QoL, individuals should be able to isolate those aspects of

HrQoL/QoL which are important to them and rate their importance. When devising this measure there were two groups; a healthy sample and a patient sample (suffering from irritable bowel syndrome and peptic ulcer disease). The first step of the instrument design was a semi-structured interview in which QoL *cues* for *each individual were elicited.* This formed the basis for the QoL evaluation. Interestingly enough health was not mentioned by every individual and was less frequently mentioned in patient sample! The findings of McGhee et al (1991) suggest that to conceptualise QoL as predominantly health-related may be mistaken.

Despite being largely focused upon the subjective views of the respondent there are a group of rating scales such as the Quality-Adjusted Life-Year (QALY) (Williams 1985) and Quality of Well-Being Scale (Kaplan et al 1984) which express QoL as a trade-off between health status and life expectancy. A single-score is the resultant value and a financial value can be placed upon it. These measures can then be used to make decisions relating to the allocation of health resources.

Anne Bowling (Bowling 1991) in her overview of HrQoL/QoL/Health Economic measures outlines some of the criticisms levelled at them. Firstly, they have not been adequately tested for their validity and reliability. Secondly, "sufferers" of the diseases assessed rarely complete the scales; usually "experts" complete them. This term includes doctors, nurses, medical and nursing students. Research has shown that there is a poor correlation between expert and patient QoL ratings in three disease states; cancers (Slevin et al 1988), elderly subjects (Pearlman and Uhlmann 1998) and ADI (Foster et al 2002). Thirdly, an underlying assumption is that health economic ratings are rational and that value judgements are not being made. Fourthly, that distilling QoL into one score is problematic, in practice QoL is multidimensional. Finally, linking to the point about rational versus value judgements is the likelihood that disease suffers may assign greater value than someone assessing a hypothetical disease state. For example a frail and pained elderly person may feel that "such an existence is as valuable to them as someone else's apparently healthy state."

Subject Burden

One of the aspects that should be considered before deciding what instruments to use and data to collect is the burden placed upon the subject. Once more this involves a "trade-off", on this occasion between length and depth of investigation (Berzon 1998). When assessing the acceptable level of burden the following issues need to be considered; the number of items, time taken to complete the instrument, complexity of the instrument and capabilities of the patient. Other considerations are clinician/researcher time and expense.

As a general rule longer instruments give a more comprehensive data coverage but create a greater subject burden. It follows logically therefore that shorter instruments are less comprehensive but carry a smaller subject burden.

Chapter 2

LITERATURE REVIEW

METHODOLOGY

The key-words alcoholism and Quality of Life (QoL) were entered into the Medline and BIDS databases covering the period 1966-February 2006. This returned two-hundred and nineteen articles. Further sources were used; the word alcohol(ism) was searched for in the index of the Journal of Quality of Life covering all fifteen volumes. This included abstracts from the ISOQOL (International Society for the Study of Quality of Life) conferences. As a result a further five published abstracts were found. Secondly the index of the following journals covering the last 10 years was made, checking for the word "Quality of life." These were "Addiction", " Addiction Abstracts", " Addiction Biology", "Alcohol and Alcoholism", "Drug and Alcohol Dependence", "Journal of Studies on Alcohol", "Alcoholism Clinical and Experimental Research" , " Addictive Behaviours" and "Alcohol". Using this methodology returned a further three peer-reviewed papers and three published abstracts. Also a contemporary review article (Donovan et al 2005) revealed a further 7 papers that had used quality of life in alcoholism treatment research. The same article contained a further eight articles that used the term substance use rather than alcoholism- these were excluded from the review as the analyses included both alcohol and drug users that were treated as a total sample.

Thus in total this review includes 237 published works.

ALCOHOL AND QUALITY OF LIFE RESEARCH IN CONTEXT

The search revealed articles going back as far as 1977, this is *prima facie* a mean of over 8.4 papers or abstracts annually (assuming 28 years). However one hundred and twelve (47%) papers were excluded from the review and thus the annual mean for articles considered in the review was nearly 4.5. Table 2.1 a and b lists the excluded articles and the grounds for their exclusion. The most common ground for exclusion was that the focus of the article was QoL subsequent to the development liver disease (n=16, 14%). Seven (8%) papers were not considered because they were review articles or concerned various physical conditions. These physical conditions were; tuberculosis, osteoporosis, atrial fibrilation, fetal alcohol syndrome, nephropathy, epilepsy and opthalmology. Six papers (7%) were excluded for the following reasons; because the main concern was i) the elderly, ii) pancreatitis and iii) HIV/AIDS/Hepatitis C. Five (6%) papers relating to re-integration of mentally-ill patients into the community and pension entitlement respectively were also excluded. Four papers (4%) were excluded for the following reasons i) nutrition, ii) partners and families of alcohol dependent individuals, iii) patients with carcinomas iv) cost of alcoholism to the general population, v) Epidemiological and General Population Studies, vi) existensialism and vii) conference statements/proceedings/letters. Three papers (3%) were exempted on the following grounds i) benzodiazepine use and abuse and ii) the emotional well-being of psychiatrists/physicians. Two papers (2%) were not included for six grounds i) police practices ii) role of nurses iii) juvenile delinquency and drinking in young people iv) physical and psychological rehabilitation v) neurotransmitters and biochemical markers and vi) dentistry.

There were ten papers where the subject categories could not be collapsed into any of the categories shown in table 2.1a and these are shown in table 2.1b. They ranged from the expected topics such as gambling to the more esoteric-for example, circumpolar health.

One of the papers excluded from the review was a previous review article (Foster et al 1999). The themes covered by this work were the paucity of papers, QoL in alcohol-dependent individuals, the link between QoL and comorbidity and alcoholism, QoL alcohol dependency and social environment, QoL changes associated with abstinence, minimal or controlled drinking and QoL measurements as predictors of relapse. The present review will consider the literature under the following headings;

a) Measurement and Attempts at a Definition in Alcohol Dependent Individuals
b) QoL of Alcohol Dependent Individuals
c) QoL and Psychiatric Comorbidity
d) QoL and Physical Comorbidity
e) QoL and Longitudinal Outcomes
f) QoL and Pharmacological Treatments for Alcohol Dependence/Abuse
g) QoL and the Social Environment of Alcohol Dependent Individuals
h) QoL in Alcohol Dependent Women
i) QoL and Homelessness
j) The role of Sleep in the QoL of Alcohol Dependent Individuals.

Table 2.1a. Articles Excluded From The Literature Review; Alcoholism and Quality of Life. (Four or more citations)

Categorisation	Number
QoL Subsequent to Liver Disease. Jowsey et al (2001); Duvoux (2001); Hegedus et al (2001); Bustamante Schneider and Fernadez Ramos (2001); Mejias et al (1999); Dammer et al (1998); Coffman et al (1997); Shakil et al (1997); Reeck et al (1997); Orozco et al (1994); Krom (1994); Keefe and Esquivel (1993); Orloff et al (1992); Van Theil et al (1990); Tarter et al (1984); Jarvinen et al (1981).	16
Review Article. Peters et al (2003); Poldrugo (2003); Srisurapanont and Jarusuraisin (2002); Srisurapanont and Jarusuraisin (2000) ; Hertling et al (2001); Lepine and Pilissolo (2000); Foster et al (1999).	7
Various Physical Conditions Cueto-Manzano et al (2005); Olszynski et al (2004); Streissguth et al (2004); Snow et al (2003); Devinsky (2003) Bullock et al (2001); Morales et al (1994).	7
The Elderly. Oslin et al (2004); Burke and Wengel (2003); Brymer and Rusnell (2000); Mouton and Espino (1999); Holroyd et al (1997); Tucker et al (1989).	6
Pancreatitis. Olah et al (2004); Rios and Adams(2001); Sohn et al (2000): Soran et al (2000) Miyake et al (1987); Little (1983)	6
HIV/AIDS/Hepatitis C ANAES (2002), Mathurin et al (2002) Kramer et al (2002) Gutierrez et al (2002); Moser et al (2001); Wahlstrom and Dobs (2000)	6
Re-integration of Mentally-Ill Patients into the Community. Fakhoury et al (2005); Cosden et al (2005); Lambert et al (2003); Hubschmid et al (1988); Lindholm (1983).	5
Pension Entitlement. Elton and Hornquist (1983a); Elton and Hornquist (1983b); Hornquist and Elton (1983); Hornquist et al (1983); Hornquist (1982).	5
Nutrition. Iyengar and Nair (2000); Gray (1989); Cooke (1979); Vial et al (1991).	4
Partners and Families of Alcohol Dependent Subjects. Guethmundsson and Tomasson (2002); Ryan et al (1997); Barber and Gilbertson (1997); Krawczynski et al (1993).	4
Patients with Carcinomas Itzen et al (2002); Wustrow and Mahnke (1996); Carter (1997).; Pastore et al (1990).	4
Cost of Alcoholism to the General Population. Boning (2004); Moore et al (2000); McDonnell and Maynard (1985); Ashton and Casswell (1984).	4
Epidemiological and General Population Studies. Averina et al (2005); Costa et al (2004); Rehm et al (1996); Single et al (1995).	4

Table 2.1a. (Continued)

Categorisation	Number
Existensialism. Ventegodt et al (2004a); Ventegodt et al (2004b); Ventegodt et al (2003); DuPont and McGovern (1992).	4
Conference Statements/Proceeedings and Letters Hilton et al (2001); Wiese et al (2000); Chick and Erickson (1996); Schonfield (1993).	4

Table 2.1b. Articles Excluded From The Literature Review; Alcoholism and Quality of Life. (Three or less citations)

Categorisation	Number
Benzodiazepine Use and Abuse. Vorma et al (2005); Brunette et al (2003); Talley (1990).	3
Well-being of Psychiatrists/Physicians. Gerrity (2001); Firth-Cozens (2001); Knutsen (1977).	3
Police Practices. Saunders (1998); Finn (1985).	2
Role of Nurses. Dunbar et al (1998); Counillet (1997).	2
Juvenile Delinquency and Drinking in Young People. Dedobbeleer and Desjardins (2001) ; Russell and Hardman (1980).	2
Physical and Psychological Rehabilitation. Harter et al (2002) ; Biefang and Potthoff (1995).	2
Neuro-Transmitters and Biochemical Markers Goldstein et al (2004); Wurst et al (2000).	2
Dentistry Jones et al (2003); Rogers et al (2000).	2
Gambling Scherrer et al (2005).	1
Burnout. Anonymous (1995).	1
Ear-Acupuncture. Gaa'l and Freebairn (1979).	1
Therapeutic Commentary Waddington et al (2004).	1
Psoriasis and Sex. Gupta and Gupta (1997).	1
QoL of Humanitarian Aid Workers in Bosnia. Berk (1998).	1
Single Case Study Kulikova (2004).	1
Alcohol Not Mentioned in Abstract Di Michele and Bolino (2004).	1
Animal Study Nakahara et al (2002).	1
Circumpolar Health Korolenko and Kensin D (2001).	1

Measurement and Attempts at a Definition of Quality of Life in Alcohol Dependent Individuals (ADI)

A recently published review (Donovan et al 2005) considered thirty-six studies that had used QoL as an outcome measure as it related to drinking and other substance misuse behaviour and treatment outcomes. The authors confirmed the importance of QoL measurement. For any instrument to fulfil the criterion of measuring QoL it must have three components, physical, psychological and social (Shumaker and Berzon 1995; Testa and Simonsen 1996). The National Institute of Health Working Group (National Institute of Health 1990) has attempted to outline a framework to assess the QoL of alcohol abusers. Three domains were specified. Firstly "Clinical Status" which included the amount of alcohol consumed and other issues connected to the level of dependency. Secondly "Disorder Specific Problems" which included the negative impact of alcohol as reported by the client. Finally "General Functioning" which focused upon social functioning and environmental support. One of the most important recent trends has been the attempt to establish which types of treatment are effective with various subgroups of alcohol dependent individuals (ADI) so they can be effectively "matched" (Donovan and Mattson 1994). Project MATCH is the largest clinical trial to date that tests the "matching hypothesis." Eighteen hundred ADI were randomly assigned to one of three treatments; "Twelve-Step Facilitation" (based upon the tenets of Alcoholics Anonymous), "Cognitive Behavioural Coping Skills" and "Motivational Enhancement Therapy". These individuals were followed up after three months treatment and at three months intervals up to twelve months. The outcomes were changes in drinking patterns, functional status/QoL and utilisation of treatment services (PROJECT MATCH RESEARCH GROUP 1993). One of the aims of the Project MATCH researchers was to move away from the sole use of "Hard Endpoints" such as abstinence and to introduce other outcome measures. To this end they looked at QoL (Longabaugh et al 1994) using the previously described framework (National Institute of Health 1990). However one of the important contributions of Longabaugh et al (1994) was to recommend the collection of data beyond the subjective viewpoint of the client. Objective measures were developed which examined QoL effects in the family of the drinker. This was broadened into a consideration of the QoL of the wider society, which inevitably takes the cost of alcohol abuse into consideration.

Subsequent to PROJECT MATCH the data has been used to derive a composite measure of treatment outcome (Zweben and Cisler 2003). This included the following brief quality of life measures; the mental and physical health related quality of life (Short-Form 12) (SF-12) (Ware et al 1998) and the 5-item Satisfaction with Life Scale (Diener et al 1985).

Foster et al (1999a) criticise the National Institute of Health framework and further proposals which emanated from Project MATCH on the following grounds. Firstly the lack of patient perspective, secondly limited coverage of QoL dimensions and thirdly the omission of any attempt to consider the satisfaction of individuals with their treatments. Further work has emphasised the importance of assessing the "patient's" perspective (Foster et al 2002). In that study quality of life assessment on the part of patients and clinicians were compared using the EQ-5D visual analogue scale (Brooks R with the EuroQoL Group 1996). There was not a significant relationship between patient and clinician ratings. Clinicians tended to give lower scores indicating they perceived that the quality of life in their patients was poorer than the patients did themselves. Also it indicates that the two are comparing different constructs.

A multi-centre research group based in the United Kingdom has attempted to conduct a similar trial in real life settings to PROJECT MATCH which they have termed a "pragmatic randomised controlled trial" (UKATT Research Team 2005a). The treatments being compared were social behaviour and network therapy (new) and motivational enhancement therapy (traditional). Seven hundred and forty two individuals were recruited and the follow up rate at 12 months was 689 (93%). Two generic measures of QoL were applied in the study; SF-36 (Ware et al 1993) and EQ-5D (Brooks R with the EuroQol Group 1996). The main measure of affect was the General Health Questionnaire- version 28 (GHQ-28) (Goldberg and Hillier 1987). There were no significant differences reported in the above or alcohol-related outcome measures between the two treatments. Mental health-related QoL as measured by the mental components of the SF-36 had improved significantly at 12 months. This was accompanied by reduction in alcohol consumption, alcohol problems and dependence ratings. A further paper (UKATT Research Team 2005b) showed the results of a cost benefit analysis. There was little difference between both therapies. For each one there was a fivefold saving in health, social and criminal justice costs.

A research group from Germany (Priebe et al 1998) have shown some of the difficulties encountered when measuring QoL in alcohol dependent individuals. These authors found that a strong overlap between self-rated symptoms, subjective QoL and self-rated needs in a sample of 90 newly admitted schizophrenic patients, 170 long term hospitalised schizophrenic patients, 154 alcoholic patients admitted for a short-term and 68 patients in long-term alcohol rehabilitation.

Further difficulties were shown in Powell and Crome (1999) who applied the Schedule of Evaluation of Individual Quality of Life (SEIQoL) (McGhee et al 1991) to three groups of participants; alcohol dependent individuals (n=20), controls (n=20) and patients with hip replacements (n=20). The SEIQoL allows individuals to select and weight their chosen dimensions of QoL. They found that the range of QoL dimensions nominated by ADI was much greater than controls and hip replacement patients. In consequence they concluded that applying generic QoL measures to ADI may provide less comprehensive results than doing so to other patient groups. Domains that were *less* important to ADI than hip replacement patients and controls were, personal health, finances, family health, intellectual function, social/leisure activities, family, relationships, religion, work, independence; and family/personal health, relationships, family health and independence respectively. Those domains that were *endorsed* by ADI but not the other two groups were love, life, safety, travel, drink and control of emotional reactions.

Jane Powell is also attempting to develop an alcohol-specific QALY (see chapter 1). In Foster et al (1999a) she presented some of her interim findings. Her sample of (n= 108) has had some difficulty in using a techniques described in chapter one.

In summary these writings suggest that the constructs that contribute to the QoL of ADI are broader than other patient groups. This means that it is questionable whether an alcohol-specific QoL measure can be designed which adequately encapsulates QoL in alcohol dependent individuals.

Quality of Life of Alcohol Dependent Individuals (ADI)

Arguably the first attempt to systematically measure QoL in ADI was Welsh et al (1993). They applied the Life Situation Survey (LSS) (Chubon 1987) and concluded that the QoL of outpatient (n=51) and inpatient (n=37) (predominantly female) "alcoholics" was poor. The finding that the QoL of ADI is poor is now practically universal across treatment groups. For example it has been confirmed in a group of Polish soldiers (Polak 2001). Foster et al (1998a) used the LSS and a generic QoL measure, the Nottingham Health Profile (NHP) (Hunt et al 1980) and applied them to 60 ADI following detoxification. Comparison between the total scores for these two indices indicated that 80% of the individuals scored above the equivalent general population norms for both measures. In the same study correlation coefficients were computed between the LSS and NHP sub-scores, energy, emotional reactions, social isolation, physical mobility, pain and sleep and measures of severity of alcohol dependence (Severity of Alcohol Dependence Questionnaire) (SADQ) (Stockwell et al 1979) and alcohol problems (Alcohol Problems Questionnaire) (APQ) (Drummond 1990). Stronger relationships were found between alcohol problems and QoL measures though none of the variables showed relationships that equated to a *large* effect size ($r \geq 0.5$) (Cohen 1992).

The Short-Form-36 (SF-36) (Ware et al 1993) is commonly regarded as the "gold-standard" of health status/QoL measurement (Bowling 1995), it has been applied on a number of occasions to ADI. It can be divided into mental health and physical health composites. (Ware and Sherbourne 1992). The physical health composites are physical functions, physical role limitations, bodily pain and general health. The equivalent measures that comprise the mental health composite are emotional role limitations, vitality, social functioning and mental health. Volk et al (1997) in a sample of (n=1333) American primary care patients found that ADI as assessed by DSM-IV criteria (American Psychiatric Association 1994) had a poorer QoL as assessed by the SF-36 than abusers. The QoL of DSM-IIIR (American Psychiatric Association 1987) alcohol abusers/dependents have also been compared in the Scottish SECCAT study (Socio-Economic Costs and Consequences of Alcoholism Treatment). The sample consisted of individuals recruited from the Edinburgh Alcohol Problems Clinic who were retrospectively assessed over a six- month period. The SECCAT study has been reported in two papers (McKenna et al 1996; Patience et al 1997). McKenna et al (1996) discovered that the QoL of DSM-IIIR alcohol dependents was poorer than that of abusers, and that dependents had a greater use of health care resources than abusers. Patience et al (1997) reported that greater alcohol problems (on this occasion measured by the Alcohol Related Problems Questionnaire (ARPQ) (Chick et al 1988; Chick et al 1991) was associated with a poorer QoL.

A research group based on mainland Europe also administered the SF-36 to ADI (Daeppen et al 1998). The sample was 147 DSM-IIIR alcohol dependent Swiss inpatients and outpatients. In addition to the SF-36 the following instruments were administered in a cross-sectional design, the SADQ, Hamilton Depression Scale (HDS) (Hamilton 1967) and the Addiction Severity Index (ASI) (McLellan et al 1980). The authors found that individuals perceived their problems to be more psychological than physical. There were *large* ($r \geq 0.5$) relationships between the SF-36 emotional role and mental health sub-scores and the psychiatric sub-scale of the ASI, and the SF-36 mental health sub-score and the HDS. In addition there were *large* relationships between the SADQ total score and the following SF-

36 sub-scores; general health, social functioning and vitality. No comparison can be made between Alcohol Problem scores as this variable was not measured.

An American study of (n=674) veterans (Calsyn et al 2004) has considered the relationship between the ASI and SF-36. The researchers found there were large correlations (r >0.8) between ASI medical and psychiatric composites and SF-36 summary physical and mental health sub-scores.

The contribution of the SF-36 and other factors upon QoL has been measured. Romeis et al (1999) administered a version of the SF-36 modified for telephone surveys to 1,258 male twin pair members of the US Vietnam Era Twin Registry and compared alcoholic and non-alcoholic co-twins. The only SF-36 sub-score that differentiated the two groups following statistical controls was vitality. The significant differentiating variables were physical and psychiatric problems, drug and nicotine dependence, marital status, income and severity of dependence (DSM-IIIR). There is a shorter version of the SF-36; the Medical Outcomes Study (MOS SF-20). This has the following sub-scores, physical functioning, bodily pain, role functioning, general health, social functioning and mental health (Stewart et al 1988). It was used in an American study (Stein et al 1998). The individuals (n=2688) seeking drug or alcohol detoxification and subsequent treatment, were assessed and the breakdown of primary drug problems was alcohol (38%), cocaine (38%) and heroin (24%), respectively. The SF-20 was applied at baseline; the only sub-scores where alcohol or drug use had little effect were physical functions, role functioning, health perception and pain scores. Sociodemographic factors contributed only 2-7% of the SF-20 score variance. This is in marked contrast to Romeis et al (1999) and suggests that the impact of sociodemographic factors on QoL is markedly different in heroin and cocaine users compared to ADI.

Foster et al (2004a) published findings from a study at present only available in abstract form that examined the correlation between SF-36 and NHP sub-scores in ADI. Brazier et al (1992) performed a similar study in the UK general population. Both research groups found large relationships in the equivalent energy, mental health, pain and physical functioning subs-scores but the relationships between social isolation (NHP) and social functioning (SF-36) were only moderate. This indicates that separate constructs are being measured in these variables.

The World Health Organisation have devised a generic measurement of QoL designed to be used cross-culturally –the WHOQoL. This measures physical health, psychological health, social relationships and environment. A short 26 item the WHOQOL-BREF (Murphy et al 2000) has been used in a group of alcohol dependent males (n=36) in Brazil (da Silva Lima et al 2005). Other measures used in the study were the SF-36, Symptoms Checklist (SCL-90) (Derogatis et al 1976) and Short-Form Alcohol Dependence Data scale (SADD) (Davidson and Raistick 1986). A lower level of dependence was associated with higher SF-36 and WHOQoL-BREF scores (i.e better QoL). There was an acceptable convergent validity between the SF-36 and WHOQoL-BREF. The authors concluded that the "WHOQoL proved to be satisfactory for evaluating quality of life in this sample". These findings are optimistic but clearly such a small sample size means that at best this can be seen as pilot data.

Two others measures are of note; the Brief Life Satisfaction Scale (BLSS) and the Christo Inventory for Substance Misuse Services (CISS) Recently two researchers from the University of Missouri (Lubin and Van Whitlock 2004) have shown that a the Brief Life Satisfaction Scales (BLSS) has acceptable psychometric properties. The BLSS measures 10 items and three factors emerged following analyses- these were self-satisfaction, interpersonal satisfaction and social role satisfaction. Christo et al (2000) presents validation data for the CISS. This is a one-page twenty-item outcome evaluation tool for substance misuse services including measures of quality of life related variables. These include social functioning, general health, psychological functioning, occupations and working/personal relationships.

Four studies provide some insight into the impact of the level of alcohol consumption upon QoL. Cisler and Sweben (1999) reported some of the findings of Project MATCH and measured QoL by the Purpose in Life (PIL) questionnaire (Crumbaugh and Maholick 1964). There was a linear relationship between alcohol consumption and poor QoL. Heavy drinkers had a poorer QoL compared to moderate drinkers and abstaining drinkers. The levels of alcohol problems in their population were also assessed by means of the Drinker Inventory of Consequences (Miller et al 1995). They found that there was a sub-group of heavy drinkers who did not experience alcohol-related problems, these were from higher socio-economic client groups. This is consistent with Pearlman et al (1989) and may provide some insight as to fluctuation between the level of alcohol-related problems and QoL. Foster et al (2000a) examined the impact of QoL as measured by the NHP and LSS and alcohol consumption in a group of 82 socially deprived individuals (41 men, 41 women) admitted for detoxification. The authors found that the changes in alcohol consumption were the most significant mediator in QoL scores. There were *large* ($r \geq 0.5$) associations between changes in alcohol consumption and similar changes in NHP emotional reaction sub-scores, LSS total scores and Beck Depression Inventory (BDI) (Beck et al 1961) total scores. This study will be discussed further when longitudinal studies and the QoL of alcohol dependent women are considered.

Kraemer et al (2002) recruited 213 individuals from primary care medical clinics and measured drinking quantity using the Alcohol Use Disorders Identification test. (AUDIT) (Saunders et al 1993) and measured QoL using the SF-36. Those participants who were able to decrease their drinking by 30% per month had improved SF-36 physical and mental component scores. Finally Okoro et al (2004) surveyed 99,783 current drinkers in a probability sample of US adults. A series of QoL items from the Center for Disease Control and Prevention were used. These included "perceived general health, recent physical health, recent mental health and recent activity limitations." Periodic heavy drinking defined as five or more drinks per occasion was associated with lower QoL scores.

A Canadian general population study found that (n=788, 10%) of their sample (n=8116) had a DSM-IIIR diagnosis of alcohol abuse/dependency (Sareen et al 2005). The diagnostic tool used was the University of Michigan Composite International Diagnostic Interview (CIDI) (Wittchen 1994). They also found that this was a group who were significantly likely to seek help for emotional symptoms. Furthermore help seeking was associated with a poor QoL and past year suicidal ideation. QoL was measured by six domains; main activity, family relationship, friendships, leisure activities, income and life in general.

There are four other works that are best considered at this point. One is reported as part of a review paper (Foster et al 1999a), and the others are published abstracts from Europe and the United States. Jane Powell (Foster et al 1999a) reported findings in the development and testing of an alcohol-specific QoL measure. Her sample of (n=108) ADI suggest that questions concerning withdrawal and relief drinking, alcohol-related problems, depression, self-esteem, general health, work, satisfaction with treatment, ability to communicate, concentrate and socialise all contribute to the QoL of ADI. True et al (1997) applied the SF-36 to 1204 twin members of the Vietnam Era Twin Registry. Following controls for "psychiatric/physical comorbidity, drug and nicotine dependence, combat experience, income and marital status; only the general health and bodily pain sub-scales were associated with alcoholism. This lack of a relationship with affective state and QoL suggests that findings from the Vietnam Era Twin Registry may not be generalisable beyond that population.

Popovic et al (1997) investigated the impact of certain socio-demographic variables upon QoL in a what was then a Yugoslavian population. Alcoholics who lived in towns had a better QoL than those who resided in villages, older patients were more satisfied than younger patients. A higher level of education was also associated with a better QoL.

Work from Germany (Richter et al 2002) has shown that the number of previous treatments in the 12 months prior before admission in an inpatient alcohol treatment unit (1 or less v > 1) did have an impact upon the subjective experience of quality of life.

To summarise; i) there are a number of factors that contribute to the QoL of ADI, ii) some of these vary across different groups, iii) the QoL of these individuals is uniformly poor at baseline. Most work shows that there is a relationship between poorer QoL and increasing severity of dependency/abuse. However at present research suggests that increasing severity of dependence/abuse have less impact upon the QoL than the amount of alcohol-related problems encountered. Two important riders must be put forward, firstly alcohol-related problems have been assessed by a number of different measures and secondly it has been suggested that higher sociodemographic status provided some protection against the impact of alcohol-related problems.

There is a trend for alcohol misusers to view the deficiencies in their QoL as being largely mood-related. However an American group have shown there is a strong relationship between impaired physical status and QoL, but this sample were recruited from the Vietnam-Era Twin Registry and may not be generalisable to other patient groups. Sociodemographic factors appear to be an important mediator in QoL status. There is one exception to this trend, a paper that found only a minimal contribution from sociodemographic factors to the overall variance (Stein et al 1998). However the primary drugs for over half of the sample were heroin and cocaine which suggests that the impact of sociodemographic factors upon the QoL of illicit drug users is markedly different to that of alcohol dependents/abusers. Finally the indications are that there is a strong relationship between the level of drinking and QoL.

Quality of Life and Psychiatric Comorbidity

As the previous sections have shown there is a strong link between affective status and QoL in ADI. This section largely concentrates on those papers which have considered alcohol abuse in patients with a psychiatric diagnosis. The PRIME-MD 1000 study examined the link between QoL and psychiatric comorbidity in 1000 US individuals recruited from primary care (Spitzer et al 1995; Linzer et al 1996). The SF-20 was used as the generic QoL index. Both papers found that the incidence of "reported alcoholism" was low in this setting, and the impact of alcoholism upon QoL was minimal. The authors advanced two reasons for the low incidence of alcoholism in their sample. Firstly that those "patients" who presented as alcoholics in primary care were likely to be less dependent, and secondly a number were likely to be "in denial". Thus there is a strong possibility that the incidence of alcoholism has been under-reported and therefore any conclusions must be tentative.

Three papers were found which examined QoL, alcoholism and depression. Tollefson (1990) concluded that effective treatment of depression enhances QoL and reduces the probability of secondary alcoholism and suicide. A group of German researchers (Bronisch and Hecht 1987) compared two patient samples. Firstly, forty-eight inpatients with a "brief or prolonged depressive reaction" according to ICD-9 who had attempted suicide prior to admission. Secondly twenty-four patients with the same diagnosis who had no history of prior suicide attempts. Alcoholism and suicide attempts by first degree relatives predisposed suicidal behaviour. QoL as assessed by life events in the year prior to admission, social functioning and social support did not separate the two groups. A small scale American study (Oslin 1999) is also of note. Forty-eight individuals who had recently been convicted for being under the influence of alcohol were tracked: alcohol abuse or dependence was present in 98% of the sample. Concurrent alcoholism and depression was associated in greater self-reported alcoholism than those who had alcoholism alone.

Dysthymia is subject to under-diagnosis and in consequence under-treated. In a review of the subject (Keller 1994) the following were found to be present in the majority of sufferers; major depression, alcoholism, anxiety and personality disorders. Summarising the literature Keller concluded that dysthymia can effect every aspect of a persons's QoL including their relationships with others, earning potential and mental and physical well-being. The same review also considered some diagnostic issues. The author concluded that at the time of the writing there is not sufficient data to differentiate dysthymia from major depression or to establish to what extent dysthymia should be considered to be a personality disorder, though the link with alcohol was striking.

Arguably the strongest and most prestigious evidence of the link between substance misuse and psychiatric illness is the Epidemiologic Catchment Area (ECA) study (Regier et al 1990). This study collected data from over 18,000 adults from five US communities. The main finding of note in this area was that 50% of those individuals with serious mental illness develop an alcohol or drug use disorder at some point in their lives. Weissman (1991) reviewed selected data from the ECA and concluded that panic disorder was associated with impairment in QoL. Further information on the association between panic disorders, alcohol abuse and QoL is provided by another American group of researchers (Massion et al 1993). In total 357 individuals with a current episode of panic/generalised anxiety disorder (DSM-IIIR) were examined. The individuals had a significantly impaired QoL as quantified by an emotional health rating and alcohol abuse was linked to those who had a panic disorder without agoraphobia. Trauma has been associated with high rates of alcoholism and minor depression (Warshaw et al 1993). In this study the areas of QoL which were adversely affected by trauma were role, suicide attempts, psychiatric hospitalisation, alcohol and substance abuse and depression. This was particularly true for those individuals who met the criteria for Post-Traumatic-Stress Disorder (PTSD). Another paper (Zatzick et al 2002) has confirmed the link between PTSD problems drinking and impaired SF-36 scores in patients undergoing trauma surgery who were followed-up at 12 months. The link between PTSD, alcohol abuse and impaired QoL is particularly strong in adolescents. Clark and Kirisci (1996) examined 540 adolescents (aged 12-18) from clinic and community sources. PTSD showed significant adverse effects upon psychological, physical and social functioning. In contrast alcohol misuse primarily effected the role functioning domain only. Johnson et al (2004) have examined PTSD in a population of veterans. These researchers followed 51 veterans who had combat-related PTSD over six years. The mortality rate (17%) was high and over three-quarters had had a period of hospitalisation. Most self-reported a significant improvement in all areas of life functioning other than employment. At the same time they felt better able to cope with their illness (despite high levels of symptomatology) without the need to resort to violence or alcohol use. A review paper (Kessler 2003) has confirmed the link between alcoholism social phobia/social anxiety, impaired role functioning and diminished quality of life.

There have been two papers that have considered alcoholism, QoL and Bipolar affective disorder. The studies were conducted in the Canada and the US respectively. The Canadian study (Kusznir et al 2000) measured sixty-one individuals with a diagnosis of bi-polar disorder and assessed quality of life by the Occupational Performance Questionnaire (OPQ) and Community Functioning Scale (CFS). A third of the sample were not functioning adequately as assessed by the OPQ and a history of alcoholism or alcohol abuse was associated with poorer CFS scores.

Coryell et al (1998) examined 113 individuals with bipolar affective disorder at different time intervals over 15 years. The areas of QoL included employment, household duties, friendships, overall satisfaction, marital adjustment and recreational activities. Baseline "active alcoholism" was associated with poor short-term outcomes but this was not a significant predictor in a regression analysis performed at the end of the study. Though it should be noted that the group with alcoholism and bi-polar affective disorder was small (n=10), thus it is not surprising that statistical significance was not reached. The two significant variables associated with a poor long-term outcome were "poor optimal function in the five years before baseline assessment" and "the persistence of depressive symptoms over two subsequent years."

The study previously reported which first used the WHOQoL-BREF (da Silva Lima et al 2005) also provides noteworthy data in this sphere. The sample was 36 Brazilian men (mean age 46) from community and residential treatment centres. It considered the link between severity of dependency as measured by the SADD (Davidson and Raistrick 1986) and psychiatric symptomatology. A higher level of dependency was associated with more psychiatric symptoms. The most common symptoms were related to obsessive compulsive and depressive disorders and paranoia.

Dixon et al (1999) studied 719 American individuals with schizophrenia, and found an incidence of drug or alcohol use of 31%. The Dixon group have published two papers whereby they examined the QoL (overall life satisfaction) of their participants using the Lehman Quality of Life Interview (LQOLI) (Lehman 1983, 1988). This QoL interview assessed QoL using eight domains; living situation, family relations, social relations, leisure activities, work, finances, safety, legal problems and health. They found no association between current physical medical conditions and the presence of an alcohol or drug use disorder and overall life satisfaction. In contrast, alcohol and drug disorders were associated with depression and psychoticism (Dixon et al 1999). The second paper (Dixon et al 1998) used a naturalistic design to follow-up 268 individuals over 1 year. The sample was divided in three; past substance abusers in remission at baseline (n=70), current substance abusers (n=109) and non-substance abusers (n=89), once more QoL was assessed by the LQOLI. During follow-up current abusers at baseline were more likely remit to substance use and use alcohol to excess, otherwise there were no difference between QoL scores in the three groups. The authors concluded that a substantial proportion of subjects with past substance use were in "stable remission."

Another American group (Sullivan et al 1995) has attempted to identify risk factors for rehospitalisation in a seriously mentally ill population. The authors concluded these were medication non-compliance and alcohol abuse. The extent of outpatient service use, access to care and QoL were not associated with outcome.

Finally a German study (Bullenkamp and Voges 1994) discovered that frequent alcohol use was reported in 12.5% of mentally ill individuals who lived in five therapeutic homes in Mannheim. This sample of 136 frequent alcohol users was older men who had a lower dosage of neuroleptic medication. There was no relationship between alcohol use, age of onset of disease, rehospitalisation and general life satisfaction.

In summary there is a strong link between psychiatric comorbidity, alcohol abuse and QoL. Alcohol abuse is linked to a high probability of remission to psychiatric illness and consequently a diminution in QoL status, but the relationship of alcohol abuse to outcome is stronger than QoL scores. If psychiatric illness is unrecognised in these individuals then it is likely that QoL will deteriorate. In contrast careful supervision and treatment results in an optimistic prognosis.

Quality of Life and Physical Comorbidity

There has been one published randomised controlled trial that has evaluated a treatment aimed at ADI with a physical comorbidity (Willenbring and Olson 1999). This group compared the outcomes of a group given integrated outpatient treatment (IOT) with a "standard" alcohol treatment approach. The IOT was aimed at those individuals who were medically ill and declined physician referrals. One hundred and fifty male veterans with severe medical complications caused by alcoholism and recent drinking were randomised to either an IOT or a standard alcoholism and medical treatment group (control), they were followed up at two years. This was an older sample, the mean ages (SD) for the two groups were as follows IOT- 52.8 (11.5), Controls 57.2 (10.0) ($p < 0.05$). A number of individuals from both groups had died in the interim but the difference was not significant (IOT 18%, Control group 30%). Seventy four percent of the surviving 38 IOT were abstinent compared to 17 out 36 (47%) surviving from the control group ($p=0.02$). There were no differences in the symptoms of alcohol dependence, quality of life or life problems. The authors concluded that both treatments were "surprisingly effective in inducing abstinence" and the IOT required "further refinement and testing."

The present search revealed surprisingly few studies or papers that had examined the link between QoL, physical comorbidity and ADI. However a review examining the link between alcohol and cancer exists (Lundberg and Passik 1997). The authors pointed to two areas where this is particularly pertinent in ADI; psychiatric comorbidity and poor nutritional status. Both these factors mean that compliance with treatment regimes is often compromised.

The scores of individuals with lung, bladder, head and neck cancers and ADI have been compared (Foster et al 1999b) using a symptoms checklist designed for cancer patients (deHaes et al 1990). The scores of ADI were greater (i.e. worse) by a factor of up to 2.5. There are a number of qualifications to these findings, firstly the sample of ADI is small (n=60) compared to the cancer groups (> 127). Secondly the comparisons are from previously published data (deHaes et al 1996), thus controls for important confounders such as affective scores could not be made.

American researchers (Levine et al 2005) have examined facial trauma, life satisfaction and a number of psychological conditions including alcoholism and general drinking. Facial trauma was defined as a facial laceration of 3cm or greater or a fractured facial bone requiring an operation within the past 6-24 months. A retrospective analysis found a significant association between facial trauma, poor life satisfaction, a higher incidence of alcoholism and binge drinking. Other conditions associated with facial trauma included greater unemployment, more marital problems, jail terms, a lower attractiveness rating and a higher incidence of post traumatic stress disorder.

A study of 46 individuals reported data following traumatic injury and an alcohol/other drug inpatient stay at six months. (Baier Manwell et al 2005) The majority (61%) had been abstinent within the past 7 days and reported no binge drinking within the past 30 days. Half the sample met the criteria for current depression and there was a significant up take of health care facilities including five hospitalisations and 206 inpatient visits. In addition there was a lifetime incidence of 72 alcohol-related injuries, 74 motor vehicle crashes and 88 "other legal events"

The Donovan et al (2005) review revealed a number of additional studies that had compared QoL of alcoholics with other "chronic disease conditions". One of these was Carrington et al (1996) This study consisted of a postal survey of 18 alcoholic and 85 non-alcoholic patients who had received a liver transplant found no differences in QoL inventory scores between the two groups. Though the differences in sample sizes should be noted. The two other papers are both related to individuals recruited from American primary care settings. Firstly a study of 51 DSM-IV alcohol abusers/dependents (Johnson et al 1995) showed that this group had more impaired QoL scores (SF-20) and a greater level of psychiatric co-morbidity than those individuals without psychiatric disorders. Finally Morgan et al (2003) compared SF-36 scores of 104 DSM-IV alcohol dependents seeking outpatient treatment with US general population norm scores. There were significant differences in SF-36 sub-scores compared to US general population norms in the following sub-scores: physical role, general health, vitality, social functioning, emotional role and mental health. (in order of increasing statistical significance). The ADI group had poorer QoL scores.

Quality of Life and Longitudinal Outcomes

As early as 1979 (Hamilton 1979) reported an improvement in self-reported QoL as a result of detoxification from alcohol. There have been a number of studies that have investigated the impact of abstinence on QoL following treatment. Rather and Sherman (1989) interviewed 114 members of Alcoholics Anonymous (AA) (62% male) with a mean length of abstinence of 4.6 years. Two sobriety factors emerged, QoL (contributing 23% of the variance) and desire to drink (11.6% of the variance): enhanced QoL correlated with a longer period of abstinence. In a study of German alcoholics who had been abstinent for four years (Mann et al 1997), QoL was assessed by the Munchner-Lebensqualitats-Dimensionen-Liste. This is divided into four domains; somatic aspects, psychic aspects, social life and everyday life. Each showed a significant improvement in consequence of prolonged abstinence. Chaturvedi et al (1997) interviewed 50 male Indo/Asian ICD-10 alcoholics undergoing alcohol treatment. The authors reported that an improvement in QoL might influence long-term recovery. The areas of QoL endorsed by the participants were job-related, social functioning, and the personal such as peace of mind, reputation, self-respect, religious, altruistic acts and sensation seeking.

Amodeo et al (1992) have found that improvements in consequence of abstinence are not linear. They measured QoL using the Purpose in Life Questionnaire (PIL) (Crumbaugh et al 1970) and Life Satisfaction Scale (Bradburn 1969) in 60 men. The sample was divided into three categories; firstly 3-12 months abstinence (n=13) (short), 13-42 months abstinence (n=26) (moderate) and 43 months-9 years abstinence (n=21) (long). Those individuals in the moderate group had the best QoL scores. These findings suggest improvements in QoL lessen over time, though the small sample means that any findings are at best tentative.

We have studied a sample of socially deprived ADI from inner-city London who were detoxified through a voluntary sector alcohol detoxification unit and found a less consistent picture (Foster et al 1998a). There were significant improvements in LSS, depression (Beck Depression Inventory) (BDI) (Beck et al 1961), and Rotterdam Symptoms Checklist (RSCL) (deHaes et al 1990) physical and psychological symptom scores as a result of not relapsing to heavy drinking at three months. In the main generic QoL measure (NHP) there were two sub-scales which showed a deterioration in QoL scores, even in non-relapsing individuals, sleep and pain. This suggests that a short period of abstinence may uncover problems that have up to detoxification been hidden by alcohol use. Three limitations should be noted, the comparatively small sample, the short follow-up period, and whether findings from the voluntary sector can be generalised to other treatment settings.

In an effort to build on the Foster et al (1998a) study a further twenty two individuals were recruited so that were equal number of men (n=42) and women (n=42). Foster et al (2000 b) describes the results of applying the LSS (Chubon 1995) at three month follow-up. Only two individuals were lost to follow-up and one had died in the interim period. Sixty three per cent had relapsed to heavy drinking and LSS scores both significantly changed as a result of both remission from heavy drinking and relapse. The LSS variables that were improved as a result of remission from heavy drinking were as follows: appetite, sleep and self-esteem. Similarly those LSS variables that had deteriorated as a result of relapsing to heavy drinking: these were mood/affect, public support and work/life role.

There are two research groups who have provided data concerning the link between controlled drinking and QoL. Gual et al (1999) conducted a naturalistic study of 850 ADI from a treatment unit in Catalonia, following up their participants over three years. Once more the sample was divided into three comparison groupings; abstainers (n=371), controlled drinkers (n=55) and heavy drinkers (n=323). These categorisations were assessed according to the level of drinking during the last three-years of the study. The cut-off point for controlled drinking was 12 units of alcohol per week for both men and women. The QoL domains assessed were morbidity, alcohol-related problems, psychological and social functioning. The sample was predominantly married and employed. In addition having a collateral informant at a stable home address was a condition of recruitment. Abstinent individuals had significantly better outcomes than controlled and heavy drinkers on medical, socio-economic and psychological measures. Heavy drinkers had significantly poorer outcomes than controlled drinkers, whose outcomes closely mirrored those of heavy drinkers in the physical health domains. In contrast, social behaviour in controlled drinkers followed the profile of abstainers. Any conclusions concerning controlled drinking and QoL are tentative. This was a naturalistic study and the sample size was small. However the authors state that in their clinical experience this reflects clinical reality in Catalonia.

The second group (Watson et al 1996) were based in the United States. These were compared two groups (n=51 in each) from Alcoholics Anonymous (AA), (controlled/limited drinkers and abstainers) at 48 weeks. The definition of controlled drinking followed that proposed by Maisto et al (1979); i.e. no more than 42 ounces of ethanol over 4 weeks (an average of 1.5 ounces per day) over four weeks. The QoL data examined were risk of jailing, detoxification or job loss. The controlled/limited drinkers consumed 16 times as much alcohol as abstainers and were four times more likely to regress to an unacceptable level of drinking. There was no difference in the QoL outcomes between the two groups.

Watson and his researchers have also contributed another paper (Watson et al 1997) which has examined the link between QoL and extent of attendance at AA four weeks after treatment. On this occasion the sample was (n=150) male alcoholic veterans, once more the time frame was 48 weeks and the QoL dimensions were also as before. There was a four-way comparison as follows; Non-participants (n=38), this was no AA attendance, occasional attendance (n=48) equated to 1-4 meetings during the four weeks immediately following treatment, moderate (n=37) was 5-8 meetings and frequent (n=27), 9 or more meetings over the same time period. Frequent jailing was inversely associated with the non-participation group compared to moderate and occasional participants, all other QoL differences were not significant. Occasional and moderate attendance was associated with better outcomes than non-attendance but frequent attendance was not associated with an additional improvement in any outcomes.

A more recent study examining the impact of AA and quality of life has been conducted in the UK (Gossop et al 2003). One hundred and fifty participants who were resident at an alcohol treatment unit were surveyed at baseline and 80% were followed up at six months in a community setting. Quality of life was measured by the LSS (Chubon 1995). Frequent AA attendance following discharge was associated with improved drinking and quality of life outcomes compared to infrequent/non-attenders of AA. Further evidence to support greater encouragement of the use of AA is provided by a French-Canadian study (Kairouz and Dube 2000). These authors found that a greater period of abstinence supported by AA was associated with a "greater subjective experience of well-being."

AA is a form of mutual–help and this form of "treatment" has been subject to research. Kingree and Thompson (2000) considered the six months outcomes of a group of "adult children of alcoholics" (ACOA) with substance abuse problems who were assigned to either ACOA-specific mutual help meetings or substance abuse education classes. The ACOA showed significantly better outcomes- in particular they perceived themselves as having "better status" and this was accompanied by a reduction in depression and substance use.

A small-scale Norwegian study (n=28) (Berglund et al 2004) found that quality of life as assessed by mental well-being was improved by a 28 day Minnesota inpatient treatment programme. Though clearly the small sample size limits any conclusions that can be drawn from these findings. Furthermore the authors concede that the improvements shown may largely be a result of adjustment to treatment or their social sitaution.

A smaller Swiss study compared a group of individuals from an alcohol unit who were given "civil commitment" (n=17) and followed up at four years with a group age and sex – matched randomly selected patients from the alcohol unit (Bourquin-Tieche et al 2001). Civil commitment (CC) is a process whereby a judge " decides whether a person who is alleged to be mentally ill should be required to go to a psychiatric hospital or accept other mental health treatment. A CC is not a criminal conviction and will not go on a criminal record. http://www.oregoncounseling.org/LawRights/CivilCommit.htm This study notwithstanding the small sample size gives some support for increased use of CC. Compared to the age and sex matched sample the CC had better alcohol related and quality of life four year outcomes. Quality of life was again measured by the SF-36.

A number of studies have examined various QoL measures as predictors of relapse. Hoffman and Miller (1993) followed up 1918 American individuals in alcohol or drug treatment at 12 months. Abuse of drugs other than alcohol was associated with poor outcomes after controlling for sex and age. This was especially true for intravenous drug use. For all participants emotional distress, relationship difficulties, family problems, financial difficulties, craving and being around others who used alcohol or drugs made the commitment to abstinence difficult, and these were all predictive of relapse. The present author has been part of a group that has tested QoL measures as predictors of relapse (Foster et al 1998b). The baseline predictors of three month relapse in a group of 60 ADI admitted for detoxification at a voluntary sector alcohol detoxification unit, were NHP sleep sub-scores, number of cigarettes, social class and Irish ethnicity. Prescription of analgesia was also associated with relapse. Every 10 points scored on the NHP sleep sub scale increased the chances of relapse by an odds ratio of 1.4. This finding led to further work exploring the relationship between sleep and outcome (described shortly). For every ten cigarettes smoked there was an increased likelihood of relapse of 2.2. Members of social classes IV/V (lower) were 12.3 times as likely to relapse as individuals from social classes I/II (higher). Irish individuals (n=13) were 10.5 times more "at risk" of 3 month relapse than other sampled ethnic groups. Finally being prescribed analgesia in the 12 months prior to baseline assessment put these individuals at 4.5 times of greater risk of 3 months relapse. Interestingly the NHP pain sub-score was not associated with relapse but further insight into the relationship between pain and outcome is provided in Foster et al (1999 b). This paper contained an analysis of the changes in scores in a symptom checklist originally designed for cancer patients (RSCL) in the aforementioned sample. The only variable that showed significant changes in consequence of relapse and non-relapse was sore muscles. Two baseline symptoms of physical pain; sore muscles and sore eyes were both associated with SADQ and APQ-Core scores.

The validity of self-reported sobriety and collateral reports has been tested in 171 former individuals at a 28-day inpatient programme in Richmond Virginia (Wolber et al 1990). There was a ninety-two percent agreement, and acceptable convergent validity was shown in the areas of "quality of sobriety", familial, occupational, social and emotional adjustment. Yersin et al (1999) found that the SF-36 was a more useful indicator of the effects of a change in drinking status than the ASI. Their sample consisted of 46 ADI recruited from a Swiss alcohol specialist unit who were followed up at 6 months. In the abstinent patients 7 (88%) dimensions of the SF-36 produced a significant improvement compared with 2 (29%) in the ASI. The results were not so conclusive in the case of drinkers, only 3 (38%) SF-36 dimensions showed significant changes compared to only the alcohol use dimension of the ASI. Some caution must be noted regarding these findings, the sample size is small and most of the respondents were of a high socio-economic status.

There have been two naturalistic studies that have used QoL measures as part of battery of outcomes to test the efficacy of treatments of differing lengths (Trent 1998; Foster et al (2000c). Trent (1998) followed-up a sample of 2,823 ADI from the US navy's alcohol treatment programme for 12 months. One group remained for four weeks and another six weeks. The QoL measure used was the Quality of Life Enjoyment and Satisfaction Questionnaire (Q-LES-Q) (Endicott et al 1993). The author concluded that the programme could be standardised to four weeks without an adverse impact upon outcome. The second paper (Foster et al (2000c) compared QoL outcomes as measured by the RSCL, LSS, and NHP and the BDI and GHQ-12 (Goldberg 1972) as measures of affective disturbance in two groups both consisting of 32 ADI. The first were admitted to a voluntary sector alcohol detoxification unit for a detoxification lasting up to seven days. The second group could remain for a further 21 days. No demographic variables separated the two groups, and the only significant differentiating variable following a logistic regression was recreational cannabis use (this was associated with the greater likelihood of a longer stay). The participants were followed up at 3 months, there was not a significant difference between the changes in scores of the two groups, but the outcomes in the 7- day only group were positive whereas all the outcomes for the other group were negative.

There is now a body of work concerning the efficacy of screening and brief interventions in harmful and hazardous drinkers. One recently published study (Crawford et al 2004) applied the EQ-5D in a clinical trial conducted in an accident and emergency setting. Two groups of participants (n=599) were compared, those who received an information leaflet only versus those given an information leaflet and an appointment with an alcohol worker. Follow-up data was collected at 6 and 12 months. The group referred to the alcohol worker had superior outcomes at both follow-up time points. There were no quality of life differences between the two comparison groups at any time point. This may relate to the design of the EQ-5D but it should be noted that this was not a group of dependent drinkers. Many would not have encountered sufficient problems from their drinking to perceive it as affecting their quality of life.

Brief interventions are thought to be particularly applicable to a primary care setting. Work conducted in Boston US (Samet et al 2003) applied quality of life measures (the physical and mental component summaries of the SF-36) to a group of ADI (n=199) who participated in a randomised controlled trial. The intervention was part of the HELP study, and took the form of linkage to a primary care clinic during detoxification (PCC) versus controls. PCC resulted in a significant difference in primary care linkage at 12 months, but the changes in QoL scores were not significant. Similar work investigating the impact of brief interventions from Pittsburgh (Conigliaro et al 2000) found that unemployment rather than race was associated with the “clinical indicators of alcohol problems” and poorer QoL scores.

In summary, there is an improvement in QoL in consequence of abstinence though its impact varies across different sociodemographic and treatment groups. This improvement is non-linear and tends to tail-off over time. There is also an improvement that results from controlled drinking though this is not as great as abstinence and most samples of controlled drinkers are small. Attendance at AA is linked to an improvement in outcomes but there is no evidence as yet that greater attendance yields superior outcomes. Various aspects of QoL and generic QoL measures have been shown to predict outcome. Finally QoL measures have been used to assessed the efficacy of longer treatments v shorter treatments. The two papers in question have confirmed the findings of Miller and Hester (1986) who concluded that longer or more intensive programmes failed to produce any significant benefits.

Quality of Life and Pharmacological Treatments for Alcohol Dependence/Abuse

There is now an emerging body of evidence relating to quality of life (QoL) and various pharmacological treatments for alcoholism. The evidence for the efficacy in clinical trials of two opioid antagonists – Naltrexone and Nalmefene has been subject to systematic review and published in the Cochrane database (Srisurapanont and Jarusuraisin 2005). The authors reviewed the findings of 29 randomised controlled trials and concluded that the evidence for the efficacy of Naltrexone was questionable beyond 12 weeks and that Nalmefene should not been used in the alcohol-related treatments. Furthermore they reported that there was minimal evidence to date relating to patient satisfaction, HrQoL, costs benefits or mortality. An Australian study has compared the impact of a 12 week cognitive behaviour therapy programme (CBT) only versus CBT + naltrexone in consecutively recruited ADI (Feeney et al 2004). There were 43 participants in each group but 73 participants (54%) refused to take any medication. The QoL measure used was the SF-36 and mood was assessed using the GHQ-28. On completion of the programme there were significant improvements in seven SF-36 sub-scores and GHQ-28 total scores. The SF-36 sub-score that did not show a significant improvement was vitality. Naltrexone did not confer any additional benefit.

The first study to consider Disulfiram that included the term QoL as a key word was Wilson et al (1984). One hundred and twenty "alcoholic volunteers" received either a 800mg, 1200 mg or 1600 mg Disulfiram implant. All groups had increased sobriety rates and enhanced QoL at two-year follow up though no dose response was found.

Acamprosate has a chemical structure similar to amino neurotransmitters such as gamma-amino butyric acid (GABA) and glutamate. It is thought to reduce craving for alcohol by stabilising the imbalance of these neurotransmitters. There is now a large body of work from clinical trials using Acamprosate that have applied QoL measures, most of these are multi-centred and have been conducted by the New European Treatment Study Group (ETSG). Morgan et al (2004) provides the most comprehensive account of this clinical trial and once more the QoL measure used was the SF-36. The ETSG recruited individuals from five European countries and tracked three and six-month outcomes of those treated with Acamprosate and psychosocial support. (There was no control group). Baseline data was collected from 1216 individuals with a mean age of 43, more than three-quarters of the sample were males and SF-36 scores were well below equivalent general population norms. (i.e. poorer) The sub-scores where this was most marked were physical and emotional role limitations and social functioning. In addition predictors of baseline SF-36 total scores were assessed using a linear regression analyses. The most important predictors were Severity of Alcohol Dependence scores, employment status, psychiatric history, quantity and frequency of alcohol consumption, attendance at Alcoholics Anonymous, global health status, age, gender and level of education. Three months data was collected from 686 (56%) participants,- the equivalent follow-up six month follow-up rate was 497 (48%). Significant improvements were observed in all SF-36 sub-scores at three months. The changes between three and six months were minimal. Predictors of QoL after treatment completion were "the SF-36 baseline profile", followed by abstinence duration. This study confirms the link between reducing alcohol consumption/achieving abstinence and improved QoL, though it should be noted that the drop-out rates in this study were high and any data beyond baseline is likely to be skewed towards producing positive outcomes. Ansoms et al (2000) and Fuchs and Riebenfeld (2002) provide data from the from the Belgium /Luxembourg and Swiss arm of the ETSG. In each case all SF-36 sub-scores improved over the six months follow-up period.

A French study (Acamprosate et Repercussions Economiques et Sociales- ARES) (Kiritze-Topor et al 2004) compared 422 DSM-IV participants recruited from primary care centres comparing the twelve month outcomes of those participants randomised to the Acamprosate group (n=348, 82%) with a control group The primary outcome measure was the number of Alcohol related problems as measured by the Alcohol-Related Problems Questionnaire (ARPQ) (Chick et al 1988; Chick et al 1991). QoL was measured by the SF-36. The final analysis used was "intention to treat". At 12 months the Acamproaste group had fewer alcohol problems and higher SF-36 scores than controls.

Work in the United States (Johnson et al 2004) has found that Toprimate a fructopyranose derivative improved drinking and quality of life outcomes following a 12 week clinical trial. Quality of life was assessed by the Quality of Life Enjoyment and Satisfaction Scale (Q-LES-Q) (Endicott et al 1993).

A review article published in the early 1990s (George 1994) suggested that integrating serotonin reuptake inhibitors (SSRI) into a treatment package in alcohol-related disorders would result in improved outcomes and an enhanced quality of life.

The majority of work in this field has involved testing Acamprosate and the work indicates that as an adjunct to other treatments it can produce positive QoL outcomes. However the main study in the field (ETSG) has a number of important limitations that mean it may only be suited for certain ADI population sub-groups. There was no control group and the drop out rate was high. Thus those with less positive outcomes were not assessed. Other pharmacological treatments which have produced positive QoL outcomes albeit in rather piecemeal trials have been SSRI, Toprimate, Disulfiram and Naltrexone. Three Cochrane database reviews have now been conducted concerning the efficacy of Naltrexone and these have questioned efficacy beyond 12 weeks. The same reviews concluded that Nalmefene should not be used in alcohol related treatments.

Quality of Life and the Social Environment of Alcohol Dependent Individuals

This is an area where the overlap between the other parts of this review is particularly marked. To some extent whether these articles appear here or elsewhere is arbitrary. Claus et al (1999) examined the substance abuse recovery processes of 7,092 individuals and compared first and previous treatment subjects. They entered the following into a discriminant function analysis, age, gender, ethnicity, marital status, years of schooling, and a number of instruments including the ASI, Readiness to Change Questionnaire (Heather et al 1993), psychological status and a 15 item QoL measure. This analysis accounted for only 6.5% of the variance, thus the authors concluded that change occurred through multiple unmeasured processes. However they drew two other conclusions, firstly alcohol and drug problems were not the best predictors of returning to treatment/assessment, those individuals with a decreasing QoL status and a readiness to change were most likely to re-initiate treatment contact. Secondly "contemplators" (Prochaska and DiClemente 1986) were less satisfied with their QoL than others in different "Stages of Change" including "precontemplators". The explanation provided for this finding was that pre-contemplators were aware of fewer problems.

In the late 1980's two Australian writers (Grichting and Barber 1989) found that quality of family life and past and current parental drinking were related to alcohol and drug consumption. Humphreys et al (1997) recruited and followed-up 395 previously untreated alcoholics at three and eight years. There was a similar number of men and women. Greater attendance at AA predicted 3 year remission, lower depression scores and higher quality relationships with friends, spouse/partner predicted a positive 8 year outcome. A conceptual model of the social environment of ADI has been formulated (Beattie et al 1993). It has four components; alcohol-relevant affiliative support, general affiliative support, alcohol relevant support in the workplace and general support in the workplace. This was tested on outpatient alcoholic clients (n=148) from a private non-psychiatric hospital who were followed up at 18 months. Social support had a stronger relationship to outcome than alcohol consumption and the authors felt that environmental variables were an important determinant in outcomes for this treatment group. More recently (Beattie 2001) conducted a meta-analysis of the link between social relationships and drinking outcomes. The author concluded that the effect was "variable, inconsistent and weak."

A group of Swedish researchers have published five papers in the series "Abuse of alcohol - Disability pension – Quality of life", two of these are noteworthy in this context (Hornquist and Elton 1983; Hornquist et al 1983). The sample in both papers consisted of 56 alcohol abusers. Those abusers granted pensions reported positive changes in alcohol consumption, psychiatric status, self-rated well-being, and nutritional status. For this grouping their social situation and daily activities remained constant (Hornquist and Elton 1983). The second paper from the study found that the following variables were related to overall deterioration on being granted the pension, an abrupt change after a previously active life, longer education, middle age, passivity, social confinement and psychiatric status. In contrast self-related well being, remaining intellectual resources and lower alcohol consumption were associated with a good outcome (Hornquist et al 1993).

The same researchers have looked at the correlates to loneliness in their samples, once more there are two papers which have resulted from their endeavours (Hornquist and Akerlind 1987; Akerlind et al 1987). In the former 95 alcohol abusers were tested over a two-year period. The lonely abuser was marked as being discontented, indolent and passive. The writers concluded that the link between "loneliness and lack of self-esteem was extraordinarily marked." Intellectual testing was not associated with loneliness (Hornquist and Akerlind 1987). Finally Akerlind et al (1987) examining the same individuals found that the external social situation as assessed by amounts of contacts or social network was not linked to the perception of loneliness. This was more closely associated with the quality of existing relationships rather than quantity.

QUALITY OF LIFE OF ALCOHOL DEPENDENT WOMEN

The earliest paper found in the search concerning this subject was French (Gillet et al 1991). These researchers studied one hundred and seventy eight women (mean age 41) over a period ranging from one and a half to six years, over sixty percent were married, one-third working and sixty per cent had been dependent upon alcohol for less than 5 years. Fifteen per cent of the sample was lost to follow up, and a further twelve percent of the sample died. The most frequent causes of death were suicide and complications arising from alcoholism. Over twenty percent of the sample was abstinent throughout and an improvement was reported in forty-five percent of the sample. "Absence of marital life" and a greater baseline alcohol intake were related to poor outcome.

A German study (Rudolf and Priebe 1999) has examined QoL in 70 alcohol dependent women at six-month follow-up. The structure of QoL varied according to age, job situation, finances, age of admission and perception of alcohol dependence and subjective QoL predicted relapse. A later paper using the same data set (Rudolf and Priebe 2002) confirmed the link between depressive symptoms and poor quality of life scores using baseline data only. Those areas of quality of life where the relationship was most marked were "family situation", "life as a whole", "the need for greater support" and more negative consequences of alcoholism. However the small sample size means these findings must be treated with caution. Women are more likely to present to alcohol services with affective disturbances (Gomberg 1993), Foster et al (2000a) provides further support for this. We recruited a further 22 women than the samples described in Foster et al (1998a) so that there were an equal number of men and women (42 each). Following a logistic regression of all baseline variables there were four variables which significantly differentiated the two groups. Two of these were indicators of affective disturbance: GHQ-12 scores, (Goldberg 1972) and the prescription of antidepressants during the previous twelve months. Furthermore women were more likely to be in a higher social class and drink less alcohol in a typical week at baseline assessment. Three-month outcomes were also tracked, gender did not contribute significantly to any outcomes including relapse rates, and QoL. The only significant total sample change was a reduction in the amount of alcohol consumed in a typical week. The reduction in alcohol consumption was significantly related to changes in the following QoL measures, NHP emotional reaction sub-scores, LSS and BDI scores.

An American study (Spalding and Metz 1997) using the same number of AA attending women and men (n=44 in each group) who had a mean length of sobriety of 64 months examined the impact of spirituality in the alcoholism recovery process. QoL was measured using the Satisfaction with Life Scale. The constructs measured were- satisfaction with life, depression, self-esteem and sense of symbolic self. Women had a higher QoL and were more likely to use "collaborative coping." Poorer QoL scores was associated with women with lower perceived social support. In all participants a longer period of sobriety was related to higher QoL scores, providing more support for AA in alcoholism treatment in certain groups.

Whilst Gillet et al (1991) found a relationship between suicide and alcoholism, a Finish group have found an association between alcohol and homicide (Eronen 1995). One hundred and twenty-seven homicide offenders were examined over a 13-year period. This group had 10-fold higher odds ratio than the female general population for having schizophrenia and personality disorder. There were "substantially higher odds ratios" for alcohol abuse/dependence and antisocial disorder.

A study conducted in Tubingen (Germany) (n=22) has looked at the profile of homeless women (Torchalla et al 2004). Most had become homeless as a result of domestic violence and were reluctant to seek help from treatment services. There was a high prevalence of psychiatric disorders (71%) and the leading disorder was substance abuse/dependence (43%). The frequency of anxiety disorders and schizophrenia were 35% and 12% respectively. Multiple disorders were present in thirty five percent of the sample.

In summary the affective disturbance, in particular anxiety and depression is marked in alcohol dependent women and this has a major impact upon their QoL.

Quality of Life and Homelessness

The majority of studies in this area to date have been conducted in the United States. Braucht et al (1995) followed-up 323 homeless individuals most of whom were alcoholics and found that QoL improved with abstinence. Most of this improvement occurred within the first six months, thereafter it slowed down. The two other papers related to "older homeless persons". One of these (Elias and Inui 1993) employed a qualitative methodology. These authors found that the experience of shelter in their group (n=35) was linked to their self-perception and reduction in alcohol consumption. Shelter provided safety, support, community and an opportunity to regain sobriety. Finally Cohen et al (1993) examined (n=130) individuals in a program for elder homeless persons and followed them up at three years. Forty-one had been experienced psychotic symptoms or a psychiatric inpatient admission at baseline. The remainder (n=89) had not experienced any psychotic symptoms or psychiatric admissions at baseline assessment. Those individuals who were not mentally ill had significantly better outcomes; including more service contacts, enhanced well-being and higher rates of sobriety.

In addition to the above studies a Canadian review from the Institute of Health Promotion Research, Vancouver has confirmed the link between alcoholism, poor quality of life and social exclusion in this group and provided recommendations for policy makers and future research. (Frankish et al 2005)

The Role of Sleep in the Quality of Life of Alcohol Dependent Individuals

An American study of (n=8,870) individuals from the Vietnam Era Twin Registry assessed their self-reported sleep during the previous month by means of a postal questionnaire (Fabitsitz et al 1997). There was a high degree of alcohol consumption and the following sleep problems were present in at least 48% of the sample, waking often, waking tired/worn out, trouble falling asleep and awakening early. Alcohol consumption was associated with a high risk of sleep problems and the authors concluded that there were strong associations between sleep disturbance, alcohol consumption and diminished QoL.

The Nottingham Profile (NHP) sleep sub-scale has been used in a number of studies by the present author and his colleagues. In Foster et al (1998b) it was found to be the most significant predictor of relapse at three-months in a sample (n=60) of socially deprived alcohol-dependent individuals from inner city London. A further paper (Foster and Peters 1999c) describes another analysis where the effects of the five NHP individual sleep variables were tested in the same sample. Sleep latency as measured by the variable "It takes me a long time to get to sleep" was a significant predictor of relapse and the perception of sleeping badly "I sleep badly at night" was associated with a poor 12-week outcome. The correlations between the NHP sleep score and depression as measured by the BDI were also investigated and a significant relationship was found. In contrast there was not a significant association between the NHP sleep sub-score and severity of alcohol dependence SADQ and APQ-Core scores.

The NHP sleep sub-score has also been tested in a group of currently drinking moderately dependent (Potamianos et al 1984) outpatients from inner-city London (n=52) (Foster et al 2002). Over half of the individuals reported sleep disturbance in the following three NHP sleep individual variables: sleep latency; (n=29, 56%); sleeping poorly; (n=36, 69%) and early morning awakening, (39,75%). In addition to the five NHP sleep variables the HADS (Zigmond and Snaith 1983) and EQ-5D were applied. The participants were followed-up at three months. The follow-up rate was 90%. At baseline the sleep parameters were related to HADS but not EQ-5D scores. By three months ten (21%) had returned to sensible drinking levels (Royal College of Psychiatrists 1986) but there was no improvement in HADS, EQ-5D or NHP sleep scores.

Work from the same group has considered quality of life and self-reported sleep as measured by the EQ-5D and Pittsburgh Sleep Quality Index (PSQI) (Buysee et al 1989) in a group of ADI resident in a unit using the Minnesota treatment model (Cohn et al 2003). Affective status was also assessed by the HADS. Each individual had been alcohol free for at least 10 days prior to assessment. Measurements were taken from the participants (n=57) at baseline and 12 weeks, just prior to completion of the programme. Sleep disturbances are known to continue long after drinking has stopped (Vitiello 1997) thus it was not surprising that over ninety per cent of the sample suffering from impaired sleep at baseline. Forty percent of the sample provided 12-week data. HADS Depression and EQ-5D scores had improved significantly but HADS Anxiety and PSQI scores had not.

More recently there has been some interest in treatment for chronic insomnia. A review has tentatively suggested that there is some evidence for the effectiveness of cognitive behavioural therapy in alcoholism. (Smith et al 2005)

To summarise these studies have emphasised the importance of self-reported sleep disturbance as an indicator of clinical outcomes, largely because sleep disturbances continue long after drinking has stopped. The link between sleep disturbance and anxiety/depression in the group is striking.

CONCLUSION

This review has shown that QoL is not a discrete concept. Issues such as social environment, psychiatric and physical comorbidity, polydrug use, sleep, level of dependency/abuse and consumption are intrinsically linked to the QoL of ADI. Present research points to these phenomena having a greater impact on QoL scores rather than vice versa. Generally the QoL of ADI is poor and worsens as a result of continued drinking, conversely an improvement results from abstinence or controlled drinking. Quality of life measurements have been used as part of programme evaluation and the likelihood is that this will become a growing trend as the limitations of using "hard endpoints" become apparent.

Part Two: Pilot Work

Chapter 3

PILOT STUDY

Before the main study two pieces of pilot work took place. The first of these was a small project designed to establish the best mode of follow-up. The second was a larger project that formed the basis of the current project. This has been published in two papers (Foster et al 1998a; Foster et al 1998b).

STUDY A

Five participants were given follow-up clinics appointments to see the author for a research interview. Despite being offered travel expenses only one attended for their visit. Therefore the decision was taken that unless the participant had any objections follow-up visits would take place at home. This method was applied in Study B and the study described in the current monograph.

STUDY B

Brief Description of Research Participants and Methods Used

Sixty participants were studied (39 males, 21 females). Baseline data was collected and then they were followed up at three months. The following questionnaires were administered (except where otherwise stated these will be described more fully in the chapter four)

Baseline Only

Alcohol Problems Questionnaire (APQ) (Drummond 1990)
Severity Alcohol Dependence Questionnaire (SADQ) (Stockwell et al 1979)

Baseline and Follow-Up

Beck Depression Inventory (BDI) (Beck et al 1961)
Life Situation Survey (LSS) (Chubon 1987)
Short-Form General Health Questionnaire (GHQ-12) (Goldberg 1972)
Nottingham Health Profile (NHP) (Hunt et al 1980)

Rotterdam Symptoms Checklist (RSCL) (deHaes et al 1990)

RESULTS

Fifty-eight (97%) participants were successfully followed-up and 32 (62%) participants had relapsed to heavy drinking at 12–week follow-up (Chapter four provides a definition of the relapse criterion used).

a) Alcohol dependence was associated with a poor QoL. In most measures 80% or more of the individuals scored above their equivalent general population norms.
b) There were significant changes in baseline and 12-week scores resulting from relapsing/non-relapsing in the following variables; LSS, BDI, RSCL physical and psychological symptom scores and NHP energy sub-score.
c) There was no association between any of the study measures and time taken to relapse. The major predictors of relapse were (in order of increasing statistical significance) Irish nationality, lower social class, greater number of cigarettes smoked and disturbed sleep.
d) The study described in the rest of the monograph which is an extension of Study B tests whether
    i) these findings are generalisable to other settings and
    ii) applicable to a larger sociodemographically diverse sample followed-up over a longer period.

MODIFICATIONS TO THE PROTOCOL USED IN STUDY B

The main modifications were an extension of the follow-up period to twelve months incorporating assessment at three, six and twelve months. In addition the sample was increased to 240 and recruited from six different treatment centres in total. (These will be described in chapter four). There were also changes in the measurements. Instead of the two measures of disturbance in mood used in Study B: (the BDI and GHQ-12); the GHQ-28 was substituted. The GHQ-28 was specifically designed for research purposes and had four sub-scales that incorporated domains of interest to the research team; somatic disturbance, anxiety and insomnia, social dysfunction and severe depression. There were two other additional changes to the protocol used in Study B. Firstly to add the "gold standard" of QoL measurement (Bowling 1995) ; the Short-Form-36 (SF-36) (Ware et al 1993) to the battery of questionnaires. Secondly the addition of a measure of area-based measure of social deprivation, this was the Jarman Index (Jarman 1983).

Part Three: Participants and Methods

Chapter 4

DESCRIPTION OF THE STUDY CENTRES

The total participant sample consisted of 240 (178, 74% males; 62, 26% females) DSM IV (American Psychiatric Association 1994) alcohol dependent individuals (ADI) aged 18-65 recruited from six different treatment centres. There was only one exclusion criterion. This was being unable to give informed consent due to cognitive deficits; the author assessed this. Each treatment centre and will now be briefly described in turn. Foster (2004b) describes the literature of studies that have attempted to evaluate treatment effectiveness in each of these treatment modalities.

VOLUNTARY SECTOR ALCOHOL DETOXIFICATION UNIT (VOL SEC)

This was the centre where the Study B (described in chapter three) took place. Forty (22, 55% males, 18, 45% females) were consecutively recruited who had not been included in the Foster et al (1998a) and Foster (1998b) studies. Each individual had been drinking heavily prior to admission. Most were self-referrals and admitted because they fulfilled the criteria for residential detoxification; either a lack of social support, a history of previous withdrawal seizures or several attempts at community detoxification. Baseline assessment took place 4-5 days after admission.

The philosophy of the unit was to offer a service to individuals who in the past have found it particularly difficult to access statutory services such as women, homosexuals, and those individuals from the ethnic minorities, though in practice the majority of the service users were single white men. The treatment regime offered is comprehensively described in Foster et al (2000c). After-care was provided by the local community alcohol services or some individuals moved on to further residential rehabilitation.

MEDICAL WARDS (MED WARD)

Forty (36, 90% males, 4, 10% females) individuals were randomly recruited from four medical wards. There was no fixed treatment or aftercare protocol. Each individual was admitted after assessment in an accident and emergency department to one of three medical teams. The mode of recruitment was as follows. The author first telephoned the ward to ascertain whether any "alcoholics" were admitted. Thus the eligibility criterion in this instance was an individual who was identified as being an alcoholic by general medical or nursing staff. This centre was chosen because it represented a non-specialist treatment modality where ADI are commonly treated whilst being acutely physically unwell. Treatment consisted of whatever was provided by the medical or nursing teams as part of their routine care (no standardised psychiatric after-care). ADI were discharged back into the community

Private Sector (Priv Sec)

Forty participants (26, 65% males, 14, 35% females) were recruited consecutively from an inpatient unit (Inpatients) (n= 30, 75%) situated on the outskirts of London and an outpatient unit (Outpatients) based in Central London (n=10, 25%). These centres form part of a group of alcohol and drug dependency clinics. The private sector was chosen for two reasons; firstly to date external evaluation of private sector treatments is rare. Secondly the previously described study centres had both been largely socially deprived individuals, using the private sector provided the opportunity of examine the treatment of less deprived-ADI.

The regime offered to inpatients was a high dosage tapered detoxification with the aim of a quick discharge, usually 4-5 days. Outpatients were prescribed a 7-10 day tapering dose of diazepam. Many inpatients were seen for their baseline assessment on the day of discharge. Inpatients were seen by a qualified nurse daily and during the first two days of the detoxification they were checked every 30 minutes. Whilst on the unit there was an optional occupational therapy programme. Individuals were discharged back into the community. There was a strong recommendation that each individual was prescribed Disulfiram/Antabuse for at least the first three months after discharge. The rationale is that this allows the individual to remain in the presence of alcohol-cues without the alcohol-coping response as an option-thus learning and self-efficacy are promoted (Brewer 1993).

National Health Service Alcohol Specialist Ward (Alc Ward)

This was a sample of forty (29,73% male, 11,27% female) consecutive individuals recruited from inner and outer London. Each individual was admitted for 2-6 weeks during which they would have a medication-assisted detoxification. This was tapered according to the judgement of the medical and nursing teams, with reference to a score on the Clinical Withdrawal Assessment for Alcohol scale (CIWA) (Sullivan et al 1989). The reason for inclusion was that it represented a specialist evidence-based treatment modality designed for ADI. The treatment regime is described in Martinez Raga et al (2002). After-care was either provided by the local community alcohol services, a four week day programme (described later in this chapter under the heading Community Alcohol Services) or some individuals moved on to further residential rehabilitation.

Minnesota Project (Minn Proj)

This was a residential Minnesota project run by the voluntary sector and based in inner-city London. The centre was chosen because the Minnesota method is used in many rehabilitation centres in both the United Kingdom and in particular the United States. Despite this there have been very few attempts to evaluate their treatment efficacy or cost effectiveness, and as such it was chosen for the study. Forty individuals (32, 80% male, 8, 20% female) were selected on a convenience basis in this sample. All but three resided in a London Borough, the others were from rural areas of England.

Before admission residents were expected to be at least four days alcohol free. The programme was up to thirteen weeks in length. All the counselling staff were themselves either former opiate or alcohol dependent individuals who had been both drug and alcohol free for over two years. The Minnesota method of alcohol and drug treatment is based upon the first four steps of Alcoholics Anonymous; thus abstinence was a pre-requisite of participation. Attendance in outside AA/NA meetings was encouraged. For a description of the philosophy and practice of Minnesota Programmes see Cook (1988). There was strong recommendation that thirteen weeks was an insufficient period for individuals to tackle their alcohol problem and the preferred mode of after-care was referral to another rehabilitation unit (second stage).

Community Alcohol Services (Comm Alc)

This study centre was chosen as it represented a treatment modality where was the likely typical patient profile was a less severely alcohol dependent individual. Forty (n=33, 83%) male and (n=7,17%) females) individuals selected on a convenience basis who attended a day programme run by a National Health Service community alcohol services based in outer London. All individuals were at least seven days alcohol-free at commencement of the day-programme. The day programme lasted for four weeks and each session was run by either a qualified psychiatric nurse, psychiatrist, or invited outside speakers. Sessions that comprised the day programme included relapse prevention, avoidance of high-risk situations, relaxation, optional alcohol anonymous meetings and planning for the weekend/how we coped over the weekend groups. During the group programme there were no concurrent individual counselling sessions. At the end of the programme six individual sessions of counselling were offered based on the principles of brief motivational interviewing as formulated by Miller (1983) and operationalised in Rollnick et al (1992). They were discharged as out-patients under the supervision of a consultant psychiatrist.

Chapter 5

STUDY MEASURES USED

BASELINE ONLY

Alcohol Problems Questionnaire (APQ)

This is a scale designed in order to "develop a comprehensive questionnaire to measure alcohol-related problems, and so to explore the relationship between problems and dependence" (Drummond 1990). A subsequent paper (Williams and Drummond 1994) describes additional validation studies. There are 44 questions in total, but only the first 23 were completed. The remaining questions concerned employment, marriage, and children. They were not completed, as they were not applicable to the majority of the sample. The core of this questionnaire (which was used as it was relevant for most individuals) concerns alcohol related problems in the following areas; friends, finances, police, and physical or psychological difficulties, which have taken place in the past six months. This is an easy form to complete with each question being answered yes or no. Every positive response is assigned a score of 1 and the range of possible scores is 0-23. In a sample of 103 inpatient and outpatient male and female problem drinkers (Drummond 1990) the mean APQ score was 11.16 (SD=4.5).

Severity of Alcohol Dependence Questionnaire. (SADQ)

The Severity of Alcohol Dependence Questionnaire was devised by Stockwell et al (1979) and based upon the elements of the alcohol dependence syndrome as postulated by Edwards and Gross (1976). Before administration an individual is asked to visualise a period of recent heavy drinking within the last six months. There are 20 items divided into the following sections; physical symptoms of alcohol withdrawal, affective symptoms of withdrawal, craving and relief drinking, typical daily alcohol consumption and reinstatement of symptoms after heavy drinking following a period of abstinence.

Each item has four possible responses "never or almost never", "sometimes", "often" and "always or nearly always", scored 0,1,2,3 respectively. The maximum potential score is 60. In a review article (Stockwell et al 1983) it was described as "a widely used, reliable and valid instrument to measure alcohol dependence". The same paper outlined scores of > 30 as equating to severe dependence. Potamianos et al (1984) further subdivided the scores as follows

0-15	Mild Dependence
15-30	Moderate Dependence.

BASELINE AND FOLLOW-UP QUESTIONNAIRES

Life Situation Survey (LSS)

This scale measures several quality of life indicators from the perception of the interviewee thought to be applicable and relevant to those with chronic illnesses. There are 20 items scored on a Likert-type rating scale where individuals are asked to "Rank their opinions on a continuum of agreement and disagreement" (Bowling 1991). These include work, leisure, financial situation, environment, self-esteem, security, public support, autonomy, and social support amongst others. Each item has scores ranging from 1-7; therefore the range is 20-140. Scores in excess of 100 reflect a good quality of life and those less than 90 are associated with a poor quality of life. Guidance for completion of the LSS is contained in Chubon (1995). A further paper (Chubon 1987) gives an account of its development.

General Health Questionnaire (GHQ 28)

The General Health Questionnaire is a self-administered questionnaire, which measures changes in psychiatric status over the past few weeks; it is not a diagnostic instrument and was developed by Goldberg (1972). A handbook (Goldberg and Williams 1988) explains its design development and operation. There are five forms of the questionnaire with 60, 30, 28, 20 and 12 questions respectively. The 28-item version was chosen for this study because it is specifically designed for research purposes and has four validated sub-scales, somatic symptoms, anxiety and insomnia, social dysfunction and severe depression (Goldberg and Hillier 1979). The same paper recommends a cut-off point for "psychiatric caseness" of GHQ-28 scores > 4.5 (range of scores 0-28).

Each item has four possible responses to each question which can be coded according to a Likert-rating 0-1-2-3 or alternatively 0-0-1-1. Goldberg and Hillier (1979) could see little advantage in the Likert rating as the correlation between the two methods is 0.92-0.94 (Banks 1983), therefore the 0-0-1-1 method was adopted for this study. The questionnaire has been described as "Offering a leading example of how a health measurement should be developed, thus resulting in a high degree of validity markedly higher than rival methods" (McDowell and Newell 1987).

Rotterdam Symptoms Checklist (RSCL)

This questionnaire was designed by deHaes et al (1990) as a quality of life (QoL) measurement in which the physical and psychological symptoms of cancer are assessed. Many of the symptoms listed are also present during alcohol detoxification; such as lack of appetite, worrying, difficulty sleeping, diarrhoea, shivering tingling in the hands and feet and dry mouth. There has been only one paper that has used these indices with ADI written by the present author (Foster et al 1999b).

Raw scoring is on a Likert scale; there is one neutral response and three others increasing in severity- each item is scored 1-4. There are 30 questions, so the possible range of scores is 30-120. However for normative/other treatment comparisons each sub-scale is converted into a percentage score. de Haes et al (1996) provides the details for this transformation and the original validation studies which produced normative data for the RSCL. The equation for the transformation is as follows;

raw scale score-minimum raw score/maximum-minimum score x100.

The transformed scores for the physical and psychological sub-scales are used throughout this monograph. A general population study conducted in Rotterdam (n=201) produced a mean psychological symptom score of 9.9 (SD=9.0) and the equivalent statistics for physical symptoms were 17.0, 18.1 (Mean, SD).

Nottingham Health Profile (NHP)

The Nottingham Health Profile is a self-administered questionnaire that takes about 10 minutes to complete. It was designed to measure "Perceived health problems and the extent to which such problems affect daily activities." (Hunt et al 1994) An account of its development is contained in Hunt et al (1980), and the latest published handbook is Hunt et al (1994). The profile was originally divided into two parts, the second element assesses the demand for health care and its use is no longer recommended.

Part One contains 38 items divided into six subsections. The figure in brackets denotes the number of questions in each sub group:- physical mobility (8), pain (8), sleep (5), social isolation (5), emotional reactions (9), and energy level (3). Each of these statements is weighted. The weights were calculated from the results of a community sample (n=1200) of approximately equal numbers of men and women, aged 18-74 representative of patient and non-patient populations. The sample was asked to assess the relative seriousness of each item in comparison to others within the same group (McKenna et al 1981). An individual section can be scored 0-100 (higher scores indicate greater health problems), giving a possible total score for the profile of 600.

The main advantage of the Nottingham Health Profile is its high reliability and validity (Hunt et al 1994). As a result of the validation studies a great deal of normative demographic data is available. One study of 2173 male and female general practice patients in the Nottingham area (Hunt et al 1985) produced a set of normative age scores. The figures quoted below are the age norms for the 40-44 age group, the range containing the mean age of the study sample.

Energy	11.3
Pain	5.8
Emotional Reactions	10.2
Sleep	12.4
Social Isolation	4.3
Physical Mobility	3.3

This was chosen as our main generic subjective QoL measure for Study B (see chapter three) (Foster et al 1998a; Foster et al 1998b). However those studies revealed there to be a fundamental deficiency when applying this indices to alcohol dependent subjects.

Why Two Measures of HrQoL Were Used

The NHP produced a high number of zero scores, which makes statistical comparison in longitudinal studies difficult. Therefore the SF-36 was chosen as the main generic subjective QoL indicator for the present study. Unfortunately the SF-36 does not have a Sleep sub-scale. In Study B (see chapter three) this was the most significant predictor of relapse and the research team wished to ascertain whether this result was replicated to across a number of other settings, stable over a longer period and repeated in a larger sample. A paper comparing the NHP with the SF-36 in a United Kingdom sample (Brazier et al 1992) found that overall the relationship between their equivalent indices was strong. There was however one exception to this the SF-36 Social functioning and NHP Social isolation sub-scale did not have acceptable correlations. This study is particularly concerned with how these two sub-scales operate across different centres, in a larger study sample and over a longer follow-up period, thus both measures are of interest.

Short-Form Thirty Six (SF-36)

The SF-36 is “rapidly becoming the generic health status measurement of choice” (Bowling 1995) and is now being increasingly used worldwide. There is a free handbook, which gives an account of its development (largely in the United States) and scoring system (Ware et al 1993). There are eight main sub-scales and one additional scale; reported health transition. The eight main sub-scales are as follows with the number of individual items being shown in brackets; Physical functioning (10), Social functioning (2), Physical role limitations (4), Emotional role limitations (3), Mental health (5), Energy/vitality (4), Pain (2), General health perceptions (5) and Reported health transition (1).

Details of the raw scoring system is contained in Ware et al (1993), for normative comparisons each sub-scale is transformed into a percentage score, the aforementioned handbook provides the equation for this transformation it is as follows;

raw score-lowest possible raw score/highest possible raw score x100.

The percentage i.e. transformed score is reported throughout in this monograph. Higher scores denote a better QoL and the range of transformed scores is 0-100. Jenkinson et al

(1993) provides normative United Kingdom data. This study consisted of 9332 subjects recruited through the computerised registers of the family health services authorities (community general medical practice). The response rate was 72%. Data was provided for five age sub-samples; Table 5.1 presents means and standard deviations of the normative sample in the age range 35-54 (n=2271) (1039 male, 1232 females) because this corresponds to the mean age of the present study sample. There were a number of incomplete responses to each item which were not entered into the analysis, so number of responders are also presented.

Table 5.1. SF-36 Sub-Scale United Kingdom Norm Scores for the Age Range 35-54

Variable	n	Mean	SD
Physical Functioning	993	91.9	14.5
Social Functioning	1009	90.5	17.0
Physical Role Limitations	1008	89.5	25.5
Emotional Role Limitations	1008	86.0	28.6
Mental Health	990	75.0	16.1
Energy/Vitality	1001	63.5	18.6
Pain	1008	85.6	19.7
General Health Perceptions	998	74.1	18.5

The normative total SF-36 score for the age range 35-54 was 656.1. No normative data was presented for the Reported health transition sub-score.

Other Baseline Assessments

The base line assessment was carried out 4-5 days after admission to each study unit. The author met with the interviewee, presented information about the study, answered any queries, obtained written informed consent and administered the previously described outcome measures. The interview lasted approx 45 minutes in total.

Socio-demographic data was collected, this included age, gender, ethnicity, social class, marital status, work status and a social deprivation score. (The index finally used to measure social deprivation will be described in *Social Deprivation*). Social class was assigned in accordance with the then United Kingdom definitions contained in the Registrar General's classification of socio-economic status (Office of Population Censuses and Surveys 1991). Present and last employment was the assigning variable for men and for women employment of spouse or father was applied if they were not working or had not worked themselves. Since conducting the study the categorisations have been reviewed and amended (Office of National Statistics 2001). Individuals were also asked to provide information concerning cigarette dependency, family history of alcoholism, previous treatment experiences, past and present alcohol use and the extent of use of prescription and illicit drugs.

Social Deprivation

The Jarman Index (Jarman 1983) produces a social deprivation score according to the Local Government electoral ward (an administrative unit equating to a population of approx 20,000) in which the individual resides. Jarman scores were collected for the total sample and higher scores are indicative of a greater level of deprivation. Details of the precise methodology employed to obtain a score are contained in Jarman (1983). The Jarman Index is based upon the weighting of the following eight census variables using the 1991 population census figures. These are elderly persons living alone, children/infants under five years of age, one parent families, unskilled persons (social class V), unemployed persons, overcrowded accommodation, number of persons changing address within one year and those persons from ethnic minorities. The composite score is called an underprivileged area score and positive scores denote socially “privileged” areas.

Follow-Up Assessment

Individuals were followed up at 12 weeks, 26 weeks, and one year. At this visit the RSCL, LSS, GHQ-28, NHP and SF-36 were re-administered. In addition at each visit the researcher completed a Time-Line Follow-Back (TLFB) (Sobell et al 1988). The TLFB asks an individual to recount and quantify their drinking pattern(s) by reference to anniversary dates and normal routine. Dependent on the results of the TLFB the subjects were sub-divided into two comparison groups; relapsers (R) and non-relapsers (NR) according to their status at each follow-up visit.

Relapse Criteria

Relapse was defined as the consumption of at least 21 units of alcohol for males and 14 units of alcohol for females over a 7 day period at anytime during the follow-up period in accordance with the recommended levels of sensible drinking (Royal College of Psychiatrists 1986). Drinks were allocated their strengths according to guidelines laid down by the Health Education Authority (Health Education Authority 1995). In the United Kingdom one unit is the equivalent of 8-10 grams of alcohol (Paton 1996).

Chapter 6

DATA ANALYSIS

INTRODUCTION

Throughout this monograph there will be short summaries of the statistical methodologies used to address each question. The aim of this chapter is to summarise the techniques used.

POWER CALCULATION

The results of the correlations from the pilot study (see chapter three) (Foster et al 1998a) were used to perform the power calculation for the present study. Two hundred and twenty individuals was sufficient to detect a significant association with a 80% power at the 5% level when the value of the correlation co-efficient was at least 0.19. In the pilot study much greater correlations than this were found e.g. $r=0.59$ between log-transformed SADQ and APQ-Core scores and $r=0.41$ between transformed SADQ and RSCL physical symptom scores.

PRESENTATION OF STATISTICS

Prevalence data is presented and categorical variables were tested by two-tailed *Chi-*Square/Fishers exact tests-dependent upon whether there were five or more participants in each cell. Parametric findings were presented with means and standard deviations and medians and range values were used for non-parametric distributions. To account for multiple testing the cut-off point needed to reject the null-hypothesis was $p \leq 0.01$. Unless otherwise stated this was used throughout.

Thus in order to conclude statistical significance two criteria had to be met:

a) An unadjusted significance level of $p \leq 0.01$

b) Significance at $p \leq 0.01$ after controlling for confounding factors.

"Between Group" Differences

These compared those participants who relapsed (criterion already defined in chapter five) at three, six and twelve months and those who were re-detoxified during the study period with those who had not relapsed at the aforementioned time-points or been re-detoxified. Initially the following univariate tests were used, (dependent upon the type of variable and spread of the data) two- tailed *Chi*-squared/Fishers exact, Mann Whitney "U" or Independent Sample "t" tests. To establish the predictors of relapse at all three time points and predictors of re-detoxification, a categorical variable e.g. relapse at 12 months "Yes" or "No" was entered into a Forward-Stepwise Logistic Regression as the dependent variable. Each regression model will be described in the text. By this method the computer only selects the significant variables so when using the Forward-Stepwise methodology significance was taken as $p \leq 0.05$. These results were all accompanied by odds ratios and 95% confidence intervals. A General Factorial ANOVA established whether any of the study variables were linked to the time taken to relapse and time taken to re-detoxification using only those individuals who had relapsed at the end of the study period or been re-detoxified respectively.

In addition an intention to treat analysis was performed on relapse rates, predictors of relapse at each time point and days to relapse. The methodology used was that described in the previous paragraph with a worse possible scenario being assumed. Thus all participants lost to follow-up were assumed to have relapsed and that this took place on the day following their last known day of non-relapse.

"Within Group" Changes

Those participants who relapsed during the study and those who did not were subdivided into two groupings, relapsers and non-relapsers. Firstly a Repeated Measures ANOVA was carried out entering relapse at 12 months "yes" or "no" as the "between-subjects" factor. This ascertained whether the change in 12 month scores were significantly different for the two groups. If so it was possible to conclude that participants came from separate samples and further investigations could be performed. The changes between baseline and 12 month scores were then investigated and tested by a Repeated Measures ANOVA. The regression/ANOVA model used will be fully described in the text. To recap statistical significance was only concluded if significance ($p \leq 0.01$) was maintained after controlling for all confounding factors.

Two other tests were also carried out

i) *Non-Relapse group only:* Two-tailed Wilcoxon tests were performed on the "within group" differences in Baseline/3month, 3/6 month, 6/12 month scores to establish whether there was a linear improvement in QoL/QoL-related variables over the study period.
ii) *Relapse group only:* The aim was to establish whether the change in QoL scores for each variable was significantly linked to time taken to relapse and re-detoxification respectively. To test the difference in baseline and 12 month scores each QoL/QoL-related variable was entered into a linear regression in turn as an independent

variable. There were no other confounders entered, days to relapse or days to re-detoxification were the dependent variables respectively. Both the independent and dependent variables were log-transformed if there was a non-gaussian data-spread.

Quality of Life Burden

This was calculated by comparing the baseline scores of the total sample to published peer-reviewed norms. The number and percentage of those scoring beyond the norm scores were then ascertained.

PART FOUR: RESULTS

Chapter 7

SOCIODEMOGRAPHIC AND CONSUMPTION-RELATED FINDINGS

TOTAL SAMPLE CHARACTERISTICS

The sociodemographic characteristics for the total sample of 240 individuals are shown in Table 7.1. Nearly three-quarters (n=178, 74%) were male and the mean age was 42.6 years (SD=10.0). There was no significant difference between the ages of male and female alcohol dependent individuals (ADI) (42.0, 18-65 Median, Range,) (42.0, 23-65, Median, Range,) (Male : Female) (Two-tailed Mann Whitney "U" test) (U=5360, p=0.737). Seventy one percent (n=170) were White English and just over one fifth of the total sample were of Celtic origin i.e. individuals born in Scotland, Ireland or Wales. The majority (n=162, 67%) were either single or divorced and living alone (n=124, 52%). One hundred and sixty six individuals (69%) were unemployed and 157(65%) individuals were in social classes III, IV and V (Semi-skilled unskilled manual/non-manual workers) combined. The mean Jarman index score was 21.0 (SD=18.4).

Table 7.1. Sociodemographic Data for the Total Sample (n=240)

Age (Years)		**Living Arrangements**	
Mean	42.6	Alone	124 (52%)
SD	10.0	Family Unit	105 (43%)
		Other	11 (3%)
Gender		**Employment Status**	
Males	178 (74%)	Unemployed	166 (70%)
Females	62 (26%)	Employed	61 (25%)
		Housewife	8 (3%)
		Other	5 (2%)
Ethnicity		**Social Class**	
White English	172 (72%)	I	7 (3%)
Celtic*	50 (21%)	II	75 (31%)
Other#	18 (7%)	III	68 (28%)
		IV	47 (20%)
		V	43 (18%)

Table 7.1. (Continued)

Marital Status		Social Deprivation (Jarman Index)	
Single	93 (39%)	Mean	21.0
Married	69 (28%)	SD	18.4
Divorced	74 (31%)		
Other	4 (2%)		

Key: * Celtic= Irish, Scottish and Welsh individuals. # Other= White European, Australian, American, Black British, Black Afro-Caribbean and Asian individuals.

Alcohol History and Consumption Outcomes

The median units (see chapter five for a definition of unit) of alcohol consumed in a typical week prior to assessment was 201 (32-610 Range). Seventeen (6-50 Range) was the median age of commencing drinking (weekly) and the statistics for age of weekly intoxication were as follows- (21, 11-58, Median, Range). The mean age of first contact with alcohol services was 35.3 (SD=10.8). The final variable relating to this was the numbers of days alcohol free at the time of baseline assessment. The median statistic for this was 7.0 (4-56 Range).

Miscelleanous Other Baseline Outcomes

Prescription Drug Use

One hundred and ninety (80%) ADI had been prescribed any of the following drugs over the past twelve months; vitamins, benzodiazepines, analgesia, antidepressants, antibiotics, antacids, bronchodilators, antihypertensives, chlormethiazole, anticonvulsants neuroleptics, laxatives and cough medicines. Vitamins were the most commonly prescribed drug (n=96, 40%). The following categories of drugs were prescribed to over 30% of the sample; viz. benzodiazepines (n=88, 37%), analgesics (n=82, 32%), antidepressants (n=74, 31%) and antibiotics (n=74, 31%).

Illicit/Unprescribed Drug Use

A proportion of the sample (n=91, 38%) had used illicit/unprescribed drugs within the past twelve months. Drug using individuals (Users) were likely to be younger than non-drug users (Non-Users) (38.0, 8.8, Mean, SD) (45.2, 9.6, Mean, SD) (years) (Users : Non-Users) (Independent Sample "t" test) ($t=5.91$, $p < 0.001$). The most prevalent drug used was cannabis (n=76, 32%) followed by unprescribed tranquilizers (n=49, 20%).

Tobacco Use

The majority of individuals, 184 (76%) were current smokers. When asked how soon after waking up they would smoke their first cigarette the individuals replied as follows: less than 5 minutes (n=121, 66%); 15-30 minutes (n=34, 19%); 30 minutes to 1 hour (n=10, 5%) and greater than one hour (n=20, 10%). A linked question was "How difficult would you find it to go without smoking for the whole day" , yielded four possible responses: very difficult (n=115, 63%), fairly difficult (n=34, 18%), fairly easy (n=18, 10%) and very easy (n=17, 9%). The median age for starting smoking was 14 years (0-40, Range) and the statistics for the number of cigarettes smoked daily at baseline assessment was (17.5, 0-80, Median, Range).

Family History and Related Variables

One hundred and forty (58%) of the sample had a family history of "alcoholism" (self-defined) in one of the following categories: mother, father, brother, sister, child, grandparent, aunt, uncle and cousin. One hundred and twenty (50%) had a history of first degree relatives with "alcoholism" (father, mother, brother, sister and child) and seventy-one (30%) had second-degree relatives with a family history of "alcoholism". Twenty-nine (13%) of the total sample had a partner with an alcohol problem. Females (n=19, 66%) were 2.3 times more "at risk" of having a partner with an alcohol problem than males (Two-tailed *Chi*-squared test) (*Chi*-squared= 26.9, df=1, $p < 0.001$).

Previous Treatments

One hundred and eighty two (76%) of the sample had received a previous alcohol-related treatment. Of these one hundred and twenty nine (54%) had experienced a residential detoxification and 90 (38%) a community alcohol detoxification. For the purposes of this study "residential detoxification" includes detoxification in statutory or voluntary sector alcohol detoxification units, in acute psychiatric wards, general hospital medical wards and in prison. A further one hundred and one individuals (42%) had been in receipt of non-detoxification treatment. This included outpatient group or individual treatments. It did not include attendance at Alcoholics Anonymous meetings. Thirty-nine (21%) ADI had a previous residential treatment only, eighteen (10%) had a community detoxification only and twenty-one ADI (11%) had non-detoxification treatment only.

Chapter 8

BASELINE QUALITY OF LIFE AND RELATED OUTCOMES

The median and range statistics for baseline quality of life (QoL) and related outcomes are shown in table 8.1. Over half (n=130, 52%) had SADQ scores > 30 and thus fulfilled the criteria of severely alcohol dependent individuals (ADI) (Stockwell et al 1983). The mean APQ score in a sample of 103 inpatient and outpatient male and female drinkers during which the APQ was designed was 11.16 (Drummond 1990). In the present sample (n=153, 64%) had APQ scores > 11. Two hundred and four (85%) of the total sample had baseline GHQ-28 scores > 4.5 which is the threshold for psychiatric caseness (Goldberg and Hillier 1979). Chubon (1995) recommended that scores below 90 are indicative of a poor life situation. One hundred and ninety three (85%) of the total sample had scores < 90.

Table 8.1. Baseline Quality of Life and Related Outcomes

	Median	Range
Alcohol Problems (APQ-Core)	12	2- 22
Severity of Alcohol Dependence (SADQ)	32	2- 60
Psychological Scores (RSCL)	52	0-100
Physical Scores (RSCL)	32	1- 88
General Health Questionnaire 28 (GHQ-28)	16	0- 28
Life Situation Survey (LSS)	74	25-127
Nottingham Health Profile		
Physical Mobility	0	0-100
Pain	22.9	0-100
Energy	39.2	0-100
Emotional Reactions	31.5	0-100
Sleep	50.4	0-100
Social Isolation	38.9	0-100
Total Score	229.1	0-539
Short-Form -36		
Physical Functioning	85	0-100
Role Functioning	25	0-100
Pain	51	0-100
General Health	35	0-100

Table 8.1. (Continued)

	Median	Range
Vitality	35	0- 95
Social Functioning	50	0-100
Emotional Role	16.5	0-100
Mental Health	40	0-100
Total Score	355	31-781
Reported Health Transition	4	1- 5

QUALITY OF LIFE BURDEN OF THE STUDY SAMPLE

This is presented by comparing the mean scores of the present sample to published general population norms for the equivalent study indices. The results are shown in table 8.2a and 8.2b, and both tables should be read in combination. When considering the extent of the QoL burden the most useful measurement to describe is the percentage of individuals scoring beyond the population norms for each variable. There was only one variable with less than half of the individuals scoring above (i.e. worse than) the general population norms; this was physical mobility (NHP). The following variables had at least eighty percent of the total sample scoring above their equivalent population norm score (in order of decreasing QoL burden); vitality, physical functioning and bodily pain (all SF-36 sub-scores), General Health Questionnaire-28 total scores, sleep, social isolation, and emotional reactions, (all NHP sub-scores) and Life Situation Survey total scores. Furthermore there were six measurements where 90% or more individuals scored beyond their general population norms (again in order of decreasing QoL burden), SF-36 total scores, psychological symptoms (RSCL), NHP total scores, social functioning (SF-36), energy level (NHP) and mental health (SF-36).

Table 8.2a. Comparison of Published Peer-Reviewed Norms for Study Outcomes Measures for the Present Sample

	Normative Values		Sample Group (n=240)		Statistics
	Range	Mean	Range	Mean	Abnormal Scores (%)
Cigarettes per Day	N/A	14.1	0- 80	17.9	133 (55%)
SADQ	0- 60	N/A	2- 60	32.5	N/A
APQ-Core	0- 23	N/A	2- 22	12.6	N/A
RSCL					
a) Physical Symptoms	23- 92	9.9	1- 80	34.8	186 (76%)
b) Psychological Symptoms	7- 23	17.0	0-100	53.3	231 (96%)
GHQ-28	0- 28	< 4.5	0- 28	14.8	204 (85%)
LSS	20-140	> 90	25-127	73.7	193 (80%)
NHP					
Physical Mobility	0-100	3.3	0-100	15.6	114 (48%)

Table 8.2a. (Continued)

	Normative Values		Sample Group (n=240)		Statistics
Pain	0-100	5.8	0-100	30.8	174 (73%)
Energy Level	0-100	11.3	0-100	53.4	217 (90%)
Sleep	0-100	12.5	0-100	48.0	203 (85%)
Social Isolation	0-100	4.3	0-100	40.1	197 (82%)
Emotional Reactions	0-100	10.2	0-100	29.9	194 (81%)
Total Scores	0-600	47.3	0-539.4	236	229 (95%)

The literature sources were as follows; also quoted are the geographical areas where the normative data was obtained. Cigarettes per Day (Wald et al 1988) United Kingdom; RSCL (DeHaes et al 1990) Rotterdam Holland; GHQ-28 (Goldberg and Hillier 1979) London and Manchester, England; LSS (Chubon 1995) South Carolina USA and NHP (Hunt et al 1994) Nottingham England. There were no published peer-reviewed normative data for the SADQ or APQ-Core scales.

Table 8.2b. Comparison of Published Peer-Reviewed Norms for the Short-Form 36 Sub-Scores and Total Scores and the Present Sample

	Normative Values		Sample Group (n=240)		Statistics
	Range	Mean	Range	Mean	Abnormal Scores (n, ;%)
Physical Functioning	0-100	91.9	0-100	73.5	208 (87%)
Role Functioning	0-100	90.5	0-100	39.2	189 (79%)
Bodily Pain	0-100	85.6	0-100	50.9	203 (85%)
General Health	0-100	74.1	0-100	40.0	186 (76%)
Vitality	0-100	63.5	0- 95	34.3	210 (88%)
Social Functioning	0-100	90.5	0-100	47.8	225 (94%)
Emotional Role	0-100	86.0	0-100	34.6	189 (79%)
Mental Health	0-100	75.0	0- 96	41.6	217 (90%)
Total Scores	0-800	656	31- 781	361	231 (96%)
Reported Health Transition	1-5	N/A	1 - 5	3.5	N/A

The normative data comes from Jenkinson (1993). The geographical areas where the participants were recruited were as follows; Berkshire, Buckinghamshire, Nottinghamshire and Oxford (United Kingdom). There was no published normative data for the reported health transition sub-score.

Chapter 9

RELAPSE RATES/PREDICTORS OF RELAPSE

INTRODUCTION

In this chapter the relapse rates of the whole sample and relapse as a predictor of outcome were investigated. Follow-up rates are also reported. The differences between relapse and non-relapse scores are reported at three time points, three months, six months and one year. Initially univariate differences are described, tested by either *Chi*-squared, Mann Whitney "U" or Independent Sample "t" tests. In the tables medians and range scores are presented because the data spread for the majority of variables was non-gaussain. Where appropriate means and standard deviations are shown accompanied by the results of parametric testing. Finally the sociodemographic and QoL/QoL-related variables were all entered into a Forward-Stepwise Logistic Regression accompanied by any variables which showed a noteworthy impact upon outcome after univariate testing ($p \leq 0.05$). Variables at the $p \leq 0.05$ level were entered into the regression because this has traditionally been regarded as the cut-off point to reject the null-hypothesis. For the purposes of the study they were regarded as *prima facie* predictors and were entered so that their impact upon outcomes could be assessed. By entering them in the regression the chances of a Type I error (i.e. false positive) were reduced. The results of these regressions show the significant predictors of outcome with accompanying odds ratios and 95% Confidence Intervals. For these regressions $p \leq 0.05$ was acceptable as the cut-off by which to reject the null hypothesises as only these variables were selected by the computer and controlling for the effects of confounding factors was inherent in the process.

RELAPSE DATA THROUGHOUT THE STUDY

The overall follow-up rate was (n=232, 97%) at three months, (n=231, 96%) six months and (n=228, 95%) at twelve months respectively. In the results that are primarily reported no assumption has been made as to the relapse status of those subjects lost to follow-up. However an intention to treat analysis (ITT) was performed according to the principles described in the *Data Analysis* (chapter 6). The total-sample relapse rates (not ITT) were as follows; three months (n=116, 50%), six months (n=142, 61%) and twelve months (n=163, 71%).

Univariate Baseline Differences Between the Relapse/Non Relapse Groups

For each of these analyses the results reported do not assume a relapse status in individuals lost to follow-up. However an ITT analysis was also performed and this is briefly summarised at the end of each section.

Three Months

In order to undertake this analysis the social class, ethnicity and marital status variables were collapsed as shown in table 7.1. A categorical variable consisting of individuals who lived alone, in a family unit, in an institution or had some other living arrangement was collapsed to form a composite living arrangements variable. The differences between the relapse (R) and non-relapse (NR) groups were not significant in the following demographic variables; ($p > 0.02$) (in order of increasing probability) gender, age, marital status, living arrangements and ethnicity. There were three sociodemographic variables that had significant univariate differences. Firstly higher Jarman scores, (living in an underpriviledged area) were associated with relapse ((+)28.8, (–) 17.6 – (+) 49.7, Median, Range) ((+) 16.0, (–) 25.2 – (+) 49.7, Median, Range) (Relapse : Non Relapse) (Two-tailed Mann Whitney "U" test) ($U=4172$, $p < 0.001$). Secondly unemployment was linked to outcome (Two-tailed *Chi*-squared test) (*Chi*-squared=10.7, df=1, p=0.002). Ninety-two (57%) of the R group were unemployed at baseline and forty-seven (66%) individuals who were employed had not relapsed at three months. Finally there was a link between social class and three month outcome (Two-tailed *Chi*-squared test) (*Chi*-squared=15.7, df=2, $p < 0.001$). Alcohol dependent individuals (ADI) in Social Classes I and II (Professional and Managerial Occupations) were likely to have had a positive outcome (n=54, 66%). In contrast, those individuals from Social Classes IV and V (n=56, 64%) (Unskilled Manual/Non-Manual Occupations) were more likely to have relapsed to heavy drinking at three months.

The number of units consumed weekly, age of initiation to drinking/drinking weekly and age of first contact with alcohol services showed no significant differences between the R and NR groups ($p > 0.06$). However a longer period alcohol free (days) at the time of baseline assessment was associated with not relapsing to heavy drinking at three months (6, 2-56, Median, Range) (9, 2-56, Median, Range) (Relapse : Non Relapse) (Two-tailed Mann-Whitney test) ($U=4753$, $p < 0.001$).

Not being prescribed any drug within the past twelve months was significantly related to a positive result (Two-tailed *Chi*-squared test) (*Chi*-squared=8.25, df=1, p=0.006); thirty (70%) individuals in the NR group had not been prescribed any drugs. The prescription of vitamins was the only category of drug linked to three months outcome (Two-tailed *Chi*-squared=11.1, df=1, p=0.001). Sixty (63%) individuals who were prescribed vitamins relapsed to heavy drinking at three months follow-up. Illicit drug use was not associated with outcome (Two-tailed *Chi*-squared test) (*Chi*-squared=1.52, df=1, p=0.273). Finally family history and the number of previous treatments did not differentiate the R and NR groups ($p > 0.4$ for both variables).

Table 9.2a shows the "between group" differences in median and range scores at three-month follow-up for the ordinal QoL and QoL-related variables. Also shown, as legends to the table are the equivalent parametric data where appropriate. The variables which showed significant "between group" differences were as follows (in order of decreasing significance); bodily pain, general health (SF-36), pain (NHP), physical symptoms (RSCL), SF-36 total scores, NHP total scores, sleep (NHP), GHQ-28 , physical abilities (NHP) and physical functioning (SF-36).

There were noteworthy differences between the previously reported results and in the ITT analysis. These concerned previous alcohol-related treatment and GHQ-28 total scores. In the ITT sample the relapse group had significantly more previous alcohol-related treatments (n=124) (3, 0-80, Median, Range) (n=116) (1, 0-62, Median, Range) (Relapse : Non-Relapse) (U=5657, $p < 0.001$). This related to residential treatments only (1.5, 0-45, Median, Range) (0, 0-45, Median, Range) (Relapse : Non-Relapse) (U=5045, $p < 0.001$). The difference in the number of previous community detoxification and non- detoxification treatments between the R and NR groups was not significant ($p > 0.7$ on both occasions). For GHQ-28 total scores there was no longer a significant "between group" difference following testing in the ITT comparison groups (16.5, 0-28, Median, Range) (14.5, 0-28, Median, Range) (Relapse : Non-Relapse) (U=5847, p=0.012).

Six Months

There were three sociodemographic variables, which produced significant differences between the R and NR groups at six months follow-up; Jarman Index, living arrangements and social class.

Firstly living in an underpriviledged area (Jarman Index) was associated with relapse ((+) 27.4, (–) 18.0 – (+) 49.7, Median, Range) ((+) 16.6, (–) 25.2 – (+) 49.1, Median, Range) (Relapse : Non-Relapse) (Two-tailed Mann Whitney "U" test) (U=4329, $p < 0.001$). Secondly the composite living arrangements variable revealed the following significant difference (Two-tailed *Chi*-squared test) (Fishers exact test statistic, df=4, p=0.005). Further investigation showed that the difference related to individuals who lived alone at baseline assessment. Thus the baseline living alone variable was tested and this produced the following significant findings (Two-tailed *Chi*-squared test) (*Chi*-squared=11.0, df=1, p=0.001). Eighty-six (72%) individuals who lived alone had relapsed to heavy drinking at six months. Finally individuals in Social Classes IV/V had a poor six month outcome (Two-tailed *Chi*-squared test) (*Chi*-squared=10.0, df=2, p=0.007). Of the individuals from Social Classes IV/V, sixty-five (74%) were in the relapse group. All other sociodemographic differences were $p > 0.05$.

Neither the "any prescription drugs" (*Chi*-squared=4.2, df=1, p=0.053) or the "any illicit drugs" variables (*Chi*-squared=0.70, df=1, p=0.481) produced any "between group" differences after two-tailed *Chi*-squared tests. However being prescribed vitamins during the twelve months prior to baseline assessment was again associated with relapse (Two-tailed *Chi*-squared test) (*Chi*-squared=8.48, df=1, p=0.004). Sixty-nine (73%) individuals who were prescribed vitamins had relapsed to heavy drinking at six months. The differences between the R and NR groups concerning any other category of drug (prescribed/illicit) were $p > 0.05$.

None of the alcohol history variables revealed any significant differences, but the number of units of alcohol consumed weekly at baseline, and length of time alcohol free at baseline assessment both produced significant findings after two tailed Mann Whitney "U" tests. A greater number of units consumed (210, 56-609, Median, Range) (168, 32-610, Median, Range) (Relapse : Non-Relapse) (U=4984, p=0.007) and a shorter period alcohol free (days) at the time of baseline assessment (6, 2-56, Median, Range) (9, 2-56, Median, Range) (Relapse : Non-Relapse) (U=4929, p=0.004) were associated with relapse to heavy drinking.

The total number of previous alcohol-related treatments was not significantly related to outcome (Two-tailed Mann-Whitney test) (U=5101, p=0.013). However there was a significant association with numbers of previous residential treatments and relapse to heavy drinking, after non-parametric testing (1, 0-45, Median, Range) (0, 0-45, Median, Range) (Relapse : Non-Relapse) (U=4616, $p < 0.001$). Similar tests regarding the numbers of community alcohol detoxification and non-detoxification treatments were both $p > 0.5$. The difference in the family history variable between the R and NR groups was not significant ($p > 0.1$).

Table 9.2b shows the six months "between group" differences in the QoL and QoL-related variables. There were four significant differences (in order of decreasing significance); bodily pain (SF-36), physical symptoms (RSCL), pain (NHP) and NHP total scores.

Once more an ITT analysis was carried out. There was one additional significant univariate finding. ADI who had relapsed reported significantly higher (poorer) NHP sleep scores than those who did not (n=151) (55.4, 0-100, Median, Range) (n=89) (38.5, 0-100, Median, Range) (Relapse : Non-Relapse) (U=5390, p=0.01).

Twelve Months

At the end of the follow-up period there were two sociodemographic variables which showed a significant between group differences; Jarman scores
((+) 26,6, (–)18.0 – (+)49.7, Median, Range)
((+) 16.6, (–) 25.2 – (+) 48.6, Median, Range) (Relapse : Non-Relapse) (Two-tailed Mann Whitney "U" test) (U=3639, $p < 0.001$) and social class (Two-tailed *Chi*-squared test) (*Chi*-squared=9.24, df=2, p=0.009). Seventy-three (83%) of the participants from Social Classes IV/V had relapsed and fifty (64%) from Social Classes I/II had *not* relapsed to heavy drinking at the end of the study. All other sociodemographic differences were $p > 0.05$.

The weekly number of units of alcohol at baseline was significantly associated with outcome (210, 56-610, Median, Range) (161, 45-420, Median, Range) (Relapse : Non-Relapse) (Two-tailed Mann Whitney "U" test) (U=3754, $p < 0.001$). However by the end of the study the significant protective effect provided by a greater length of time alcohol free at baseline assessment was lost (6, 2-56, Median, Range) (7, 2-56, Median, Range) (Relapse : Non-Relapse) (Two-tailed Mann Whitney "U" test) (U=4434, p=0.052). All alcohol history related variables and family history differences were $p > 0.07$.

"Any prescription drug use" (*Chi*-squared=0.15, df=1 p=0.708) and "any illicit drug use" (*Chi*-squared=0.41, df=1, P= 0.880) were both not related to outcome by the end of the study period. However there was still a trend for the prescription of vitamins in the 12 months prior to baseline assessment to be associated with a negative outcome though statistical significance cannot be inferred any longer (Two-tailed *Chi*-squared test) (*Chi*-squared=4.10, df=1, p=0.034). Seventy-four (80%) individuals prescribed vitamins during the study had relapsed to heavy drinking.

Significant differences were also present concerning the previous alcohol related treatments variables after non-parametric tests. The differences in total number of previous treatments was not significant (2, 0-80, Median, Range) (1, 0-11, Median, Range) (Relapse : Non-Relapse) (U=4331, p=0.030). However the number of previous residential treatments did show a significant "between group" difference (1, 0-45, Median, Range) (0, 0-8, Median, Range) (Relapse : Non-Relapse) (U=4110,p=0.006) both were associated with a negative outcome. Previous community alcohol detoxification or non-detoxification treatments were both not associated with outcome.

Table 9.2c shows the difference in scores between the relapse and non-relapse groups at 12 months in QoL and QoL-related outcomes. There were four significant differences (in order of decreasing statistical significance), bodily pain sub-scores (SF-36), pain (NHP), physical symptoms (RSCL) and role function (SF-36).

The ITT results showed some differences to the previously reported findings. Significance relating to the social class was no longer present (*Chi*-squared=7.9, df=2, p=0.019) and the trend reported concerning prescription vitamins was no longer of borderline significance (*Chi*-squared=3.4, df=1, p=0.076). The numbers and percentages of individuals who had not relapsed in the collapsed social class variables were as follows; I/II (n=28, 44%), III (n=22, 33%) and IV/V (n=15, 23%). Forty-five of the NR group were prescribed vitamins in the 12 months prior to baseline assessment compared to 77 in the R group. Finally there was one additional significant finding to those variables shown in table 9.2c, this concerned the SF-36 reported health transition sub-score (n=175) (4, 1-5, Median, Range) (n=64) (3, 1-5, Median, Range) (Relapse : Non-Relapse) (U=4497, p=0.01). Lower reported health transition scores indicate a better health status

Table 9.1 provides a summary of all the significant findings during the study for those variables not shown in tables 9.2a-c. Only those individuals who were followed-up successfully (i.e. not ITT) were included in table 9.1.

Table 9.1. Summary of Significant Univariate findings for Non-QoL/QoL-related variables

Variables	Follow-up Periods		
	Three Months	Six Months	Twelve Months
Age	No	No	No
Gender	No	No	No
Ethnicity*	No	No	No
Marital Status*	No	No	No
Living Arrangements*	No	Yes	No
Social Class*	Yes	Yes	Yes
Unemployment	Yes	No	No
Jarman Index Scores	Yes	Yes	Yes
Baseline Number of Units of Alcohol Consumed	No	Yes	Yes
Age of Starting Drinking	No	No	No
Age of Regular Intoxication	No	No	No

Table 9.1. (Continued)

Variables	Follow-up Periods		
Age of First Contact with Alcohol Services	No	No	No
Shorter Length of Time Alcohol-Free at Baseline	Yes	Yes	No
Family History Score	No	No	No
No Prescription Drugs During Previous 12 months	Yes	No	No
No Illicit Drug Use During Previous 12 months	No	No	No
Prescription of Vitamins During Previous 12 months	Yes	Yes	No
Number of Previous Alcohol-Related Treatments	No	No	No
Number of Previous Residential Alcohol-Related Treatments	No	Yes	Yes

This table only relates to those subjects followed-up at each time-point. Yes= Significant Finding, No=Non-Significant Finding. Significance taken as $p \leq 0.01$. * Denotes composite variables.

Table 9.2a. Comparison of Baseline Scores of Relapse and Non-Relapse Group at Three Months

	Relapse (n=116)		Non-Relapse (n=116)		Statistics	
	Median	Range	Median	Range	Stats	p
Number of Cigarettes	20.0	0- 80	17.0	0- 60	6351	0.457
SADQ	35.0	2- 60	30.0	2- 60	5433	0.011
APQ-Core	12.0	3- 22	12.0	2- 22	6022	0.166
Physical Symptoms (RSCL)	39.0	4- 88	26.0	1- 88	5075	< 0.001
Psychological Symptoms (RSCL)	57.0	0-100	52.0	0-100	6104	0.221
GHQ-28	17.0	0- 28	15.0	0- 28	5359	0.007
Life Situation Survey	71.0	36-103	76.0	25-127	5413	0.011
Nottingham Health Profile						
Physical Abilities	10.6	0-100	0	0-100	5451	0.007
Pain	32.6	0-100	15.9	0-100	5056	< 0.001
Energy Level	60.8	0-100	39.2	0-100	6123	0.233
Sleep	60.3	0-100	50.3	0-100	5315	0.005
Social Isolation	40.1	0-100	38.2	0-100	5949	0.126
Emotional Reactions	38.7	0-100	30.0	0-100	6218	0.318
Total Scores	249	7-539	192	0-523	5205	0.003
Short-Form Thirty Six						
Physical Functioning	75.0	5-100	90.0	0-100	5361	0.007
Role Functioning	25.0	0-100	50.0	0-100	5586	0.020
Bodily Pain	41.0	0-100	62.0	0-100	4734	< 0.001
General Health	35.0	0- 77	45.0	0-100	4882	< 0.001
Vitality	30.0	0- 85	40.0	0- 95	5860	0.089
Social Functioning	40.0	0-100	50.0	0-100	5846	0.083
Emotional Role	0	0-100	33.0	0-100	6682	0.924

Table 9.2a. (Continued)

	Relapse (n=116)		Non-Relapse (n=116)		Statistics	
Mental Health	40.0	0- 92	40.0	4- 96	6521	0.648
Total Scores	315	35-776	389	31-781	5179	0.002
Reported Health Transition	4.0	1- 5	3.0	1- 5	5453	0.011

Key: SADQ =Severity of Alcohol Dependence, APQ= Alcohol Problem Questionnaire, RSCL=Rotterdam Symptoms Checklist. All the results are shown following two-tailed Mann Whitney "U" tests. The following are the equivalent parametric results where appropriate after two-tailed Independent Sample "t" tests; a) SADQ (34.9, 14.4, Mean, SD) (29.9, 14.2, Mean, SD) (Relapse : Non Relapse) (t= –2.70, p=0.007), b) APQ-Core (12.7, 4.1, Mean, SD) (11.8, 4.3, Mean, SD) (Relapse : Non Relapse) (t= –1.54, p=0.124) and c) Life Situation Survey (70.8, 15.6, Mean, SD) (76.9, 17.2, Mean, SD) (Relapse : Non Relapse) (t=2.83, p=0.005). Significance was taken as $p \leq 0.01$.

Table 9.2b. Comparison of Baseline Scores of Relapse and Non-Relapse Group at Six Months

	Relapse (n=142)		Non-Relapse (n=89)		Statistics	
	Median	Range	Median	Range	Stats	p
Number of Cigarettes	19.0	0- 80	16.0	0- 43	6177	0.772
SADQ	33.0	2- 60	30.0	2- 57	5388	0.060
APQ-Core	12.0	3- 22	12.0	2- 22	5740	0.240
Physical Symptoms (RSCL)	35.0	3- 88	25.0	1- 80	4808	0.002
Psychological Symptoms (RSCL)	57.0	0-100	52.0	0-100	6095	0.650
GHQ-28	16.0	0- 28	14.0	0- 28	5281	0.036
Life Situation Survey	72.0	36-118	74.0	25-127	5468	0.092
Nottingham Health Profile						
Physical Abilities	10.6	0-100	0	0-100	5248	0.019
Pain	32.6	0-100	14.8	0-100	4875	0.003
Energy Level	60.8	0-100	39.2	0-100	5967	0.464
Sleep	53.7	0-100	38.5	0-100	5112	0.014
Social Isolation	42.0	0-100	35.3	0-100	5520	0.104
Emotional Reactions	38.1	0-100	29.9	0- 90	5290	0.036
Total Scores	246	7-539	192	0-523	4980	0.007
Short-Form Thirty Six						
Physical Functioning	80.0	5-100	90.0	0-100	5290	0.036
Role Functioning	25.0	0-100	50.0	0-100	5767	0.244
Bodily Pain	41.0	0-100	62.0	0-100	4733	0.001
General Health	35.0	0- 80	40.0	0-100	5168	0.020
Vitality	35.0	0- 95	35.0	0- 90	5968	0.477
Social Functioning	50.0	0-100	50.0	0-100	5849	0.338
Emotional Role	0	0-100	33.0	0-100	6229	0.854
Mental Health	40.0	0- 92	40.0	4- 96	6038	0.569
Total Scores	329	35-776	384	13-781	5332	0.046
Reported Health Transition	3.6	1.2	3.3	1.2	5205	0.020

Key: SADQ =Severity of Alcohol Dependence, APQ= Alcohol Problem Questionnaire, RSCL=Rotterdam Symptoms Checklist. All the results are shown following two-tailed Mann

Whitney "U" tests. The following are the equivalent parametric results where appropriate after two-tailed Independent Sample "t" tests; a) SADQ (33.9, 14.6, Mean, SD) (29.9, 13.9, Mean, SD) (Relapse : Non Relapse) (t= –2.07, p=0.040), b) APQ-Core (12.5, 4.1, Mean, SD) (11.8, 4.5, Mean, SD) (Relapse : Non Relapse) (t= –1.25, p=0.201) and c) Life Situation Survey (72.2, 16.3, Mean, SD) (76.4, 17.2, Mean, SD) (Relapse : Non Relapse) (t=1.85, p=0.066). Significance was taken as $p \leq 0.01$.

Table 9.2c. Comparison of Baseline Scores of Relapse and Non-Relapse Group at Twelve Months

	Relapse (n=163)		Non-Relapse (n=65)		Statistics	
	Median	Range	Median	Range	Stats	p
Number of Cigarettes	18.0	0- 80	16.0	0- 43	5047	0.574
SADQ	33.0	2- 60	29.0	2- 57	4343	0.034
APQ-Core	12.0	3- 22	11.0	2- 22	4640	0.143
Physical Symptoms (RSCL)	35.0	3- 88	22.0	1- 72	4077	0.007
Psychological Symptoms (RSCL)	57.0	0-100	52.0	0- 90	4933	0.417
GHQ-28	16.0	0- 28	13.0	0- 28	4320	0.030
Life Situation Survey	74.0	38-118	74.0	25-127	4656	0.154
Nottingham Health Profile						
Physical Abilities	10.6	0-100	0	0-100	4496	0.054
Pain	32.6	0-100	14.8	0-100	4115	0.007
Energy Level	60.8	0-100	39.2	0-100	4785	0.241
Sleep	50.9	0-100	38.5	0-100	4300	0.025
Social Isolation	40.1	0-100	39.0	0-100	5065	0.603
Emotional Reactions	38.7	0-100	26.9	0- 90	4623	0.134
Total Scores	238	7-539	183	0-523	4210	0.016
Short-Form Thirty Six						
Physical Functioning	80.0	5-100	90.0	0-100	4445	0.056
Role Functioning	25.0	0-100	50.0	0-100	4189	0.010
Bodily Pain	42.0	0-100	62.0	0-100	3889	0.002
General Health	35.0	0- 90	47.0	0-100	4358	0.036
Vitality	35.0	0- 95	40.0	0-90	4811	0.279
Social Functioning	50.0	0-100	50.0	0-100	4931	0.413
Emotional Role	0	0-100	33.0	0-100	4842	0.276
Mental Health	40.0	0- 92	44.0	4- 96	4799	0.266
Total Scores	337	35-776	411	31-781	4152	0.011
Reported Health Transition	4.0	1- 5	3.0	1- 5	4187	0.011

Key: SADQ =Severity of Alcohol Dependence, APQ= Alcohol Problem Questionnaire, RSCL=Rotterdam Symptoms Checklist. All the results are shown following two-tailed Mann Whitney "U" tests. The following are the equivalent parametric results where appropriate after two-tailed Independent Sample "t" tests; a) SADQ (33.6, 14.6, Mean, SD) (29.0, 13.5, Mean, SD) (Relapse : Non Relapse) (t= –2.20, p=0.028), b) APQ-Core (12.5, 4.1, Mean, SD) (11.5, 4.1, Mean, SD) (Relapse : Non Relapse) (t= –1.56, p=0.121) and c) Life Situation Survey (72.8, 16.0, Mean, SD) (76.8, 18.4, Mean, SD) (Relapse : Non Relapse) (t=1.66, p=0.099). Significance was taken as $p \leq 0.01$.

PREDICTORS OF OUTCOME

These were ascertained after a Forward-Stepwise Logistic Regression inserting all the previously described demographic variables (unless otherwise stated), those ordinal variables presented in tables 9.2a-c (these are referred to as QoL/QoL-related variables) and any other measures tested at a $p \leq 0.05$ level after univariate examination. As only the significant variables were selected by the computer on this occasion significance was taken as $p \leq 0.05$.

Three Months

NHP and SF-36 composite scores were not entered into the regression because they represented a series of variables measuring different constructs. In addition there were four NHP and SF-36 sub-score variables with correlations $r > 0.86$ as follows.

Energy (NHP) Vitality (SF-36)
Emotional Reactions (NHP) Mental Health (SF-36)
Pain (NHP) Bodily Pain (SF-36)
Physical Abilities (NHP) Physical Functioning (SF-36)

This level of agreement indicated that the same construct was being measured. Thus in order to reduce the number of variables tested in the regression, only the one which showed the strongest univariate relationship was included NB a smaller "U" statistic indicated a greater effect. Thus for example in Table 9.2a the SF-36 bodily pain "U" statistic was smaller than that of the equivalent NHP pain sub-score, so the SF-36 variable was included in the final regression model

The following variables were entered into the final regression model; (number of variables is shown between parentheses); sociodemographic (8), length of time alcohol free (1), any prescription drugs (1), prescription of vitamins (1), number of cigarettes smoked daily (1), APQ-Core total score (1), SADQ total score (1), RSCL physical and psychological symptoms (2), GHQ total score (1), LSS total score (1), NHP sub-scores (3) and SF-36 sub-scores (8); this was 29 variables in total. The results of this regression are shown in Table 9.3a with accompanying Odds Ratios and 95% Confidence Intervals. There were three significant predictors of outcome. The most significant predictor was living in a socially underprivileged area as measured by the Jarman Index. For every 5 points on the Jarman scale the chances of relapse were increased by 1.20. Lower (i.e. greater impairment) SF-36 bodily pain scores followed this. Each ten points on the SF-36 bodily pain sub-scales increased the possibility of relapse by 0.86. The final significant predictor of outcome was prescription of vitamins during the 12 months prior to assessment. This increased the likelihood of relapse at three months by an odds ratio of 0.48.

Another regression was performed according to ITT principles. In this event the any previous treatment and any previous residential treatment variables were entered in addition to those previously described, the significant predictors were as before.

Six Months

For this regression eight sociodemographic variables were entered into the regression as before. In addition to the variables entered at three months; the number of units of alcohol consumed in a typical week prior to/length of time alcohol free at baseline assessment, prescription of vitamins and number of previous residential treatments were also included in the final model. Five NHP and six SF-36 variables were entered according to the principles described at three months. Thus on this occasion there were 30 independent variables. Table 9.3b presents the findings of this analysis. Two of the significant predictors at six months follow-up were sociodemographic factors. Again living in an underprivileged area (i.e. Jarman Index scores) was the most significant predictor of relapse. The odds ratio for every 5 points on the Jarman scale was 1.14. Living alone was the next strongest predictor of relapse, with an odds ratio of 0.48. Lower SF-36 bodily pain scores at baseline (i.e. greater pain) also predicted a poor outcome. For every 10 points on the SF-36 bodily pain scale the chances of relapse were increased by an odds ratio of 0.90.

Having established that living alone was a significant predictor of six-month outcomes the impact of social functioning/isolation and affective status at six months upon this result were investigated. The SF-36 social functioning and NHP social isolation sub-scores both showed significant "between group differences following two-tailed Mann-Whitney "U" tests viz; social functioning (SF-36) (37.5, 0-100, Median, Range) (73.7, 0-100, Median Range) (U=4593, $p < 0.001$) (Alone : Not Alone), social isolation (NHP) (n=118) (44.5, 0-100, Median, Range) (n=110) (22.5, 0-100, Median, Range) (U=4446, $p < 0.001$) (Alone : Not Alone). Affective disturbance was assessed by GHQ-28 scores, this variable also showed significant "between group" differences (17,0-28, Median, Range) (14, 0-28, Median, Range) (Alone : Not Alone) (U=4671, $p < 0.001$).

No further variables were entered into the ITT analysis and the significant predictors were as shown in table 9.3b.

Twelve Months

For this regression the length of time alcohol free and any prescription drugs were not entered. However as prescription of vitamins in the twelve months prior to baseline assessment had an association with outcome ($p < 0.05$) this was still included. There were two additional variables inserted at this time point; the number of previous residential alcohol-related treatments and units of alcohol consumed in a typical week prior to baseline assessment. Also four NHP and seven SF-36 variables were entered. In total, the end of study regression comprised 29 variables. The results are shown in table 9.4c.

Higher Jarman Index scores was the most significant predictor relapse with an odds ratio of 1.14 for every 5 points on the scale. *Jarman scores were the only variable to predict relapse at all three time points.* This was followed by number of previous residential treatments. There was an odds ratio of 1.28 for every treatment episode prior to baseline assessment. The final predictor at the end of the study was units of alcohol consumed in a typical week prior to baseline assessment. Every 10 units of alcohol consumed increased the likelihood of relapse by an odds ratio of 1.04 at 12 month follow-up.

For the ITT regression prescription of vitamins was omitted from the final model, however the significant predictors were as shown in table 9.4c.

Table 9.3. Predictors of Relapse/Non-Relapse at Different Follow-up Periods

a) Three Months

	R	SE	df	Significance	Odds Ratio	95% Confidence Interval
Jarman Index	0.219	0.01	1	< 0.001	1.20	1.10-1.30
SF-36 Bodily Pain	(–)0.139	0.01	1	0.004	0.86	0.78-0.95
Prescription of Vitamins	(–)0.112	0.30	1	0.013	0.48	0.27-0.86

The Odds Ratios refer to every 5 points on the Jarman index, every 10 points for the SF-36 Bodily Pain score, and the chances of being prescribed vitamins during the previous 12 months.

b) Six Months

	R	SE	df	Significance	Odds Ratio	95% Confidence Interval
Jarman Index	0.169	0.01	1	< 0.001	1.14	1.06-1.23
Living Alone	(–)0.119	0.29	1	0.011	0.48	0.27-0.85
SF-36 Bodily Pain	(–)0.092	0.10	1	0.031	0.90	0.81-0.99

The Odds Ratios for Jarman and SF-36 scores are as above. The Odds Ratio for living alone refers to the greater likelihood of relapsing whilst living alone at the time of baseline assessment.

c) 12 Months

	R	SE	df	Significance	Odds Ratio	95% Confidence Interval
Jarman Index	0.159	0.01	1	0.003	1.14	1.04-1.23
Previous Residential Treatments	0.135	0.09	1	0.009	1.27	1.06-1.52
Units of Alcohol	0.120	0.01	1	0.015	1.04	1.00-1.07

The Odds Ratio relates to Jarman Index is as 3 and 6 months. Units of alcohol refers to every 10 units of alcohol at baseline assessment and previous residential treatment relates to one previous treatment. For all three tables significance was taken as $p \leq 0.05$.

The Relationship Between Time to Relapse and Study Measures

In order to establish this a custom built General Factorial ANOVA was used (described in *Data Analysis-chapter six*) entering the log-transformed days to relapse as the dependent variable. The initial ANOVA only related to those individuals known to have relapsed during the twelve month study period (n=163). A relapse was deemed to have occurred at the point when 21or 14 units of alcohol (male and female respectively) had been consumed during one week i.e. this could be in one day. Even if this quantity had been exceeded for one day only during the study, the participant was treated as having relapsed. The median number of days to relapse in this sample was 35, (2-344, Range). Again the aim was to minimise those variables entered into the regression so the strength of the relationships for the equivalent SF-36 and NHP domains were tested by a computation of Spearmans *rho* correlation coefficients. The results are shown in Table 9.4. There were no statistically significant relationships (all r < 0.5). In consequence of this series of tests, the SF-36 physical functioning, and NHP pain/energy /SF-36 mental health sub-scales were entered into the model.

Thus the following baseline variables were finally entered (number of variables shown in parentheses), sociodemographic measures (8), alcohol history (3), alcohol consumption (1), length of time alcohol free (1), family history score (1), any previous prescription (1) illicit (1) drug use within the past twelve months, prescription of vitamins (1) during the same period, previous alcohol related treatments (4), number of cigarettes (1), SADQ total scores (1), APQ-Core total scores (1) RSCL physical and psychological symptom scores (2), GHQ-28 total scores (1), LSS total scores (1), NHP sub-scores (4) and SF-36 sub-scores (7); 39 variables in total. Total NHP and SF-36 scores were not included in the final model for reasons previous stated.

There was only one variable which was significantly associated with time to relapse, this was the length of time alcohol-free (F=11.1, p=0.001). However individuals who were recruited from the Minnesota project and community alcohol services samples drank significantly less prior to baseline assessment. The treatment programmes for the Minn Proj and CAS groups were 3 months and 28 days respectively and abstinence was a condition of continued treatment. Therefore the ANOVA was repeated, on this occasion omitting length of time alcohol free. In this ANOVA there was only one significant finding, the Jarman Index (F=10.3, p=0.002). Living in a socially disadvantaged area (Jarman index scores) was associated with a shorter time taken to relapse.

An ITT analysis was also performed assuming that for those individuals lost to follow-up, relapse occurred on the day following the last known non-relapse contact. The median number of days to relapse for these 175 individuals was 36, (2-344, Range). Correlations between those NHP and SF-36 variables shown in table 9.4 were computed for the ITT sample. The trends were as before and there were no significant findings. Once more length of time alcohol-free was the only variable associated with time to relapse in the initial ANOVA (F=4.5, p=0.002). As before a secondary ANOVA model was built omitting length of time alcohol free. On this occasion Jarman Index scores showed the strongest link (F=4.9, p=0.029) but statistical significance could not be inferred.

A later regression will investigate the changes in each of the QoL/QoL-related scores. Focussing upon how these are related to the amount of time taken before relapse to heavy drinking in only those ADI successfully followed-up.

Table 9.4. Baseline Correlations for Equivalent NHP and SF-36 Sub-Scores and Days to Relapse in the Relapse Group Only (n=163)

	Days to Relapse	
	r	p
Physical Abilities (NHP)	−0.231	0.003
Physical Functioning (SF-36)	0.244	0.002
Pain (NHP)	−0.233	0.003
Bodily Pain (SF-36)	0.230	0.003
Energy (NHP)	−0.158	0.045
Vitality (SF-36)	0.132	0.093
Emotional Reactions (NHP)	−0.019	0.808
Mental Health (SF-36)	0.046	0.563

All tests were two-tailed and produced a Spearmans *rho* correlation coefficient. Significance taken as $r \geq 0.5$. There were no statistically significant relationships.

Comparison with the Results of the Pilot Study

In the pilot study (see chapter three- Study B) there were four significant predictors of relapse (in order of increasing statistical significance) Irish ethnicity, social class, number of cigarettes smoked daily and sleep (NHP). Each of these will now be considered.

A) Sleep

In the current study there was a significant difference between the R and NR groups at three months following univariate testing. However once confounders had been controlled for this was lost. A General Factorial ANOVA entering relapse/non relapse as the fixed factor was carried out to ascertain which confounders were responsible for the loss of statistical significance. The following were entered as co-variates; age, gender, ethnicity, marital status, living arrangements, social class, unemployment, Jarman Index scores length of time alcohol free, and baseline alcohol consumption. The only significant confounding factor in the ANOVA was baseline alcohol consumption ($F=11.4$, $df=11,184$, $p=0.001$).

B) Cigarettes

The number of cigarettes smoked daily failed to show a univariate difference between the two groups ($p > 0.4$).

C) Social Class

This also produced a significant "between group" difference that was lost after controlling for confounders. Unlike sleep that failed to attain univariate significance at six and twelve months, the difference in univariate social class outcome was significant at both these time-points, however confounding factors were responsible for this effect. To test this an ANOVA was employed used the identical methodology as described for sleep only on this occasion social class was the dependent variable. There were two significant confounding effects firstly Jarman Index scores ($F=18.6$, $df=10,221$, $p < 0.001$) and secondly unemployment ($F=10.1$, $df=10,221$, $p=0.002$).

D) Irish Ethnicity

Because the ethnicity variable was collapsed in order to reduce the number of variables tested by the regression, the impact of Irish ethnicity was not tested in the current study. As there were only n=28 (12%) Irish individuals in the sample and any conclusions could at best be tentative so no further analysis was performed.

Conclusion

At the end of the 12-month follow-up period there was an overall relapse rate of 71%. Prescription of vitamins in the 12 months prior to the study was associated with a poor short-term prognosis. Jarman index scores predicted relapse at all three time-points. Bodily pain as measured by the SF-36 was a significant predictor at three and six months. Living alone was a predictor of outcome at six months only. At twelve months, units of alcohol consumed in a typical week prior to baseline assessment and number of previous residential alcohol treatments were also predictors of outcome. The significant predictors of relapse were identical for those individuals successfully followed-up and others included in an intention to treat analysis.

Baseline variables that had a significant relationship with time to relapse were the length of time alcohol free and the Jarman Index. However when using an intention to treat analysis only length of time alcohol free showed a significant association with time taken to relapse.

The findings from the pilot study concerning sleep, cigarettes and social class were not generalisable to a larger more socially varied sample. Irish ethnicity was not tested because only a small percentage of the sample described themselves as having an Irish ethnic background.

Chapter 10

MISCELLANEOUS LONGITUDINAL OUTCOME MEASURES

INTRODUCTION

In the previous chapter the outcomes concerning relapse were considered. This chapter examines other non-QoL/QoL-related outcomes and considers the following including

i) Predictors of re-admission on relapse (RAOR) during the study period.
ii) Whether any variables were significantly linked to the time taken to RAOR.
iii) The use of alcohol-related community support and Alcoholics Anonymous during the study period and how this was linked to relapse and RAOR.
iv) Returning home to live alone, living in a family unit and unemployment during the study period and the impact of these upon relapse and RAOR rates.
v) The impact of drinking during the study on all the above

The RAOR analysis related to 230 individuals. Six individuals who died were known to have been re-admitted and on relapse included in the RAOR group. In total one hundred and twelve (47%) individuals were known to have been re-admitted on relapse during the twelve-month study period.

DIFFERENCES IN BASELINE SCORES : RAOR VERSUS NON-RAOR

Either two-tailed *Chi*-squared, Mann Whitney "U" or Independent Sample "t" tests were initially used to assess univariate differences. There was only one sociodemographic variable where there was a significant "between-group" difference in baseline scores. This was in Jarman index scores (28.6, (−)17.6 – (+)49.7 Median, Range) (21.7,(−)25.2 – (+)49.7, Median Range) (RAOR : Non-RAOR) (U= 4879, p=0.001). ADI who lived in a socially deprived area were more likely to be RAOR during the study period. Univariate differences in social class measures showed a trend towards predicting outcome (*Chi*-squared=8.74, df=2, p=0.013). Fifty (63%) of the individuals from the Social Classes I/II were not RAOR during the study period and fifty-three (60%) from Social Classes IV and V were RAOR during the same timespan. All other socio-demographic variables produced differences $p > 0.05$.

Neither the prescription of any drug (*Chi*-squared=4.85, df=1, p=0.040) or use of any illicit drugs (*Chi*-squared=0.013, df=1, p=0.509) were significantly associated with outcome. Prescription of vitamins in the 12 months prior to baseline assessment was however significantly related to the likelihood of RAOR (*Chi*-squared=9.08, df=1, p=0.003). Fifty-seven (60%) of those individuals who were prescribed vitamins were RAOR within 12 months of the baseline assessment.

The between group differences in alcohol consumption, alcohol history and family history were all not significant ($p > 0.05$). There was one related variable that resulted in a significant association with outcome. A shorter length of time alcohol-free at baseline assessment increased the likelihood of RAOR; (5.5,2-49, Median, Range) (8.5,2-56, Median Range) (RAOR : Non-RAOR) (U=4871, $p < 0.001$).

One other area of assessment revealed important links to outcome; this was the number of previous alcohol-related treatments. A greater number of any previous treatments was linked to a poor outcome (3,0-80, Median, Range) (1,0-21, Median Range) (RAOR : Non-RAOR) (U=4650, $p < 0.001$). The strongest relationship was with more previous residential treatment episodes (1,0-45, Median, Range) (0, 0-8, Median Range) (RAOR : Non-RAOR) (U=4615, $p < 0.001$). The link to outcome concerning the number of previous community alcohol detoxification and non-detoxification treatments were both $p > 0.13$.

Table 10.1 shows the "between group" differences in scores for QoL and QoL-related variables. There were significant findings related to the following (in order of decreasing statistical significance), physical symptoms (RSCL), GHQ-28 total scores, reported health transition (SF-36), bodily pain (SF-36), pain (NHP), role functioning (SF-36), general health (SF-36), sleep, physical abilities (NHP) and physical functioning (SF-36).

To establish which variables were able to predict RAOR within the study period a Forward Stepwise Logistic regression analysis was employed. The following variables were entered into the regression model (number of variables are shown between parentheses). Firstly Sociodemographic measures; these comprised of age, gender, Jarman Index, unemployment, social class, and the following composite variables, living arrangements, marital status and ethnicity (8). Secondly QoL/QoL-related variables shown in Table 10.1, excepting NHP pain and energy sub-scores and SF-36 role functioning and mental health sub-scores, because their equivalent NHP and SF-36 subscales respectively showed a stronger relationship to outcome after univariate testing (18). Total NHP and SF-36 scores were omitted as they both represent a composite score comprising disparate variables. Thirdly any prescription drugs, (1) prescription of vitamins (1), length of time alcohol free at baseline assessment, (1) number of previous alcohol related treatments (1) and number of previous residential treatments (1) were all included because they revealed important univariate links to outcome. Table 10.2 shows the results of this regression. The most significant predictor of outcome was a greater number of previous residential alcohol-related treatments. Each residential treatment increased the risk of RAOR by 1.29. This was followed by a higher reported health transition scores (SF-36), every 1 point on the scale (range 1-5) increased the chances of RAOR by 1.60. The final predictor of outcome was the Jarman Index scores, living in an underprivileged area was associated with a negative outcome. For every 5 points on the Jarman Index scale the odds ratio was 1.13.

Table 10.1. Comparison of Baseline Scores : RAOR versus Non-RAOR

	RAOR (n=112)		Non-RAOR (n=118)		Statistics	
	Median	Range	Median	Range	Stats	p
Number of Cigarettes	15.0	0- 80	20.0	0- 60	6123	0.333
SADQ	31.0	2- 60	33.5	2- 59	5930	0.179
APQ-Core	12.0	3- 22	12.0	2- 22	6112	0.325
Physical Symptoms (RSCL)	38.5	3- 88	25.0	1- 75	4517	< 0.001
Psychological Symptoms (RSCL)	57.0	0- 100	52.0	0-100	5883	0.150
GHQ-28	18.0	0- 28	13.0	0- 28	4841	< 0.001
Life Situation Survey	72.0	36- 104	74.0	25-127	5767	0.095
Nottingham Health Profile						
Physical Abilities	10.7	10.7-100	0	0-100	5205	0.003
Pain	41.0	0- 100	14.8	0-100	4861	< 0.001
Energy Level	60.8	0- 100	39.2	0-100	5709	0.067
Sleep	61.0	0- 100	43.7	0-100	5153	0.004
Social Isolation	40.1	0- 100	38.5	0-100	6224	0.445
Emotional Reactions	48.1	0- 100	29.0	0-100	5526	0.032
Short-Form Thirty Six						
Physical Functioning	75.0	0- 100	90.0	5-100	5296	0.009
Role Functioning	22.5	0- 100	50.0	0-100	4931	0.001
Bodily Pain	32.7	0- 100	62.0	0-100	4694	< 0.001
General Health	35.0	0- 90	45.0	0-100	5045	0.002
Vitality	27.5	0- 95	40.0	0- 90	5578	0.041
Social Functioning	38.8	0- 100	50.0	0-100	5646	0.055
Emotional Role	0	0- 100	33.0	0-100	6451	0.739
Mental Health	38.0	0- 92	44.0	0- 96	5619	0.050
Reported Health Transition	4.0	1- 5	3.0	1- 5	4858	< 0.001

Key: SADQ =Severity of Alcohol Dependence, APQ= Alcohol Problem Questionnaire, RSCL=Rotterdam Symptoms Checklist, GHQ-28 = General Health Questionnaire. All the results are shown following two-tailed Mann Whitney "U" tests. The following are the equivalent parametric results where appropriate after two tailed Independent Sample "t" tests; a) SADQ (33.7, 14.7, Mean, SD) (30.7, 14.0, Mean, SD) (RAOR : Non-RAOR) (t= −1.59, p=0.113), b) APQ-Core (12.6, 4.0, Mean, SD) (11.9, 4.5, Mean, SD) (RAOR : Non-RAOR) (t= −1.20, p=0.223), , 27.1, Mean, SD) (50.8, 24.9, Mean, SD) (RAOR : Non-RAOR) and c) Life Situation Survey (71.6, 15.7, Mean, SD) (76.1, 17.3, Mean, SD) (RAOR : Non-RAOR) (t= -2.07, p=0.039). (RAOR : Non-RAOR). RAOR=Re-admission on relapse. Non-RAOR=Non-Re-admission on relapse.

Table 10.2. Forward-Stepwise Logistic Regression to Ascertain Predictors of RAOR

	R	SE	df	Significance	Odds Ratio	95% Confidence Interval
Number of Previous Residential Treatments	0.196	0.07	1	< 0.001	1.29	1.13-1.48
Reported Health Transition (SF-36)	0.185	0.13	1	< 0.001	1.60	1.23-2.04
Jarman Index Scores	0.138	0.01	1	0.003	1.13	1.03-1.48

Odds Ratios refers to the following;- *residential treatment*; one residential treatment episode, *reported health transition*; 1 point on a scale range 1-5 and *Jarman Index*; every 5 points on the Jarman index. Significance taken as $p \leq 0.05$.

The Relationship Between Study Measures and Time to RAOR

A General Factorial ANOVA established that no variables were significantly associated with time to RAOR in the regression ($p > 0.05$).

The Impact of Use of Alcoholics Anonymous Community and Residential Services

A) Between-Centre Differences

During the study period the number of individuals utilising the services named in the title on one or more occasions after leaving the relevant study unit were as follows; Alcoholics Anonymous (AA) (n=47, 20%), community services (voluntary and statutory sector including shopfronts and drop-ins) (n=87, 36%) and residential alcohol related services subsequent to treatment (n=57, 24%). On this occasion because the findings relating to AA would be of interest to an international audience the "between centre" differences are shown in Table 10.3. In order to establish the level of unadjusted statistical significance two-tailed *Chi*-squared/Fishers exact tests were used throughout. There were two significant findings, firstly concerning AA (Fishers exact test statistic, df=5, $p < 0.001$) and secondly residential services (Fishers exact tests statistic, df=5, p=0.001). ADI from the Minnesota project were the most likely to use AA on leaving the service followed by those from the NHS alcohol specialist unit and thereafter community alcohol services. This result remained significant on controlling for sociodemographic factors (R=0.240, B=0.492, SE=0.13, df=1, $p < 0.001$). Social class was also significant in the regression (R=(–) 0.150, B=(–) 0.315, SE=0.12, df=1, p=0.007). A lower proportion of individuals from Social Classes IV/V (25%) used AA in comparison to those from the other social classes. Twenty-eight percent individuals attended AA from Social Class III and 47% from Social Classes I/II. Individuals from Social Classes I/II were 1.64 (0.70-3.89, 95% CI) times more likely to attend an AA meeting subsequent to leaving the study unit than those from Social Class III. The equivalent odds ratio relating to Social Classes IV/V was 2.32 (1.06-5.06,95%CI).

The Minnesota project and voluntary sector sample groups (38%) were also the most likely to have a follow-up residential treatment. However on controlling for sociodemographic variables "between centre" statistical significance was lost (R=0.000, B=0.023, SE=0.11, df=1, p=0.829) and no confounding variables contributed significantly to the result.

Table 10.3."Between Centre" Differences Between Up-Take of Support Services During the Study Period

Study Centre	Statistics						
	Vol Sec (40)	Med Ward (40)	Priv Sec (40)	Alc Ward (40)	Minn Proj (40)	Comm Alc (40)	p
Alcoholics Anonymous	6 (18%)	1 (3%)	3 (8%)	11 (28%)	17 (43%)	9 (23%)	< 0.001
Residential Services	15 (38%)	8 (20%)	1 (3%)	12 (30%)	15 (38%)	6 (15%)	0.001
Community Services	18 (40%)	10 (25%)	8 (20%)	18 (40%)	15 (38%)	18 (40%)	0.056

Key: Vol Sec=Voluntary Sector, Med Ward= Medical Wards, Priv Sec=Private Sector, Alc Ward=NHS Alcohol Specialist Ward, Minn Proj=Minnesota Project and Comm Alc=Community Alcohol Services. Significance taken as $p \leq 0.01$. Number of individuals shown between parentheses.

This table relates to any contact with alcoholics anonymous, any contact with voluntary/statutory sector services including drop-ins and shop fronts and any residential services beyond the baseline "treatment".

B) Relapse at Twelve Months

Of the sixty-four individuals who did *not* relapse to heavy drinking at the end of the study period twenty-three (36%) attended AA during the study. Individuals who attended AA comprised only fifteen percent of the relapse group. This association was significant before adjustment (Two-tailed *Chi*-squared test) (*Chi*-squared=15.6, df=1, $p < 0.001$) (OR=0.27, 0.13-0.53, 95% CI) and after controlling for sociodemographic factors (R= 0.224, B=1.42, SE=0.39, df=1, $p < 0.001$). None of the sociodemographic confounders were significant. There was not a significant relationship in this outcome for those individuals who used community and alcohol-related residential services ($p > 0.2$). However the trend was towards poor outcomes on both occasions. An intention to treat analysis was also performed according the principles previously described, the significant results were as before.

C) RAOR During the Study Period

Once more attendance at AA was significantly associated with outcome before statistical adjustment (Two-tailed *Chi*-squared test) (*Chi*-squared=12.9, df=1, $p < 0.001$) (OR=0.27, 0.13-0.56, 95% CI) and after controlling for sociodemographic factors (R= (–)0.200, B=(–)1.33, SE=0.40, df=1, $p < 0.001$). No sociodemographic factors contributed significantly to the regression result. Thirty-four (40%) of the individuals who were not in the RAOR group used AA. In comparison; only eleven (10%) individuals who attended at least one AA meeting during the follow-up period had a ROAR episode.

Contact with community services was not associated with outcome (n=46, 70%) (n=40, 51%) (RAOR : Non RAOR) (Two-tailed *Chi*-squared test) (*Chi*-squared=1.39, df=1, p=0.149), though the trend was towards a poor prognosis. Negative outcome was even more marked in the group that had used residential services in addition to their baseline treatment (n=36, 32%) (n=21, 18%) (RAOR : Non RAOR) (Two-tailed *Chi*-squared test) (*Chi*-squared=6.55, df=1, p=0.014). This finding was of borderline statistical significance.

LONGITUDINAL DEMOGRAPHIC VARIABLES AND OUTCOME

For this section the variables of interest were as follows. Firstly returning home to live alone, in residential treatment (throughout the study period) and living in a family unit during the study period (living arrangements). Secondly the impact of unemployment or employment over 12 month follow-up on outcome (employment status). Henceforth these will be referred to as "longitudinal demographic variables." Data was only presented for those individuals where longitudinal information was known. Seven individuals were lost to follow-up and this information could not be corroborated from patient records, relatives or other professionals. Thus the following prevalence rates related to 233 individuals; returning home to live alone (n=116, 50%), residential treatment throughout (n=9, 4%), living in a family (n=108, 46%), employed at any time during the study, including part-time work (employment) (n=73, 31%) and unemployed throughout the study (unemployment) (n=160, 69%). All these were categorical variables and thus all univariate tests were two-tailed *Chi*-squared/Fishers exact tests.

The Association Between End of Study Relapse Rates and Longitudinal Demographic Variables

Those individuals who returned home to live alone during the study period were significantly more likely to relapse at 12 months (*Chi*-squared=12.5, df=1, p=0.001) than those individuals who did not live alone. Ninety-six (59%) of these individuals had relapsed by the end of the study. Not surprisingly each individual who had remained in alcohol-related treatment throughout did not relapse (Fishers exact test statistic, df=1, $p < 0.001$). Twenty-one (33%) individuals who were living in a family unit had not relapsed during the same period. There was not a significant link between living in a family unit and relapsing by the end of the study (*Chi*-squared=3.4, df=1, p=0.076).

In order to control for sociodemographic differences, the longitudinal variables, where available, were substituted for their equivalent baseline measures. Thus in this regression unemployment rates during the study were entered in preference to the baseline unemployment measure, and either returning home to live alone, in a family unit or in treatment throughout variables replaced the composite living arrangements variable.

Returning home to live alone showed a significant trend following statistical controls (R=(–)0.140, B= (–)1.15, SE=0.41, df=1, p=0.004). After controlling for sociodemographic factors the remaining in treatment throughout variable was not significant (R=0.000, B=15.2, SE=160, df=1, p=0.924).

The link between relapse at the end of the study and employment (*Chi*-squared=13.7, df=1, $p < 0.001$) and unemployment (*Chi*-squared=24.1, df=1, $p < 0.001$) were significant before statistical adjustment. Only thirty-eight employed individuals (23%) relapsed to heavy drinking, in contrast the equivalent figures for those unemployed were (n=125, 77%).

Statistical significance was maintained for both variables on controlling for sociodemographic factors as follows; employment (R=0.192, B=1.36, SE=0.36, df=1, $p < 0.001$) and unemployment (R= (–) 0.210, B= (–) 1.47, SE=0.37, df=1, $p < 0.001$). In both regressions age was a significant contributor. Younger individuals were more likely to be employed during the study period (n=72) (39.2, 9.5, Mean, SD) (n=161) (44.0, 9.8, Mean, SD) (Employed : Unemployed) (Two-tailed Independent Sample "t" test) (t=3.44, p=0.001). The relevant regression statistics for the age variable were as follows;employment (R= (–)0.150, B= (–) 0.05, SE=0.01, df=1, p=0.004) and unemployment (R=0.146, B=0.056, SE=0.02, df=1, p=0.005).

Rates of RAOR and Longitudinal Demographic Measures

The trends concerning the living arrangements variable for RAOR mirrored those of relapse. The link between living in a family unit and RAOR was not significant (*Chi*-squared=3.9, df=1, p=0.063). In contrast returning to live alone (*Chi*-squared=8.92, df=1, p=0.004) and remaining in treatment (*Chi*-squared=8.81, df=1, p=0.003) were both significantly linked to outcome. Sixty-eight (61%) individuals who returned home to live alone were RAOR during the study period, and none of those who remained in treatment throughout required another detoxification. After controlling for sociodemographic factors the association between returning home to live alone during the study period and RAOR was significant (R=(–) 0.124, B= (–) 0.999, SE=0.38, df=1, p=0.003). Little confidence however can be placed on the finding relating to treatment throughout the study after controlling for sociodemographic confounders. (R=0.000, B=13.8, SE=131, df=1, p=0.916).

Employment (*Chi*-squared=22.4, df=1, $p < 0.001$) and unemployment (*Chi*-squared=24.1, df=1, $p < 0.001$) were both significantly associated with RAOR during the 12 month follow-up period. Only seventeen (15%) individuals who were employed had a RAOR, whereas ninety-four (85%) of the individuals who were in the RAOR group came from those individuals who were unemployed throughout. Both these findings remained significant on controlling for sociodemographic factors; employment (R=0.213, B=1.45,, SE=0.35, df=1, $p < 0.001$) and unemployment (R=(–) 0.225, B=(–) 1.52 SE=0.35, df=1, $p < 0.001$). The only significant confounding association was age. Employed individuals were significantly younger. The relevant univariate statistics have already been presented.

"Controlled Drinkers" v Abstainers: Longitudinal Outcomes

For these sets of analyses only, the non-relapse group at 12 months was subdivided into two groups. Those who drank during the study but did not relapse because their drinking either remained "controlled" or took the form of a self-limiting lapse (controlled drinkers) (CD) and those who were abstinent throughout (abstainers). The "controlled drinking" sample consisted of 21 (32%) (Males 17, Females 4) individuals. There was a statistically significant difference in the amount of units consumed during the 12 month study period between the controlled drinkers and abstainers (Two-tailed Mann Whitney "U" Test) (U=0, $p < 0.001$).

The median units of alcohol consumed over 12 months by the CD sample was 132 (6.75-928 Range).

The difference in uptake of AA, community and residential alcohol-related services was also investigated. There were no statistically significant differences ($p > 0.036$ throughout). Finally the longitudinal living arrangements and employment status variables were tested. On this occasion there were also no significant findings (> 0.25 throughout).

Drinking During the Study

a) Differences Between Relapsers and Non-Relapsers

The 12 months drinking data related to 224 individuals only. This does not include the 12 individuals lost to follow-up and a further four who died during the study period. The causes of death were as follows; head injury sustained whilst intoxicated, Hepatitis B, Liver Cirrhosis and suicide.

The median units of alcohol consumed for the total sample during the study was 3380 (0 - 26,504, Range). There was a statistically significant difference between the relapse and non-relapse groups (5419, 96-26,504, Median, Range) (0, 0-928, Median, Range) (Relapse : Non Relapse) (Two-tailed Mann Whitney U test) ($U=56$, $p < 0.001$). Sixteen (10%) individuals included in the relapse sample relapsed for short periods only and then were RAOR.

In order to conclude statistical significance in relation to the amount of alcohol consumed during the study; in addition to the eight baseline sociodemographic variables, baseline weekly units (units), SADQ, APQ and GHQ-28 scores were entered into a General Factorial ANOVA as covariates to test for their confounding effects.

After doing so the difference between the relapse and non-relapse groups remained significant ($F=188$, $df=13,165$, $p < 0.001$). There were no significant confounding effects.

b)The Link Between Drinking During the Study and Uptake of Alcoholics Anonymous, Community and Residential Services

Attendance at *any* AA meeting during the study had a significant association with less alcohol consumed during the study period before statistical adjustment (units of alcohol consumed) (68, 0-10,701, Median, Range) (3680, 0-26,504, Median, Range) (AA : Non-AA) (Two-tailed Mann Whitney “U” test) ($U=1996$, $p < 0.001$) and after controlling for confounding factors ($F=14.0$, $df= 13,165$, $p < 0.001$). Once more units at baseline was a contributing factor ($F=9.6$, $df=1$, $p=0.002$). The use of community ($p > 0.1$) and residential services ($p > 0.6$) were not significantly linked to outcome. However units contributed significantly to both regressions ($p < 0.001$ on both occasions).

c) Alcohol Consumption and Longitudinal Demographic Variables

Those individuals who returned home to live alone (Alone) during the study period had a significantly poorer outcome compared to those who did not (Not Alone). (4928, 0-26,504, Median, Range) (801, 0-16,403, Median, Range) (Alone : Not Alone) (Two-tailed Mann Whitney “U” test) ($U=3767$, $p < 0.001$). Significance remained on controlling for confounding factors ($F=6.8$, $df=12,166$, $p=0.01$). Units also contributed significantly to this regression ($F=11.8$, $df=1$, $p=0.001$). In this regression the longitudinal variables returning home to live alone, remaining in a treatment programme throughout, returning to a family unit, employment and unemployed were all entered in turn as a Fixed Factor in a General Factorial ANOVA.

Unsurprisingly remaining in a treatment programme was associated with an excellent result after two-tailed Mann Whitney “U” tests ($U=181$, $p < 0.001$). Abstinence was a condition of continued residence so by definition those who remained in treatment did not drink. Those individuals not in treatment throughout drank a median of 3449 (0-26,504, Range) units. Perhaps of greater surprise is that this finding was maintained on controlling for sociodemographic factors ($F=19.1$, $df=12,166$, $p < 0.001$). The trend for baseline units to be associated with outcome continued ($F=10.6$, $df=1$, $p=0.001$).

Returning to live in a family unit was also associated with a good prognosis before statistical adjustment (1150, 0-16,403, Median, Range) (4180, 0-26,504, Median, Range) (Two-tailed Mann Whitney “U” test) ($U=4440$, $p < 0.001$). However on controlling for confounding factors statistical significance was lost ($F=3.8$, $df=12,166$, $p=0.054$). Units was once more significant in the regression ($F=11.9$, $df=1$, $p=0.001$)

Not surprisingly the unadjusted trends concerning unemployment and employment during the study period were identical and significant following two-tailed Mann Whitney “U” tests; viz. (4390, 0-26,504, Median, Range) (645,0-25,200, Median, Range) (Unemployment : Employment) ($U=3249$, $p < 0.001$); (646, 0-25200, Median, Range) (4285, 26504, Median, Range) (Employment : Unemployment) ($U=3231$, $p < 0.001$). Significance remained after controlling for confounders regarding both variables. Units contributed significantly to both regressions (the unemployed group drank more). All the relevant results are presented below.

a)Controlling for Confounding Factors- Unemployment ($F=10.7$, $df=13,165$, $p=0.001$); Employment ($F=7.0$, $df=13,165$, $p=0.009$).

b)Contribution of Units- Unemployment ($F=14.5$, $df=1$, $p < 0.001$); Employment ($F=14.0$, $df=1$, $p < 0.001$).

CONCLUSION

One hundred and twelve (47%) individuals were re-admitted on relapse (RAOR) during the study period. The predictors of RAOR were number of previous residential alcohol related treatments, SF-36 reported health transition sub-scores and Jarman Index scores. Forty-five (20%) individuals attended at least one Alcoholics Anonymous (AA) meeting subsequent to leaving the original study unit. Individuals who were in programmes where AA was encouraged i.e. the Minnesota project and NHS alcohol specialist ward were the most likely to attend AA during the study. AA attendance was significantly associated (after statistical controls) with a positive outcome in relation to end of study relapse rates, likelihood of RAOR and units of alcohol consumed. In comparison the relationship to these study outcomes for individuals who used alcohol related residential and community services during the study was poor.

Following statistical controls unemployment was associated with a greater likelihood of relapse or RAOR. Controlled drinkers and abstainers were compared. No longitudinal variables differentiated the two groups. The only factor that did so was the units of alcohol consumed during the study period. Returning home to live alone and unemployment were associated with greater consumption of alcohol during the study. Employment was associated with lesser consumption of alcohol. The only significant confounding variable related to these effects was the amount of units of alcohol consumed weekly prior to baseline assessment.

Chapter 11

Building of the Regression Model

Hypotheses

A regression model was built to test two hypotheses

i) whether relapse to heavy drinking results in a poor quality of life
ii) whether sustained abstinence or controlled drinking results in a good quality of life.

Rationale for the Co-Variates Chosen

The co-variates were chosen for the following reasons in order to test for their confounding effects

a) Sociodemogaphic variables: Previous literature had suggested that sociodemographic variables were intrinsically linked to the QoL of ADI. The intention was to assess whether this was the case, and if so to what extent.
b) Any baseline variables which were predictors of relapse or RAOR .
c) SADQ, APQ-Core, RSCL sub-scores, LSS and GHQ-28.
d) Empirical findings suggested that social environment was important in the outcomes of ADI. Those variables relating to this measured in the current study were included in the regression model
e) Significant predictors of 3 months outcome from the pilot study other than Irish ethnicity because the number of Irish participants was small.

Statistical Testing

A repeated measures ANOVA entering relapse at 12 months "yes" or "no" as the "between subjects" factor was used to ascertain whether there was a significant difference between changes in 12 month study scores. This analysis related to the ordinal QoL/QoL-related variables and compared those individuals who relapsed at 12 months (R) and those who had not (NR). In order to test for this scores were log transformed in those variables with non-parametric distributions. The results of the raw-score differences are shown in table 11.2. There was only one variable where there was not a significant between group difference i.e. the number of cigarettes smoked daily.

The rest of the results section of this monograph is largely devoted to the "within group" changes of the R and NR groups at baseline, three, six and twelve months. In these analyses the intention was to build a regression model to examine as many baseline confounders as possible, and statistical significance will only be concluded if significance remains after controlling for all these factors.

The Variables Entered into the Final Regression Model

Eight sociodemographic variables were entered. These were age, gender, ethnicity, marital status, social class, living alone, unemployment and Jarman index scores.

Other variables were included because they had been significant predictors in the previous regression analyses. These were: previous alcohol-related residential treatments, pain (SF-36), units of alcohol consumed in a typical week prior to admission, prescription of vitamins during the 12 months prior to baseline assessment and reported health transition (SF-36). For comprehensive analysis the baseline SADQ, APQ-Core, RSCL physical and psychological sub-scores, LSS and GHQ-28 scores and QoL/QoL-related variables were tested. Humphreys et al (1997) confirmed the importance of social and familial environment in eight-year outcomes for ADRP. A British paper (Brazier et al 1992) found that the level of agreement between the social isolation (NHP) and social functioning (SF-36) sub-scores was weak in a general population sample. Thus both were included in the final regression model.

In the pilot study (see chapter three- Study B) for this work (Foster et al 1998b) sleep as measured by the NHP and number of cigarettes smoked daily were significant predictors of relapse at 12 weeks. So these two were included to assess their impact over a longer time span and with a larger sample. Table 11.1 lists all the baseline variables included in the final regression model.

Table 11.1. Baseline Predictors Included in the Final Regression Model

Age
Gender
Ethnicity*
Social Class*
Marital Status*
Living Alone
Jarman Index Scores
Unemployment
Pain (SF-36)
Units of Alcohol Consumed in a Typical Week prior to Admission
Prescription of Vitamins in the 12 months prior to Admission
Number of Previous Alcohol-Related Residential Treatments
Reported Health Transition (SF-36)
Severity of Alcohol Dependence (SADQ)
Alcohol Problems Questionnaire (APQ)
Rotterdam Symptoms Checklist-Physical and Psychological Sub-Scores (LSS)
Life Situation Survey (LSS)
General Health Questionnaire-28 (GHQ-28)
Social Isolation (NHP)
Social Functioning (SF-36)
Sleep (NHP)
Number of Cigarettes Smoked Daily

* denotes composite variable. NHP=Nottingham Health Profile, SF-36=Short-Form 36.

Table 11.2. Comparison of Baseline Scores of Relapse and Non-Relapse Groups at Twelve Months

	Relapse (n=159)		Non-Relapse (n=65)		Statistics	
	Median	Range	Median	Range	F	p
Number of Cigarettes	20.0	0- 80	18.0	0- 60	0.9	0.352
Physical Symptoms (RSCL)	55.0	0- 99	13.0	0- 75	75.6	< 0.001
Psychological Symptoms (RSCL)	86.0	0-100	29.0	0-100	57.8	< 0.001
GHQ-28	21.0	0- 28	1.0	0- 27	91.9	< 0.001
Life Situation Survey*	57.0	21-119	100.0	41-130	122	< 0.001
Nottingham Health Profile						
Physical Abilities	19.9	0-100	0	0-100	8.3	0.001
Pain	53.6	0-100	0	0-100	20.4	< 0.001
Energy Level	67.9	0-100	24.0	0-100	20.8	< 0.001
Sleep	77.6	0-100	12.5	0-100	11.3	0.001
Social Isolation	44.5	0-100	0	0-100	12.7	< 0.001
Emotional Reactions	62.2	0-100	7.0	0-100	20.8	< 0.001
Total Scores	293	100-484	129	12.9-405	11.9	0.001
Short-Form Thirty Six						
Physical Functioning	70.0	0-100	95.0	0-100	18.9	< 0.001

Table 11.2 (Continued)

	Relapse (n=159)		Non-Relapse (n=65)		Statistics	
Role Functioning	0	0-100	100.0	0-100	8.0	0.005
Bodily Pain	32.0	0-100	82.0	0-100	30.9	< 0.001
General Health	25.0	0- 85	70.0	0-100	57.8	< 0.001
Vitality	20.0	0- 95	65.0	0- 95	50.5	< 0.001
Social Functioning	25.0	0-100	87.5	0-100	43.2	< 0.001
Emotional Role	0	0-100	100.0	0-100	11.7	0.001
Mental Health	24.0	0- 96	76.0	0-100	60.2	< 0.001
Total Scores	234	11-763	624	24-774	73.3	< 0.001
Reported Health Transition	5.0	1- 5	1.0	1- 5	98.8	< 0.001

Key: RSCL=Rotterdam Symptoms Checklist. All the results are shown following log-transformation (unless otherwise indicated) and thereafter a Repeated Measures ANOVA. * Scores did not require log-transformation. Significance taken as $p \leq 0.01$.

Chapter 12

"NON-RELAPSE" SAMPLE: "WITHIN-GROUP" SCORES

INTRODUCTION

There were significant differences in baseline and 12 month scores in all QoL/Qol-related variables except number of cigarettes smoked daily between the relapsers and non-relapsers. The "within group" changes in scores for the non-relapse group (n=65) at 12 months only are reported. There are two areas of investigation in this chapter and the analysis used will be briefly described.

a. "Within Group" Changes. Unadjusted statistical significance was ascertained by a Repeated Measures ANOVA. The dependent variables were log-transformed should this be required. This was the case when there were non-parametric distributions. If unadjusted significance was established then those variables listed in the previous chapter were entered as co-variates to test for their confounding effects.
b. Wilcoxon tests were used to investigate the extent of the improvements in all total scale scores over three different periods; i) Baseline-3months, ii) 3-6 months and iii) 6-12 months.

DIFFERENCES BETWEEN BASELINE AND 12-MONTH SCORES

These results are shown in Table 12.1. The majority of variables showed significant differences in scores before statistical adjustment. Each questionnaire will now be considered in turn.

i) *Rotterdam Symptoms Checklist.* Both the RSCL sub scores lost statistical significance following controls for confounding factors; viz. physical (F=1.08, df=1,40, p=0.303), psychological (F=1.12, df=1,32, p=0.296). There was one significant confounder for physical symptom scores, this was social class (F=8.1, df=1, p=0.007). Membership of Social Classes IV/V was associated with a smaller decrease in scores (negative scores indicate an improvement in health status); (n=28, 43%) ((–) 13, (+) 5– (–) 72, Median, Range) (Social

Classes I/II), (n=22, 34%) ((–) 7, (+) 16,– (–) 45 Median, Range) (Social Class III), (n=15, 23%) ((–)2, (+) 28 – (–) 15, Median, Range) (Social Classes IV/V).

ii) *General Health Questionnaire-28*: Following log-transformation and adjustment for confounders statistical significance could no longer be concluded concerning the decrease in GHQ-28 scores (F=0.095, df=1,18, p=0.294). There were no significant confounding variables.

iii) *Life Situation Survey*: The significant difference in Life Situation scores was lost following a Repeated Measures ANOVA (F=1.76, df=1,44, p=0.192). Baseline NHP social isolation scores contributed significantly to the ANOVA (F=8.01, df=1,44, p=0.007). There was a significant Spearmans *rho* correlation for the change between LSS scores and baseline NHP social isolation scores (r= (–) 0.51, $p < 0.001$).

iv) *Nottingham Health Profile*: There was only one NHP sub-score that was significant prior to statistical adjustment. This was emotional reactions (F=7.8 df=1,37, p=0.008). Statistical significance was lost on controlling for confounding factors (F=0.29, df=1,17, p=0.595). All confounding variables were not significant.

v) *Short-Form-36:* There were no significant changes in SF-36 sub-scores following statistical controls (all $p > 0.07$). However social class contributed significantly to two variables, viz. general health (F=11.8, df=1,42, p=0.001) and social functioning (F=7.53, df=1,38, p=0.009). Firstly general health, Social Classes IV/V were associated with a smaller improvement in health status; (n=28, 43%) ((+) 27, (–) 21 - (+) 70, Median, Range) (Social Class I/II), (n=22, 34%) ((+) 7, (–) 20 - (+) 53, Median, Range) (Social Class III), (0, (–) 20 - (+) 25, Median, Range) (Social Class IV/V).

Secondly social functioning; individuals from Social Classes IV/V had a median improvement of zero

((–) 62.5 – (+) 55, Range) compared to the following statistics relating to Social Classes III ((+) 37.5, (–) 20 – (+) 100, Median, Range) and I/II ((+) 37.5, (–) 37.5 – (+) 100, Median, Range).

APQ-Core scores also contributed significantly to the change in social functioning scores (F=7.91,df=1,38, p=0.008). Fewer alcohol problems were associated with a smaller increase (i.e deterioration) in social functioning scores. Finally fewer previous residential alcohol treatments (including hospital admissions) were associated with a smaller increase (deterioration) in reported health transition scores (F=8.42, df=1,46, p=0.006).

Table 12.1. Comparison of Baseline and 12-month scores in the Non-Relapse group (n=65)

	Baseline		12 Months		Statistics	
	Median	Range	Median	Range	F	p
Number of Cigarettes	16.0	0- 43	18.0	0- 60	1.6	0.213
Physical Symptoms (RSCL)	22.0	0- 90	13.0	0- 75	23.2	< 0.001
Psychological Symptoms (RSCL)	52.0	1- 72	29.0	0-100	24.3	< 0.001
GHQ-28	13.0	0- 28	1.0	0- 27	58.1	< 0.001
Life Situation Survey*	74.0	25- 127	100.0	41-130	35.1	< 0.001
Nottingham Health Profile						
Physical Abilities	0	0- 100	0	0-100	1.2	0.295
Pain	14.8	0- 100	0	0-100	3.9	0.061
Energy Level	39.2	0- 100	24.0	0-100	5.5	0.025
Sleep	38.5	0- 100	12.5	0-100	2.7	0.112
Social Isolation	38.5	0- 100	0	0-100	2.4	0.134
Emotional Reactions	33.0	0- 100	7.0	0-100	7.8	0.008
Total Scores	183	0- 523	129	12.9-405	1.1	0.302
Short-Form Thirty Six						
Physical Functioning	90.0	0- 100	95.0	5-100	4.2	0.044
Role Functioning	50.0	0- 100	100.0	0-100	3.9	0.056
Bodily Pain	62.0	0- 100	82.0	0-100	13.5	0.001
General Health	47.0	0- 100	70.0	0-100	25.0	< 0.001
Vitality	40.0	0- 90	65.0	0- 90	27.2	< 0.001
Social Functioning	50.0	0- 100	87.5	0-100	21.7	< 0.001
Emotional Role	33.0	0- 100	100.0	0-100	17.6	< 0.001
Mental Health	44.0	0- 92	76.0	0-100	38.0	< 0.001
Total Scores	411	35- 727	624	24-774	29.1	< 0.001
Reported Health Transition	3.0	1- 5	1.0	1- 5	50.2	< 0.001

Key: RSCL= Rotterdam Symptom Checklist. All the results shown following a Repeated Measures ANOVA. The F statistic is quoted on each occasion. Unless an * is shown the statistics are the results following log-transformation of data. Significance taken as $p \leq 0.01$.

What Is Pattern in QoL/QoL Related Scores Over 12 Months?

Tables 12.2 a-c show the differences in medians for the total scores in each of the study QoL/QoL related indices at baseline, 3, 6 and 12 months respectively. There were significant health related improvements for all the indices between baseline and three months ($p < 0.001$ in each case), thereafter the picture is inconsistent. The two RSCL sub-scores and GHQ-28 total scores showed no change or virtually no change from three–twelve months. Life Situation, Short Form-36 and Nottingham Health Profile scores were all improved throughout the study period, though not to a statistically significant degree.

Conclusion

Following statistical controls the "within group" differences in scores for individuals who did not relapse during the twelve month follow-up period (n=65, %) were not significant for any of the variables tested. The improvements in total scores for QoL/QoL-related variables were not consistent over 12 months. These were significant for all variables between baseline and three months. Thereafter there were no changes in scores or they were minimal.

Table 12.2. "Within Group" Changes For Three Different Follow-up Periods in Non-Relapsing Individuals (n=65)

a) Baseline and Three Months

	Baseline		Three Months		Statistics	
	Median	Range	Median	Range	Z	p
RSCL Physical Symptoms	22.0	1- 72	0.0	0- 71	–5.39	< 0.001
RSCL Psychological Symptoms	52.0	0- 90	29.0	0-100	–4.57	< 0.001
General Health Questionnaire-28 (GHQ-28)	13.0	0- 28	2.0	0- 28	–5.80	< 0.001
Life Situation Survey (LSS)	74.0	25-127	92.0	44-131	–5.37	< 0.001
Nottingham Health Profile (NHP)	183	0-523	90.0	0-491	–5.12	< 0.001
Short-Form-36 (SF-36)	411	31-781	594	51-764	–5.62	< 0.001

The variables relate to GHQ-28, LSS, NHP and SF-36 total scores. All tests were two-tailed Wilcoxon tests giving rise to a Z statistic. Significance taken as $p \leq 0.01$. There was a significant difference between baseline and 3 months in each of the study measures.

b) Three and Six Months

	Three Months		Six Months		Statistics	
	Median	Range	Median	Range	Z	p
RSCL Physical Symptoms	13.0	0- 72	13.0	0- 75	–0.36	0.722
RSCL Psychological Symptoms	29.0	0-100	29.0	0- 90	–1.50	0.134
General Health Questionnaire-28 (GHQ-28)	2.0	0- 28	2.0	0- 26	–1.01	0.315
Life Situation Survey (LSS)	92.0	44-131	98.0	41-133	–2.12	0.033
Nottingham Health Profile (NHP)	90.0	0-491	89	0-505	–1.44	0.150
Short-Form-36 (SF-36)	594	51-764	617	25-774	–1.94	0.053

The variables relate to GHQ-28, LSS, NHP and SF-36 total scores. All tests were two-tailed Wilcoxon tests giving rise to a Z statistic. Significance taken as $p \leq 0.01$. There were no significant differences between 3 and 6 months in any of the study measures.

c) Six and Twelve Months

	Six Months		Twelve Months		Statistics	
	Median	Range	Median	Range	Z	p
RSCL Physical Symptoms	13.0	0- 75	13.0	0- 75	−0.77	0.442
RSCL Psychological Symptoms	29.0	0- 95	29.0	0- 95	−1.06	0.287
General Health Questionnaire-28 (GHQ-28)	2.0	0- 26	1.0	0- 27	−0.46	0.647
Life Situation Survey (LSS)	98.0	41-133	100	41-130	−1.08	0.282
Nottingham Health Profile (NHP)	89.0	0-505	76	0-505	−0.81	0.505
Short-Form-36 (SF-36)	617	25-774	624	25-774	−1.07	0.286

The variables relate to GHQ-28, LSS, NHP and SF-36 total scores. All tests were two-tailed Wilcoxon tests giving rise to a Z statistic. Significance taken as $p \leq 0.01$. There were no significant differences between 6 and 12 months in any of the study measures.

Chapter 13

"Relapse Sample": "Within Group Scores"

Introductory Comments

As the study progressed a methodological difficulty emerged. One hundred and twelve (47%) individuals were re-admitted on relapse (RAOR) during the study period. How was data from these individuals to be handled? After consultation with a statistician it was decided to follow the methodology described below. Participants were seen on RAOR and asked retrospectively to complete the questionnaires, focusing on the period immediately prior to RAOR. They were shown the answers to their last data-set so that they could decide whether there had been any changes. The new results were then used for those individuals for the rest of the study period, i.e. they remained the same throughout. It is thus meaningless to consider whether the changes in scores are linear when assessing relapsing individuals.

The analyses performed upon the relapse data were similar to the non-relapse group and unless otherwise stated the methodologies used were identical.

The areas of investigation were

a) Changes in baseline and 12 month "within group" scores
b) An examination of the contribution of each QoL/QoL related variable to time taken to relapse/RAOR. To investigate this the differences in scores for each QoL/QoL-related variable were entered into a linear regression as independent variables. The dependent variable was days taken to relapse/RAOR using only the individuals who had relapsed/been RAOR by the end of the study.

"Within Group" Changes

Table 13.1 illustrates the within group changes for the relapse group. There were three non-significant differences before statistical adjustment, the number of cigarettes smoked daily and SF-36 sub-scores emotional role and role functioning. All other variables with the exception of the number of cigarettes smoked daily, Emotional Role and Role Functioning (both SF-36 sub-scores) produced significant "within group" changes. As before, each questionnaire will be considered in turn.

i) *Rotterdam Symptoms Checklist*: Neither of the changes in physical (F=0.04, df=1,135, p=0.845) nor psychological symptoms scores (F=0.24, df=1,132, p=0.630) were significant following statistical controls. There was one significant contributor to the changes in physical symptom scores, living alone at baseline (F=10.7, df=1,136, p=0.001). Relapsing ADI who lived alone had a significantly poorer outcome (increase in scores equates to deteriorating health status), (n=92) ((+) 24, (–) 26 – (+) 84, Median, Range) (n=71) ((+) 4, (–) 29 – (+) 63, Median, Range) (Alone : Not Alone) (Two-tailed Mann Whitney "U" test) (U=2066, p < 0.001).

Social Class contributed significantly to the changes in psychological symptom scores (F=6.93, df=1,132, p=0.009). Individuals from Social Classes I/II had a smaller increase (i.e deterioration) in psychological symptom scores than those from Social Classes III and IV/V respectively; viz I/II (n=51) (0, (–) 43 – (+) 71, Median, Range), III (n=40) ((+) 14, (–)76 – (+) 67, Median, Range), IV/V (n=72) ((+) 9, (–) 40 – (+) 100, Median, Range). All other contributions from the confounding variables were not significant for both sets of RSCL sub-scores.

ii) *Life Situation Survey*: The "within group" changes were not significant following statistical adjustment (F=1.76, df=1,136, p=0.187) and also no confounders made significant contributions.

iii) *GHQ-28*: The "within group" differences in GHQ-28 scores was not significant following controls (F=0.54, df=1,129, p=0.465). However baseline SF-36 reported health transition (RHT) scores contributed significantly to this result (F=9.81, df=1,129, p=0.002). A comparison was made between those relapsers who scored 1,2 and 3 (Same or Better Health Status) on the RHT at baseline and the others who scored 4 and 5 (Worsening Health Status). Individuals who reported the same or better health status had a larger deterioration in GHQ-28 scores in the event of relapse. Following non-parametric testing there was an interesting but non-significant between group difference in GHQ-28 scores between baseline and 12 months (U=2493, p=0.026). The equivalent parametric analysis produced significant "between group" differences (n=74, 45%) ((+) 5.5, 9.6, Mean, SD) (n=89, 55%) ((+) 1.14, 7.1, Mean, SD) (Same or Better Health Status : Worsening Health Status) (Two-tailed Independent Sample "t" test) (t=3.31, p=0.001).

iv) *Nottingham Health Profile*. There were no significant differences in NHP sub-scores subsequent to statistical adjustment (p > 0.35). However a significant baseline confounder was found.

Baseline LSS scores and changes in NHP emotional reaction sub-scores were related (F=6.95, df=1,122, p=0.009).

v) *Short Form-36*: Two of the "within group" changes in SF-36 sub-scores were not significant prior to statistical adjustment, role functioning and emotional role. None of the seven remaining sub-scores retained statistical significance on controlling for confounding factors (all p > 0.5). The prescription of vitamins in the 12 months prior to baseline assessment was significantly associated with changes in physical functioning scores (F=7.84, df=1,132, p=0.006). Individuals prescribed vitamins had a larger improvement in physical functioning scores. Once more univariate non-parametric testing showed a trend that approached statistical significance (U=2549, p=0.040) however parametric analysis revealed there to be significant "between group" differences (n=74,) ((+) 16.1, 22.1, Mean, Standard Deviation) (n=89) ((+) 6.7, 22.3, Mean, SD) (Vitamins : Non-Vitamins) (Two-tailed

Independent Sample "t" test) (t= (–) 2.64,p=0.009). There was one significant contributor to changes in general health sub-scores, this was living alone at baseline assessment (F=8.85, df=1, 119, p=0.004). Individuals who lived alone at baseline–had a significantly larger deterioration in general health scores (n=92) ((–) 10, (+) 17.5 – (–) 55, Median, Range) (n=71) (0, (+) 45 – (–) 80, Median, Range) (Alone : Not Alone) (Two-tailed Mann Whitney "U" test) (U=2213, p=0.002)

Finally GHQ-28 scores were significantly associated with changes in reported health transition scores (RHT) (F=8.53, df=1,138, p=0.004). The changes in RHT scores were compared between those with a baseline GHQ-28 score of equal to or less than 14 and above 14 (i.e. the cut-off point was on the midpoint of the scale). There was a significant difference between the two groups (n=56) (0, (–) 1- (+) 4, Median, Range) (n=102) (0, (–) 3 – (+) 3, Median, Range) (GHQ < 14 : GHQ ≥ 14) (Two-tailed Mann Whitney "U" test) (U=2148, p=0.008).

Table 13.1. Comparison of Baseline and 12-month Scores in the Relapse Group (n=163)

	Baseline		12 Months		Statistics	
	Median	Range	Median	Range	F	p
Number of Cigarettes	18.0	0- 80	20.0	0- 80	0.1	0.768
Physical Symptoms (RSCL)	35.0	3- 88	55.0	0- 99	56.9	< 0.001
Psychological Symptoms (RSCL)	57.0	0- 100	86.0	0-100	44.4	< 0.001
GHQ-28	16.0	0- 28	21.0	0- 28	12.7	< 0.001
Life Situation Survey*	74.0	36- 118	57.0	21-119	92.1	< 0.001
Nottingham Health Profile						
Physical Abilities	10.6	0- 100	19.9	0-100	19.8	< 0.001
Pain	32.6	0- 100	53.5	0-100	26.8	< 0.001
Energy Level	60.8	0- 100	67.9	0-100	16.9	< 0.001
Sleep	50.9	0- 100	77.6	0-100	14.5	< 0.001
Social Isolation	40.1	0- 100	44.5	0-100	19.8	< 0.001
Emotional Reactions	38.7	0- 100	62.1	0-100	16.5	< 0.001
Total Scores	238	7- 539	293	100-484	23.8	< 0.001
Short-Form Thirty Six						
Physical Functioning	80.0	5- 100	70.0	0-100	24.0	< 0.001
Role Functioning	25.0	0- 100	0	0-100	5.9	0.017
Bodily Pain	42.0	0- 100	32.0	0-100	19.9	< 0.001
General Health	35.0	0- 90	25.0	0- 85	36.3	< 0.001
Vitality	35.0	0- 95	20.0	0- 95	26.1	< 0.001
Social Functioning	50.0	0- 100	25.0	0-100	22.9	< 0.001
Emotional Role	0	0- 100	0	0-100	0.3	0.518
Mental Health	40.0	0- 92	24.0	0- 96	25.4	< 0.001
Total Scores	337	35- 776	234	11-763	56.3	< 0.001
Reported Health Transition	4.0	1- 5	5.0	1- 5	23.3	< 0.001

Key: RSCL= Rotterdam Symptom Checklist. All the results shown following a Repeated Measures ANOVA. The F statistic is quoted on each occasion. Unless an * is shown the statistics are the results following log-transformation of data. Significance taken as p ≤ 0.01.

Relationship of QoL/QoL-Related Variables to Time to Relapse/RAOR

A) Time to Relapse

For this analysis the changes in baseline and 12 month scores for those individuals who relapsed during the study period were computed for each of the QoL/QoL-related variables and these were entered following log-transformation in to a linear regression as the independent variable. There were no significant relationships in either time to relapse or time to RAOR.

Conclusion

There were no significant "within group" changes and likewise no significant associations between QoL/QoL-related variables and time taken to relapse or re-detoxification following controls for confounding factors.

Part Five: Discussion

Chapter 14

SOCIODEMOGRAPHIC FINDINGS

TAKE HOME POINTS FROM THE STUDY

These results can be distilled into four main areas. Firstly the marked contribution played by sociodemographic factors to both the cross-sectional and longitudinal findings. Secondly a number of variables were predictors of outcome; viz., living in an underprivileged area; bodily pain (SF-36); prescription of vitamins; living alone; units of alcohol consumed; number of previous residential treatments and reported health transition (SF-36). Finally those individuals who attended Alcoholics Anonymous on discharge from the original treatment unit had the best outcomes overall.

The first part of the discussion will examine each of the sociodemographic parameters used in the current study and consider their contribution to outcomes.

GENDER

Gender had a minimal impact upon outcome in this study. There was one association between gender and outcome. Women were 2.3 times more likely to have a partner with an alcohol problem compared to men; which is consistent with the literature (Wilsnack et al 1984). Gender differences did not contribute significantly to any of the longitudinal findings, which may be a function of the over representation of men in the study sample. However a recent study comparing equal numbers of men and women in a voluntary sector detoxification unit also found that gender did not contribute to any of the three month outcomes (Foster et al, 2000a).

AGE

Younger participants formed an important sub-group because they had a greater number of alcohol problems and were more likely to be illicit drug users prior to recruitment. In short they comprised a group with special treatment needs. Future research should investigate what are the needs of this group so that outcomes can be maximised and they can be “matched” to appropriate treatment regimens. The issue of "treatment matching" and how these findings contribute to it will be discussed later.

Age was significantly associated with two other findings. There was a close relationship between age and the age of first contact with alcohol services and older individuals not surprisingly, had diminished physical functioning as assessed by the SF-36.

Ethnicity

The majority of participants in this study were white British. There were a small number of participants who identified themselves as Irish, Black or Asian. Ethnicity was not connected with outcome. The only conclusion that can be drawn form the findings is that the ethnic profile is consistent with previous research conducted in the United Kingdom. (Malseed et al 1990).

Marital Status

Marital status was not significantly linked to outcome and this is in contrast to the findings relating to living arrangements.

Living Arrangements

The family unit variable did not contribute significantly to outcome. The likely protective effects of living in a family unit have to be contrasted with the increased likelihood of ADI marrying or living with a drinking partner (Schukit and Tipp 1994). As previously mentioned this is particularly pertinent for women. Living alone at baseline however was associated with a number of poor outcomes. Participants who lived alone were more dependent, had a greater number of alcohol problems, lower LSS scores and contacted alcohol services at a younger age. There were a number of differences in both NHP and SF-36 sub-scores between those individuals who lived alone at baseline and those that did not (On each occasion living alone was associated with a poorer health status.) These were as follows; firstly SF-36; pain, mental health and vitality, secondly NHP; energy, pain, physical abilities, sleep and emotional reactions. Living alone was also one of the variables built into the regression which tested "within group" changes. It was associated with deterioration in both RSCL physical symptom scores and SF-36 general health sub-scores. These findings suggest the existence of a group with specialised treatment needs which provide a challenge for clinicians; individuals who lived alone and had poor baseline physical and psychological health status. They should be treated by an alcohol-specialist service able to provide an in depth psychological and physiological assessment. A number of studies have considered the impact of loneliness upon ADI. These will be considered when the predictors of relapse are discussed, for living alone at baseline was a predictor of 6 months outcomes.

Employment/Unemployment

Unemployment contributed to the baseline findings. There was a significant difference between the 3 months relapse rates in those individuals who were unemployed and employed. However this finding was not significant following controls for confounding factors. Morgan et al (2004) found that employment status predicted quality of life status as measured by the SF-36. Data from Canada (Khan et al 2002) has examined the impact of prolonged unemployment upon alcohol abuse. In the early stages of unemployment drinking decreases but as the period of unemployment lengthens the amount of alcohol consumed, and with it concurrent problems, increase.

Previous research has investigated the association between unemployment and alcohol-dependency. Unemployment for six months or more increased the likelihood of heavy drinking in a study of young British adults by an odds ratio of 1.4 (Power and Estaugh 1990). The finding that job loss increases the chances of alcohol misuse has been confirmed in the National Longitudinal Study of Youth conducted in the United States (Dooley and Prause 1998) . Other American studies have found a significant correlation between unemployment and the development of DSM-IV alcohol-dependence (Caetano and Tam 1995) a finding that was particularly marked for young men. In this context the findings of Grant (1996) provide particular concern for these authors found that unemployment and a low level of educational attainment were barriers to alcohol treatment. Work concerning a birth cohort from New Zealand followed-up until aged 18 (Fergusson et al 1997) gives further cause for concern. These authors found that increasing exposure to unemployment after age 16 was related to increased substance abuse and higher rates of anxiety.

Social Class

Hemmingsson et al (1997) found a strong relationship between the prevalence of alcoholism and socio-economic group; this was particularly the case in men. Another Scandinavian study that examined 40,000 Norwegian conscripts over 40 years (Rossow and Amundsen 1997) published data countering this. This latter study is important because it provides evidence that alcohol abuse outweighed the advantages of social class in terms of health and mortality. It should be noted that social class categorisations in these two studies were not identical to those used in the United Kingdom, both used educational level. In the current study; in addition members of classes I/II had higher LSS (i.e. better QoL) scores than individuals from classes IV/V. The present study did not replicate the previous significant findings of Foster et al (1998b) namely that ADI from classes IV/V were 12.3 times more likely to relapse than those from classes I/II. Although there were univariate significant class differences in relapse rates at all three time points and in the likelihood of RAOR in the current study, none remained significant on further statistical controls.

Membership of classes I/II and to a lesser extent III contributed to a number of positive longitudinal outcomes. Firstly individuals from classes I/II were more likely to attend Alcoholics Anonymous (AA). Using AA was associated with excellent outcomes and these will be discussed later. Secondly participants from social classes I/II/III who did not relapse to heavy drinking had a greater improvement in RSCL physical symptom sub-scores and the

SF-36 scores related to general health and social functioning. In comparison non-relapsing individuals from classes IV/V had minimal and in some case no improvement in scores. Social Class was also significantly related to the changes in RSCL psychological symptom scores resulting from relapsing to heavy drinking. On this occasion there was little change for those individuals in Classes I/II. Those participants in Social Classes III and IV/V had a large deterioration in psychological symptom scores.

Although this discussion has concentrated upon the benefits conferred by social classes I/II mention must be made of Harrison and Gardiner (1999). This study examined alcohol-related mortality and social class within the British general population from 1988-1994. Higher mortality rates were found in the lower social class band: Men aged 25-39 in the unskilled manual classes (IV/V) were 10-20 times more likely to die from alcohol related causes than those in the professional and managerial classes (I/II). These findings contrast with earlier seminal work on alcohol-related mortality (Edwards et al 1978). The most likely explanation for this temporal shift is the reduction in the real cost of alcohol over the past twenty-five years (i.e. taking into account inflation). Cartwright et al (1978) examined the percentage changes in alcohol consumption across different social classes as defined by occupation over a nine year period, which coincided with a drop in the real price of alcohol in the UK (a trend which has continued apace to the present day). The authors found a 8% reduction in the alcohol consumption of social classes I/II and an increase in both classes III (53%) and IV/V (102%). Harrison and Gardiner (1999) concluded that the alcohol-related mortality rates now mirrors those of other psychoactive substances (Parker et al 1987) and furthermore problem use is linked to social factors such as poverty, disadvantage and social class. It seems that policy interventions including pricing aimed at reducing inequalities may be the key to reducing alcohol-related harm in the general population. Is there the political will to do so? The United Kingdom Government has recently published the *Alcohol Harm Reduction Strategy For England* (The Prime Ministers Strategy Unit 2004) this document specifically avoids measures designed to restrict availability of alcohol through price- so it would seem the answer to the previous question is "no."

Area Based Social Deprivation

This was measured by the Jarman index (Jarman 1983). It proved to be the most consistent predictor of outcomes and this will be discussed later

Summary Thoughts on the Demographic Findings

The findings from the current study demonstrate important links between sociodemographic differences and outcome in ADI, but what are the best measures to assess this? From these results it would appear that the *Jarman index* is an excellent measure to use, but unfortunately it has limitations. Like the two main other deprivation indices used in the United Kingdom (The Townsend Index , (Townsend et al 1986) and the Carstairs Index (Carstairs and Morris 1989a), the Jarman index applies to geographical areas and not to individuals, therefore Jarman scores can only contribute meaningfully to outcome studies where individuals are recruited from a wide geographical area as was the case in this study. The primary measure of individual of socio-economic status used in this study was *social class*. The current measures of social class have been criticised on a number of grounds- notably that it relates to the occupation of the spouse and has severe limitations when being applied to the elderly (Naidoo and Wills 1994). The categorisations have recently been reviewed and amended in the United Kingdom (Office of National Statistics 2001). The current study was conducted before the new categories had been publicised. It has been suggested that a better proxy for social class is educational attainment. Van Oers et al (1999) found that for both sexes higher alcohol related problems were correlated with lower educational attainment. More recently a study from New Zealand has examined young adults from birth to aged 26 (Casswell et al 2003). These authors found that quantity of drinking was linked to educational attainment at 18, 21 and 26. A lower level of education was associated with a higher level of drinking.

Assessing deprivation can at best be an approximation. Further work is needed to ascertain the optimum method of measuring "deprivation" in ADI, is it deprivation indices; social class; educational attainment; unemployment or perhaps none of these? This study confirms the importance of *sociodemographic factors to outcome*. In order to provide a context for outcome studies such parameters should be routinely used and fully reported.

Chapter 15

MISCELLANEOUS OUTCOMES

ALCOHOL CONSUMPTION AND HISTORY

Baseline alcohol consumption played an important role in predicting the amount of alcohol consumed during the study and was a significant predictor of relapse at one-year. Morgan et al (2004) using a stepwise linear regression analyses discovered that quantity and frequency of alcohol consumption predicted quality of life scores (SF-36). The impact of alcohol consumption on these outcomes will be considered later. Neither the age of commencing drinking weekly or regular intoxication made any significant contributions to outcomes.

Two study centres, the Minnesota project and community alcohol services samples had a longer period alcohol-free at baseline assessment because a period of prolonged abstinence was a condition of entry to the programme. This is an important confounder, for individuals who were only 4-5 days alcohol-free could well be still be suffering from the "psychological vegetative symptoms inherent to alcoholism which are erroneously interpreted as positive indicators of depressive illness" (Clark et al 1993). This will be reflected in their subjective valuation of QoL. Davidson (1995) found that depression scores returned to normative levels between 10 and 21 days of abstinence. Allan (1995), after reviewing the literature drew similar conclusions concerning anxiety. Thus the length of time alcohol free also had to be controlled for in addition to sociodemographic differences. Length of time alcohol free was associated with outcome at three and six months though this was not significant following the application of statistical controls. However by the end of the study the protective effect provided by length of time alcohol free was lost, even in univariate analysis.

Prescription Drugs

One hundred and ninety (80%) of the sample were prescribed any of the following drugs in the twelve months prior to baseline assessment: analgesia, tranquilizers, antidepressants, antacids, laxatives, cough medicines, vitamins, bronchodilators, antihypertensives, antibiotics, anticonvulsants, neuroleptics and chlormethiazole. Vitamins were the most commonly prescribed drugs, contributing to forty percent of total prescriptions. Benzodiazepines, analgesics, antidepressants and antibiotics were prescribed to thirty per cent or more of the sample. Not being prescribed any drugs was associated with a positive three-month outcome though this was not significant following statistical controls. However the prescription of vitamins was a significant predictor of relapse at three months. This finding will be discussed later.

Illicit Drugs Use

Just less than forty percent of the participants were illicit drug users. The most popular drug being cannabis, followed by unprescribed tranquillisers. A small minority, (less than five percent) were ecstasy users. Ecstasy use plays an integral part in the clubbing and rave culture and was unsurprisingly associated with younger individuals. Overall illicit drug use did not contribute to any study outcomes, though this provides further evidence for the emergence of a sub-group of young illicit drug users that had poor outcomes. Further evidence of the existence of this problematic sub-group is provided by an American study (Martin et al 1996) which found that simultaneous polydrug use was most likely in a group of young, unmarried males: The following were the prevalence rates for the substance combinations, alcohol and cocaine (60%), alcohol alone (51%) and cannabis/alcohol and sedatives (31%).

Tobacco Use

Previous work (Foster et al 1998b) found that the chances of relapse at three months were increased by an odds ratio of 2.2 for every ten cigarettes smoked. A similar finding was reported by Stuyt (1997) who discovered that tobacco use was associated with poor twelve months outcomes. Indeed more recent findings from Project MATCH have suggested that non-smokers are likely to initiate smoking in the context of alcohol treatment (Friend and Pagano 2004). In contrast American smoking cessation programmes have shown increased abstinence rates for alcohol and decreased heavy drinking (Bobo et al 1998). The present study did not find an association between cigarette smoking and outcome (not even an univariate one). Indeed the number of cigarettes smoked daily was the only variable that did *not* differentiate relapsers and non-relapsers at twelve-month follow-up.

It is difficult to explain the weak association between smoking and outcome in the current study. Future work should try to ascertain why smoking is heavy in the non-relapse sample at twelve months. Perhaps the key is to investigate smoking and its impact upon outcomes in more diverse samples than has presently been the case.

Family History

In her seminal review (Cotton 1979) reported that rates of alcoholism were substantially higher in the relatives of alcoholics than relatives of non-alcoholics. We found a prevalence rate of 58% of individuals with any positive family history. Genetic influences in alcoholism have been summarised by Schuckit (1999). He concluded that combined genetic factors explain around half of the alcoholism risk.

Previous Treatments

Over three-quarters of the sample had previously received either a residential alcohol-related treatment, community alcohol detoxification or non-detoxification treatment. Previous residential treatment was the most common, followed by non-detoxification and treatment and finally community detoxification. Just over forty per cent of the total sample had *ever* been given a community alcohol detoxification. This included a community day centre sample. The number of residential treatments was the most significant predictor of relapse at the end of the study and also a predictor of re-detoxification upon relapse (RAOR). This will be discussed when predictors of study outcomes are considered.

Quality of Life Burden

The Quality of Life burden refers to the deficiencies in QoL scores compared with general population norm scores for equivalent measures. Two previous studies presented similar data in ADI using normative data obtained from United Kingdom populations (Foster et al 1998a; McKenna et al 1996). The former study consisted of sixty socially-deprived male and female ADI who were detoxified in a voluntary sector residential unit situated in inner city South London. The QoL measures where published peer-reviewed data was available in that study and used in the current one were the RSCL, LSS and NHP. The authors presented both the baseline means and the percentage of individuals scoring beyond the general population norms. McKenna et al (1996) applied the Short-Form-36 (SF-36) to a sample of two hundred and twelve men and women fulfilling the criteria for DSM-IV alcohol dependence/abuse (American Psychiatric Association 1994). These individuals had been in contact with the Alcohol Problems Clinic at the Royal Edinburgh hospital during the previous 12 months (inpatients and outpatients). Their data were presented as mean SF-36 scores in the form of a graph alongside UK general population norms. ADI who were of no fixed abode were excluded from both studies. However neither excluded them on the grounds of concurrent or previous psychiatric illness.

The current sample which was more sociodemographically diverse than that of Foster et al (1998a) had a greater QoL burden i.e. poorer QoL. Data comparing the two studies is presented in Table 15.1. The percentage of individuals with LSS scores beyond the norms was identical (80%) (beyond the norms, means having a poorer QoL score than the general population norm). Fewer participants in the current study scored beyond the physical symptom norms as measured by the RSCL compared to the earlier study. Although more participants in the current sample scored beyond the norm scores for the RSCL psychological symptom sub-scores, the difference was minimal. The largest difference related to the NHP. Ninety-five percent of the present sample scored beyond the NHP total scores norms, the equivalent figure in Foster et al (1998a) was eighty-two percent. The variables where the differences were most marked were pain, energy and sleep. On all three occasions the QoL was more impaired in the current sample.

The current sample had a higher quality of life burden relating to the SF-36 than the sample of McKenna et al (1996). A comparison of the two studies is presented in Table 15.2. There was little difference in the mean physical functioning sub-score; McKenna et al's sample had the greater QoL burden. In all the other sub-scores the current sample had a greater QoL burden with differences of at least 10 points.

In both Foster et al (1998a) and McKenna et al (1996) the samples had QoL scores that were well below the equivalent general population norms. Our sample despite its sociodemographic diversity has an even poorer QoL. This is particularly marked when compared to the McKenna et al (1996) sample, why was this the case?

The key does not lie in demographic disparities. There is little difference in the mean ages, marital status and unemployment rates of the two samples. Neither can it be explained on the grounds that there was a mix of outpatients and inpatients, for this was true in both cases. Some might feel that recruiting individuals from medical wards provides an explanation for the difference. If so this is only partially the case for the inclusion of private sector patients (over one third were outpatients) was likely to have offset this.

The original cohort of participants in McKenna et al (1996) paper was 586. For varying reasons only 212 (36%) completed the SF-36. The authors compared variables in those participants who were interviewed when the SF-36 was administered and those who were not. Participants who were interviewed were more likely to have attended either group or individual sessions at the clinic over the previous six months. The QoL of those interviewed may therefore be substantially different from those who were not assessed using the SF-36. Those individuals that were interviewed in McKenna et al (1996) did not undergo detoxification prior to interview and had substantial periods of abstinence over the past 6 months. The individuals in our own sample were embarking upon a treatment episode and had been drinking for most of the past 6 months. Thus the most likely explanation for the differences in scores is related to alcohol consumption.

However a thread runs through all three studies, namely the poor QoL of ADI. The current study confirms this in both an inpatient and outpatient sample. Furthermore this sample is sociodemographically diverse, with participants from the poor inner-city, the suburbs and outer London.

Positive scores indicate a greater quality of life burden in the current study. No data was presented concerning the reported health transition sub-score in McKenna et al thus any data relating to it is omitted. Higher SF-36 scores indicate a better QoL.

Table 15.1. Comparison of the Quality of Life Burden: Current Study v Foster et al (1998a)

	Current Study (n=240)		Foster et al (1998a) Study (n=60)		Differences between Samples	
	Mean	% Abnormal Scores	Mean	% Abnormal Scores	Mean Differences	Differences in % Abnormal Scores
Rotterdam Symptoms Checklist						
Physical Symptoms	34.8	76%	39.4	89%	(–) 4.6	(–) 13%
Psychological Symptoms	55.3	96%	54.3	93%	(+) 1.0	(+) 3%
Life Situation Survey	73.7	80%	75.5	80%	(–) 1.8	0%
Nottingham Health Profile						
Physical Mobility	15.6	48%	12.3	50%	(+) 3.3	(–) 2%
Pain	30.8	73%	20.4	45%	(+)10.4	(+) 28%
Energy Level	53.4	90%	40.3	64%	(+)13.1	(+) 26%
Sleep	48.0	85%	40.4	66%	(+) 7.6	(+) 19%
Social Isolation	40.1	82%	37.9	75%	(+) 2.2	(+) 7%
Emotional Reactions	29.9	81%	45.5	85%	(–)15.6	(–) 4%
Total Scores	236	95%	197	82%	(+)39.0	(+) 13%

Positive scores indicate a greater quality of life burden in the current study. % Abnormal scores refered to those individuals scoring above the published general population norms (i.e. with a poorer QoL).

Table 15.2. Comparison of Quality of Life Burden: Current Study v McKenna et al (1996)

	Current Study (n=240)	McKenna et al (1996) Study (n=212)	Differences in Sample Scores
	Mean Score	Mean Score	Difference in Mean Score
Short-Form 36 **(SF-36)**			
Physical Functioning	73.5	72.4	(–) 1.1
Role Functioning	39.2	54.2	(+)15.0
Bodily Pain	50.9	64.4	(+)13.5
General Health	40.0	54.3	(+)14.3
Vitality	34.3	49.5	(+)15.2
Social Functioning	47.8	62.3	(+)14.5
Emotional Role	34.6	51.7	(+)17.1
Mental Health	41.6	52.3	(+)10.7
Total Scores	361	461	(+)100

Chapter 16

LONGITUDINAL FINDINGS

RELAPSE RATES

ADI were followed up at three, six and twelve months and relapse rates were calculated for each follow-up period. Nincty-three percent of the sample were successfully tracked which is an excellent follow-up rate. The United States Department of Health and Human Services consider 80% to be a reasonable follow-up rate (Gould and Luckoff 1977), so the current findings are robust. The total sample relapse rates were as follows; three months (50%), six months (61%) and twelve months (71%). This is comparable to other studies that have followed up ADI over a similar period. Hunt et al (1971) found a three-month relapse rate of 58%. Using an identical definition of relapse as the present study a three-month relapse rate of 61% was recorded (Foster et al 1998b). Our 12-month relapse rate in the present study at 70% falls between rates for two other studies (though the definitions of relapse varied). In Armour et als' (1978) study the relapse criterion of returning to pre-treatment levels was fulfilled by 50% of the sample. When the criterion was changed to the consumption of a single drink the equivalent figure was 90% (Orford and Edwards 1977).

UNIVARIATE DIFFERENCES BETWEEN THE RELAPSERS AND NON-RELAPSERS

A) Three Months

When considering these differences it is possible to make some direct comparisons with the pilot study –study B-(chapter three.) Comparisons are restricted to 3-month outcomes because the Foster et al study only followed-up the individuals for a three month period. In the current study there were significant differences between relapsers and non-relapsers in the following baseline sociodemographic variables: Jarman Index scores, unemployment rates and social class. In study B significant demographic differences were in the social class and Irish ethnicity variables. There were comparatively few Irish participants in this study thus ethnicity categorisations were collapsed in the present study and at no point did the composite ethnicity variable contribute significantly to outcome.

Length of time alcohol free at baseline also significantly differentiated relapsers from non-relapsers, although this is most likely to be a consequence of the design of the study. Participants who had a longer period alcohol-free were less likely to relapse. Individuals who came from the Minnesota project and community alcohol services samples had the greater periods alcohol-free. Continued residence in the Minnesota project and continued contact with the community alcohol services day programmes were contingent upon abstinence. Both these treatment centres showed good three months outcomes. The other categorical variable which was associated with a significant three-month univariate outcome, was the prescription of vitamins during the twelve months prior to the study; a finding that was not found in study B. It is however a finding with important clinical implications, for alongside Jarman Index and SF-36 bodily pain scores it remained significant following statistical controls. These findings will be discussed in greater depth shortly when the significant predictors of outcome are considered.

Taking the level of significance as $p \leq 0.01$ only one QoL/QoL-related variable showed a univariate "between group" difference in study B, the NHP sleep sub-scale. Five significant findings were identified in the current study in the same variables suggesting that the sample size in study B was too small to detect some significant differences. Significant "between group" differences were seen for the following QoL/QoL-related variables for the current sample (in order of increasing statistical significance) bodily pain, general health (SF-36), pain (NHP), RSCL physical symptoms, SF-36 and NHP total scores, sleep (NHP), GHQ-28 total scores, physical functioning (SF-36) and physical abilities (NHP). The majority of the variables relate to physical health status and suggest that poor physical health is a marker for early relapse, which is consistent with the poor outcomes pertaining to vitamins.

B) Six Months

To date no studies have applied both the SF-36 or NHP to ADI and followed them up beyond three months. A direct six and twelve-months comparison between this study and other work is therefore impossible. Again a number of sociodemographic variables were responsible for "between group" differences. The uinvariate significant benefits conferred by living in areas with lower Jarman Index scores (better areas) and membership of social classes I/II continued and living alone was associated with a poor outcome. Both Jarman index scores and living alone were significant after controlling for confounding factors. These will be discussed in further detail in the section considering predictors of outcome.

Two of the baseline variables relating to alcohol consumption were associated with significant "between group" differences at 6-month follow-up. Relapse was associated with drinking a greater amount of alcohol at baseline and non-relapse was associated to a greater period alcohol free also at baseline. Thus the protective effect provided by the length of time alcohol free at baseline was still present at six months. One of the tenets of the Minnesota project was that three months was too short a period to grapple with the problems of addiction. A proportion of the sample was therefore still in some form of residential unit at 6 month follow-up. Again abstinence was a condition of residence. This factor contributed in part to the protective effect provided by a greater length of time alcohol free though the present methodology cannot quantify the contribution.

Two other non QoL/QoL-related findings were of univariate significance at 6-month follow-up, namely the prescription of vitamins and the number of previous residential treatments. The prescriptions of vitamins may be an indirect index of outcome. These are prescribed by general practitioners (community based doctors) and there must be some perception that these ADI are malnourished, however it was no longer significantly associated with twelve months outcomes. The number of previous residential treatments received prior to baseline assessment was a significant predictor of twelve-month outcome and this too will be discussed later.

Fewer QoL/QoL-related univariate significant "between group" differences were evident at six months follow-up (4) compared with three months follow-up (10). The four significant differences were all related to a poor physical health status: RSCL physical symptom sub-scores, bodily pain (SF-36), pain (NHP), and NHP total scores. Following statistical controls only one variable remained significant. This was SF-36 bodily pain sub-scores. Taken in combination these findings suggest that quantifying physical health status as has been done in this study provides clinicians with useful information.

C) Twelve Months

Sociodemographic factors still showed important univariate "between group" differences in Jarman Index scores and social class at 12-month follow-up. Throughout the study individuals in social classes I/II had positive outcomes and social classes IV/V poor outcomes. However this effect did not remain significant after controlling for demographic factors.

Two other non QoL/QoL-related significant differences, alcohol consumption and the number of previous of residential detoxification treatments both remained significant after statistical controls. These will be discussed shortly. By the end of the study the protective effect provided by length of time alcohol-free at baseline was lost. This was largely related to the Minnesota project sample and one possible explanation is that a number of those who had been in extended rehabilitation had left the residential units in question and relapsed between six and twelve month follow-up. In the United Kingdom any long-term residential placement has to be sanctioned by Local Authority Social Services (see Foster et al 2003) for data concerning how these resources are allocated), who work within fixed budgets. Residential placements are comparatively expensive and funding beyond six months is rare.

None of the QoL/QoL-related variables were significant after statistical controls. However all three significant univariate differences viz.; RSCL physical symptoms, bodily pain (SF-36) and pain (NHP) relate to the poor outcomes for those with an impaired physical health status. Having a general medical hospital sample may largely explain this finding but it should be noted that this *is* the avenue of treatment for many alcohol dependent individuals.

PREDICTORS OF RELAPSE

These will be described in chronological order and were the variables that were selected by the computer following a Forward-Stepwise Logistic Regression i.e. after controlling for baseline confounders.

Three Months

There were three predictors at this time point. The most significant was Jarman Index scores, followed by SF-36 bodily pain sub-scores and prescription of vitamins (vitamins) during the 12 months prior to baseline assessment. Vitamins prescription was the only variable which was solely significant at three months. The implications of the findings concerning the other two variables will be described later.

Vitamins

Prescription of vitamins was associated with higher 3-month relapse rates (odds ratio of 0.48). The prescription of vitamins may provide important clinical information for it could be a marker for poor baseline status and an indication that early relapse is likely.

All of the drugs prescribed were in oral form and usually by community based doctors. The link between a poor nutritional status and vitamin deficiency in alcoholics particularly thiamine, B12, nicotinamide and pyridoxine was reviewed by Ryle and Thompson (1984). They point out that the consequences of vitamin deficiency can be lesser degrees of brain damage. If this is prolonged and undetected a "vitamin deficiency syndrome" develops and the damage could be irreversible. Two clinical conditions may result, firstly Wernicke's encephalopathy and secondly Korsakoffs Psychosis/Alcohol Dementia. Wernicke's encephalopathy is a consequence of thiamine deficiency. It is reversible but if not treated may lead to Korsakoffs psychosis or death. Korsakoffs psychosis is irreversible and marked by a personality change that may incorporate amnesia, disorientation and confabulation.

Oral thiamine is poorly absorbed in subjects who have been drinking heavily and are already malnourished (Hoyumpa 1983). During the 1980's "Parentrovite" was prescribed in intravenous or intramuscular forms to administer thiamine to malnourished ADI. There were a number of extremely rare adverse reactions to this, such as anaphylactic shock (Thompson and Cook 1997). In consequence the Committee on the Safety of Medicines (1989) published a warning cautioning against its routine use. As a result of this and manufacturing problems "Parentrovite" prescription virtually ceased and oral thiamine was prescribed to alcoholics who had a poor nutritional status and were therefore at a greater risk of developing Wernicke's encephalopathy (O'Brien 1995). Ramaya and Jauhar (1997) describe an increase in the incidence of Korsakoff's psychosis in the East End of Glasgow and postulate that there is a strong association between this and the movement away from the administration of intramuscular thiamine supplements. The area where Ramaya and Jauhar conducted their study was one marked by dietary neglect in socially deprived and socially isolated heavy drinkers. This is a profile that mirrors a substantial proportion of participants in the current study. There is a possibility that the oral prescriptions they received were of minimal clinical utility.

Another reason for the infrequent use of intra-muscular preparations is that the main indication for their use, Wernicke's encephalopathy, is believed to be rare. In fact its prevalence is underestimated. (Reuler et al 1985). ADI who are prescribed vitamins seem have a high risk of short-term relapse and moreover a proportion of this group may be in the process of cognitive degeneration that will not be addressed by oral vitamins. The greater use of intra-muscular preparations should be encouraged. Writing in *Current Opinion in Psychiatry* Chick (1997) called for "urgent evaluation in controlled studies" to ascertain whether greater use of parenteral thiamine could significantly prevent the development of Korsakoff's syndrome.

Six Months

Living alone at baseline was the only predictor of outcome at six months only. The SF-36 bodily pain sub-score was a predictor of both three and six month outcome. The other predictor of six-month outcome was Jarman Index scores, which was a significant predictor at all three-time points.

Living Alone

Participants who lived alone at baseline were 0.48 times more likely to relapse than individuals who did not. It has been postulated that loneliness, defined as the absence of mental and social well-being (Bell 1956) is the single most important factor in development of substance misuse (Mijuskovic 1988; Gaev 1976). In our study the measures that most approximate to an absence of mental and social well being were the General Health Questionnaire total scores, the SF-36 social functioning and the NHP social functioning sub-scales. The six month scores for each of these variables in individuals who lived alone at baseline and those who did not were compared using univariate tests. On each occasion there was a highly significant difference ($p < 0.001$). Thus there was a strong association with living alone and loneliness in this sample.

A review of the empirical work up to the end of the 1980s concerning loneliness and alcohol abuse published in *Social Science and Medicine* was undertaken by two Swedish authors (Akerlind and Hornquist 1990). They concluded that loneliness is significant in all stages of the development of alcoholism and a contributor in the growth of alcohol abuse and "an encumbrance in attempts to give it up". Alcoholics feel lonelier than most other groups (Elton and Hornquist 1983a) and this leads to feelings of non-involvement in social roles and relationships (Carman et al 1983). These feelings of loneliness are not obviously related to an individual's social situation or the number of their social contacts (Jones 1985). They seem to reflect a feeling of being lonely which manifests itself in a "sad passivity" (Rubenstein and Shaver 1982) and specifically a cluster of the following variables, indecision, lassistude and indolence (Akerlind et al 1988). This in turn sets up a barrier to change. The lonely alcoholic suffering from feelings of low self-esteem is often resigned to their fate and unable to change their life situation. Social solace can be sought in the undemanding company of other drinkers. Clearly such a situation sets up a poor prognosis.

Researchers have found that although company and meaningful social interactions are important, they fulfil only some of the recovery needs. Self-help groups such as Alcoholics Anonymous can play an important part. Being alone is an experience common to many people. Hornquist and Akerlind (1990) state that one of the key steps in the recovery process is for the individual to be "alone without feeling lonely".

There have been two important studies from the United States subsequent to Hornquist and Akerlinds's work. An examination of 92 males and 62 females recruited from rehabilitation centres found that loneliness was associated with a lack of self-esteem, marital satisfaction, job-satisfaction, and greater number of years consuming alcohol (Medora and Woodward 1991). Data from Project MATCH also indicates the importance of treatment in addressing the consequences of loneliness. In consequence of treatment friendships with drinkers decreased and non-drinkers increased (Mohr et al 2001).

Taken in conjuction with the optimistic message of Mohr et al ,Hornquist and Akerlind's review contains important messages for treatment services. Firstly many treatment programmes use groups, whilst individuals should learn to develop confidence in such a setting, for many this will be an extremely difficult transition to make. Those not able to make the transition may well leave treatment prematurely. Expectations must be realistic and programmes planned accordingly. Secondly programmes should incorporate an opportunity to practise normal social intercourse in settings other than on the ward, unit etc. If necessary a nurse or other worker could accompany the individual initially. Thirdly patients should be actively linked to community based services on discharge. All too often they are merely given telephone numbers of e.g. community drop-in services and expected to attend on leaving. This is a group with a chronically low self-esteem, thus to expect them to expose themselves to a difficult new social setting without practice, whilst ideal is probably unrealistic. Once more it should be the role of the key-worker to provide this initial link. Finally Alcoholics Anonymous can provide a structure for social support and should be encouraged by treatment services. A number of important findings concerning the use of AA emerged in this sample. These findings will be dealt with in greater depth later.

Finally a comment about solitary drinking in the general population: Demers and Bourgault (1996) found that solitary drinking was not necessarily problematic, the key variable was the quantity of alcohol consumed.

Bodily Pain

The bodily pain construct as measured by the SF-36 was a predictor of relapse at both three and six months. At three months each 10 points on the scale (range 0-100, lower scores indicate higher impairment) increased the chances of relapsing by 0.86. The equivalent increased chances of relapse at 6 months were 0.90. Highly significant differences were apparent in SF-36 bodily pain scores at 12 months between the relapse and non-relapse group, but this was not maintained once confounding factors were accounted for. Epidemiological data from the United States has found that the principal reasons for alcohol-related emergency department admissions were pain, injury and drink problems (Li et al 1998)

A number of areas have been identified where a correlation between pain and alcohol misuse exists. These include skeletal myopathy (Reilly et al 1995), acute pancreatitis (Gupta and al-Kawas 1995), epigastric pain (Glickman 1995), back pain (Gorman et al 1987) and arthritis (Blaze Temple et al 1992). The link between pain and outcome is under-explored, though one study has shown that sore muscle scores as measured by the RSCL was the only variable where the changes in scores were significant both in consequence of relapse and non-relapse to heavy drinking (Foster et al 1999b). Stewart et al (1995) found that alcoholics were more sensitive to the pain reducing effects of alcohol than controls and postulated a familial/genetic link, confirming earlier work carried out in India (Chaturvedi 1987). Projects establishing a link to dependency and pain are in their infancy but a Swedish study (Hoffman et al 1995) found that in a group of chronic pain patients, 24% met the DSM IIIR criteria for dependence. The most common was dependence on analgesia, followed by alcohol and lastly sedatives.

The findings from the current study suggest that there is a clinically important link between the subjective experience of pain and early relapse. Furthermore significant correlations between the baseline measures of SF-36 pain and RSCL physical symptom scores suggest it is a predominantly physiological construct. If a thorough physiological appraisal and some measurement of pain were incorporated into clinical assessment information could be provided as to those individuals who rate their pain highly and might be at risk of earlier relapse. However it is not that simple. The belief that there is a linear relationship between the amount of pain stimuli and how it is experienced has long been discredited (Sternbach 1978). What one person may experience as mild pain another may view as severe. Thus a clinician could feel that an individual is healthy when the individuals being assessed perceived themselves to be in a degree of pain. All the more important then that the experience of pain is explored in a baseline assessment. The SF-36 bodily pain construct includes two questions. One asks an individual to rate their pain on a scale of none to very severe. The second question measures the extent to which pain interfered with their daily functioning, with the options ranging from not at all to extremely. These two questions could easily be incorporated into routine assessments.

Twelve Months

Three variables were significant predictors of 12-month outcome. These were (in order of increasing statistical significance), Jarman Index scores (this was the only variable which was significant at all three time-points), number of previous residential treatments and alcohol consumption at baseline. The latter two were significant at twelve months only.

Alcohol Consumption

For every 10 units of alcohol consumed at baseline the odds ratio of 12 months relapse was increased by 1.04. The difference in median units consumed in the relapse and non-relapse groups was 50 units. This link to outcome is consistent with a number of studies and points to the fact that baseline alcohol consumption is a good indicator of prognosis. Eckardt et al (1982) found that alcohol consumption at eight months follow-up was statistically related to pre-treatment alcohol consumption levels; this study used a logistic regression analysis in a sample of 72 alcoholic ADI. The current study has a far larger sample and therefore greater statistical power. It also employed a logistic regression methodology.

Further evidence for this link is provided by a Norwegian study (Duckert 1993). Two samples, inpatient (n=86) (male : female ratio 4.5 : 1) and outpatients (n=92) (male : female ratio 1.6 : 1) were followed up at four years. Variables predicting alcohol consumption in the inpatient sample at follow-up were degree of social integration, alcohol consumption before the start of treatment, and male gender. In the outpatient sample only consumption before commencement of treatment was related to follow-up consumption levels.

Deborah Dawson has written widely on alcohol consumption, its link to outcome and how to measure it accurately. In this context two large-scale studies are particularly noteworthy (Dawson 2000; Dawson 1996). In Dawson (1996) the past year drinking/dependency status was investigated in 4,585 adults with a history of DSM-IV alcohol dependence. The aim was to assess whether treatment samples would reflect the course of alcoholism in the general population. Those treated were twice as likely to be abstinent, but only half as likely to be drinking without abuse or dependence. The authors concluded that treatment studies might not reflect the experiences of groups not seeking treatment. A link was found between outcome and alcohol consumption throughout the sample. Higher alcohol intake at baseline decreased the chances of abstinence or drinking without abuse or dependency. Dawson (2000) examined the link between alcohol consumption, dependence and mortality. Baseline data of (n=37,682) US adults who were at least 25 years of age was linked to mortality data from the National Death Index (n=3,586 deaths). There was no protective effect provided by light or moderate drinking amongst dependent drinkers (DSM-IV) and very heavy drinkers had a significantly increased odds ratio of mortality in comparison to past year and life time abstainers. The author postulated that three variables were implicated in the increased mortality of dependent drinkers in comparison to non-dependent drinkers (drinking comparable amounts of alcohol); longer and heavier drinking histories, more severe health problems at baseline and heavier episodic drinking.

Our findings add to these studies. The current sample was recruited from different treatment settings and with a wide demographic profile. In addition the sample size was larger than both the Eckhardt and Duckert studies and a series of confounding effects were controlled for. Findings at 12-month follow-up clearly point to an association between baseline alcohol consumption and outcome. Baseline alcohol consumption therefore should be taken into account when assessing treatment needs.

Number of Previous Residential Detoxification Treatments

At twelve-month follow-up the number of previous residential detoxification treatments was a significant predictor of relapse to heavy drinking. Each residential detoxification prior to baseline assessment increased the odds of relapsing by 1.27. This finding is consistent with research that previous residential detoxifications are also a useful clinical marker of outcome. A history of "clinic treatment" has been shown to correlate with a poor baseline status and long-term outcome (Valliant and Milofsky 1982).

Cunningham and Breslin (2004) have shown treatment utilisation increases according to the degrees of alcohol-related harm. American studies that have investigated the pathways into treatment, are particularly illuminating in this context. Timko et al (1993) found ADI with "fewer financial resources, more serious drinking problems and poorer baseline functioning were more likely to enter residential treatment". More recently (Tucker et al 2004) showed that greater psychosocial problems and higher dependency levels were associated with help seeking. This confirmed earlier findings from the same research group (Tucker and Gladsjo (1993). In the 1993 study the variables associated with treatment utilisation were greater "psychosocial dysfunction particularly in relation to inter-personal relationships and greater non-prescribed drug use."

JARMAN INDEX SCORES

The Jarman index measures the extent of social underprivilege in a local government electoral ward. This was the only variable that was a significant predictor of outcome at all three time-points. Higher scores on the index indicate a greater level of underprivilege. At 12-month follow-up the odds of relapsing were increased by 1.14 for every five points on the Jarman scale. There was a difference of 10 points between the relapse and non-relapse groups at twelve-months. In addition this variable was significantly associated with the length of time taken to relapse to heavy drinking.

The link between inequality and health in the United Kingdom was highlighted in the *Black Report* (Townsend and Davidson 1982). This was the remit of a Department of Health and Social Security working group. The report provided a detailed study of the link between mortality, morbidity and social class. There were three main findings

- "At every stage of life those in the lower social classes had higher death rates than those at the top of the social scale.
- Children born into the lower social classes had lower birth weights and a shorter stature.
- All the major diseases affected social classes IV and V more than social classes I/II" (Naidoo and Wills 1995)

In the current study there was only a moderate correlation between social class and Jarman Index scores, so other factors were contributing to the very strong link between living in an underprivileged area and outcome.

The Jarman index has been used to investigate the relationship between ethnicity, social class, unemployment, overcrowding and the standardised mortality ratio (SMR) (Sundquist et al 1996). All 192 district health authorities in England and Wales were investigated. There was a significant connection between the Jarman index score and the SMR. Additionally those areas that had a higher SMR also had a greater proportion of unskilled, unemployed and individuals living in overcrowded situations. Individuals from the "New Commonwealth and Pakistan" had a lower mortality rate, though the reasons for this were unclear.

To the author's knowledge the current study is the first project conducted in the United Kingdom that has applied the Jarman Index to ADI. The association between social deprivation and outcome in this group is striking. Our findings are confirmed by data from a non-clinical population in Holland (Droomers et al 1999). This general population study reported that excessive alcohol consumption was linked to lower educational achievement. Other significant contributors to this effect were financial problems, deprivation and income. Later work from the same group (Droomers et al 2004) revealed that individuals with a lower education level were three times more likely to drink excessively than those who were not.

Droomers et al (1999) and Harrison and Gardiner (1999) have called for targeted community interventions, both general interventions and those aimed at reducing alcohol consumption. These studies and our findings taken together make a persuasive case for a national alcohol policy. *Alcohol Concern* have published *"Proposals for a National Alcohol Strategy for England"* (Alcohol Concern 2000). They suggest a number of interventions aimed at the reduction of alcohol consumption. These were taxation and prices, controlling of licensing to discourage under-age drinking and intoxication, and finally the control of direct advertising of alcohol and indirect promotion of alcohol through for example, sponsorship of sporting events. In 2004 the strategy was finally operationalised in the United Kingdom and the reaction to it has been largely negative (Drummond 2004; Room 2004). These writers point out that it does not contain any of the policy interventions rated as "effective" by Babor et al (2003) most of which were included in the recommendations of Alcohol Concern. This should also be seen in the context that as of November 2005 it will be possible for licensees to sell alcohol twenty-four hours a day in England and Wales. However the most likely outcome will be to extend frequent drinking to midnight and beyond. Room (2004) is particularly scathing of the minimal community safeguards in the new Licensing Act 2003. The move to twenty-four opening is based upon the belief that by staggering closing times British drinkers will adopt a more continental approach to their drinking rather than continuing "binge drinking". Two authors have pointed out that the belief that continental drinking is largely unproblematic is based on assumption rather than evidence. Drummond (2000) stresses that there has been minimal research conducted concerning continental patterns of drinking and Foster (2003) concludes his review of the literature with the comment that the belief that British drinkers will adopt continental drinking habits as a "triumph of hope over experience." There are a number of bodies that are showing disquiet surrounding the change in the licensing laws. Local authorities are concerned about the likely increase in public order problems as a result of increased drinking and many police officers feel that the extra policing involved will stretch their resources to breaking point. The one thing that is certain is that the change in English and Welsh drinking practices will be closely monitored.

Interestingly the strategy says little about using population-wide strategies to address alcohol problems. Alcohol problems are seen as residing with the individual. All the more pressing that studies should be undertaken examining what are the components of underprivileged areas that contribute to such poor outcomes. Evidence can be produced for policy makers to monitor the impact of policy changes and for the treatment community; interventions can then be designed, targeted and evaluated with the aim of establishing whether they have a significant clinical impact and are cost-effective.

Chapter 17

MISCELLANEOUS OUTCOMES

In this section outcomes relating to re-admission on relapse (RAOR) and longitudinal process variables are considered. Many of the trends mirror those pertaining to predictors of relapse and these will only be briefly touched upon to avoid repetition.

WHERE WERE INDIVIDUALS RE-ADMITTED ON RELAPSE?

One hundred and twelve (47%) of ADI was re-admitted on relapse. Re-admission on relapse (RAOR) Four reasons could possibly contribute to the high numbers of subjects who were RAOR. Firstly nearly one fifth were medical re-admissions and likely to be in a medical crisis. Secondly individuals who contact treatment services had a poorer baseline status than those who did not (Timko et al 1993). The combination of this factor with the finding that a sizeable percentage of the re-admissions were in medical crisis would certainly contribute to poor outcomes. The third and fourth reasons are intuitive and would need to be tested. Thirdly it is likely that once individuals entered the "treatment system" it is easier to be re-admitted because the unit staff knew him or her. Fourthly and finally another consequence of entering the "treatment system" is that the subject learns to associate relapse with readmission for detoxification and seeks this actively, rather then attempting to cope with this in the community

Predictors of Re-Admission on Relapse (RAOR)

The predictors of RAOR mirrored those of relapse. However, it should be noted that these findings are arguably of even greater importance because re-admission by its very nature has further cost implications beyond relapse.

Only two sociodemographic variables were significantly related to outcome after univariate analysis: Jarman Index scores and social class. Of these only Jarman Index scores were significant following controls. Prescription of licit/illicit drugs, alcohol consumption/history and family history variables were not related to the likelihood of relapse on re-admission.

The most significant predictor of RAOR was the number of previous residential treatments that were recorded at baseline assessment. The link to the likelihood of these individuals being of poorer baseline status has already been discussed (Valliant and Milofsky 1982). Once more the majority of measures associated with univariate outcomes were linked to a compromised physical health status. These were in order of increasing statistical significance; physical functioning (SF-36); sleep (NHP); physical abilities (NHP); general health (SF-36); SF-36 total scores; role functioning (SF-36); NHP total scores; pain (NHP); reported health transition (SF-36); bodily pain (SF-36) and RSCL physical symptoms. There was one exception to this rule;-GHQ-28 total scores, however it should be noted that there is a somatic symptom sub-score in the GHQ-28, so to some degree it will be measuring similar constructs. Only one of the previously listed variables was significant after univariate testing following controls. This was the SF-36 reported health transition sub-score (RHT). The RHT asks the respondent to rate their health compared to one year ago on a five- point scale ranging from "Much better-Much worse." There is scope for investigation as to whether the RHT is a pre-dominantly physical or psychological construct. The associations between the RHT and GHQ-28 scores and RSCL physical symptom scores were only *moderate* ($r < 0.4$) (Cohen 1992).

Taken in combination, these findings are of importance to clinicians, service commissioners and economists. They suggest that the following variables; greater previous use of residential alcohol services and areas marked by social underpriviledge are markers for a group of ADI who if not adequately treated are likely to present an expensive health burden. No variables measured in this study were significantly associated with the length of time taken to RAOR.

Process Variables

Community/Residential Services/Alcoholics Anonymous

Process variables refer to those variables measured *during the course of the study* i.e. on this occasion the number of participants using community services (including shop-fronts and drop-ins), and attending residential alcohol-related services or Alcoholics Anonymous (AA) *following* treatment. Community services were the most common form of treatment utilisation followed by residential services and lastly AA.

In this context the outcomes of interest were rates of relapse, re-admission on relapse (RAOR) and alcohol consumption over twelve-month follow-up. The outcomes concerning those participants who used community and residential services were poor for all three variables, although not significantly so. As previously noted individuals approaching treatment services generally have a poor baseline status and this goes some way to explaining their poor outcomes.

The findings relating to those individuals who used community and alcohol-related residential services are in marked contrast to those who attended AA on at least one occasion subsequent to discharge. In our sample those ADI who attended AA had significant positive outcomes relating to relapse and RAOR rates and alcohol consumption. These remained significant after controlling for sociodemographic factors. It is estimated that one-third to one-fifth of all abstaining former frequent drinkers in Finland are AA members (Makela 1994). One of the conclusions of Project MATCH was that AA involvement should be given special consideration where there are *networks supportive of drinking* (Longabaugh et al 1998). This is profile mirrors our sample. Arguably the most robust findings in support of AA are Valliant (2003). This was a 60-year follow-up study that found prior alcohol dependence and AA attendance were the best predictors of sustained abstinence. Further work from the United States (Bond et al 2003) found that involvement in AA in the 12-36 months subsequent to treatment was associated with positive outcomes. Other important factors were the percentage of heavy/problem drinkers in the social network, and the AA support.

There has been only one UK study that has investigated the outcomes of ADI that has been reported in two separate papers (Gossop et al 2003; Harris et al 2003). The Gossop et al paper reported positive drinking and quality of life outcomes in 150 inpatients in an alcohol specialist unit at 6 months. The other paper examined the acceptability of AA to the same group of UK ADI. The authors found that there was a large variability in the responses though few were universally negative, many rejected the idea of a "higher power." This lack of UK data is a serious omission especially when put in the context of our findings.

Most information relating to AA comes from the United States where self-help organisations have a greater acceptance in the wider-culture (both treatment and beyond) than is the case for the United Kingdom. There has recently been a great interest in researching the impact of AA in the United States in larger participant samples. Two papers are of particular interest. Firstly Moos and Moos (2004) confirmed that extended contact with AA was associated with positive outcomes and another research group (Zemore and Kaskutas 2004) extended these positive outcomes to "helping in AA" i.e. active participation.

The current study can be criticised on the grounds that it represents a small, non-randomised and self-selecting sample. However there is strength in the naturalistic design, because it mirrors reality. Although the numbers are small (only one-fifth of the total sample) they are likely to represent a higher prevalence of AA attendance than would normally be expected in the United Kingdom. The Minnesota project regime is designed around the tenets of AA, and two of the other study centres, the National Health Service alcohol specialist unit and community alcohol services incorporated contact with AA routinely into their treatment programmes. These were the centres with the greatest up-take of AA on leaving treatment. This finding suggests that encouragement of AA is likely to result in greater attendance, and in consequence positive and cost effective outcomes. The costs of AA attendance are minimal, a voluntary collection is taken at each meeting; otherwise it is free.

AA is not for everybody and even in the United States "AA variously attracted and repelled different problem drinkers" (George and Tucker 1996). Even greater ambivalence on the part of potential clients in the United Kingdom is likely- some ambivalence on the part of this group has been confirmed by Harris et al (2003). An interesting finding was that even though most of our participants were in social classes III/IV/V, the greatest AA attendance occurred in social classes I/II. From clinical experience there remains one other factor that needs to be tested and if proven addressed. The ambivalence is not restricted to patients, it also extends to staff, presumably those not familiar with the research literature.

The present methodology cannot address the issue of dose-response for details were only collected relating to "any contact with AA". McCrady et al (1996) have pointed out that the picture of AA attendance is a complex one that needs greater research and the work of one group suggests that there is not a dose-response (Watson et al (1997). From this discussion it is clear that there are still many avenues for research. One such avenue would be to establish in greater depth the areas of ambivalence on the part of patients and staff (should they exist on the part of staff),perhaps there might be a role for qualitative techniques to be employed to help fulfil this aim. Another could be to design packages with the aim of encouraging a greater attendance in individuals from social classes III/IV/V. The message from this study is that positive encouragement towards AA on the part of treatment services can result in greater uptake and with it positive cost-effective outcomes. AA attendees will always self-select. However services should take steps to ensure that this self-selecting group is larger.

Returning Home to Live Alone/Family Unit/ Living in a Residential Alcohol Unit Throughout the Study

Returning home to live alone was associated with poor outcomes relating to relapse at twelve months, RAOR and alcohol consumption following statistical controls. The link to loneliness and social isolation in ADI has already been discussed. Furthermore social isolation has been postulated as an explanation for the steep rise in rates of alcohol-related diagnoses in Scotland (Chick 1997).

By definition living in a residential unit throughout was associated with non-relapse and non-RAOR (continued abstinence is often a condition of residence). Both these findings did not remain significant following statistical controls. However the finding that no alcohol was consumed by this grouping was significant even after multivariate testing, despite the relevant analysis only concerning nine individuals. Most of the participants who remained in a residential unit throughout the study came from the Minnesota project and these findings suggest that for a small number of-individuals there are significant benefits to be gained from prolonged rehabilitation. Two questions remain to be addressed by future methodologies. Firstly can this be repeated with a larger sample? Secondly are these significant benefits cost-effective?

Intuitively one might expect that returning home to live in a family unit would result in significant benefits. In fact individuals who lived in a family unit were more likely to relapse at 12 months than those that did not. In contrast they were less likely to be RAOR and consumed less alcohol over 12 months. However none of these findings were significant following statistical controls. These results are consistent with research that suggests that returning to a family is not inevitably associated with positive outcomes.

Schneider et al (1995) found that for females, being married contributed to the high likelihood of early relapse. However in males, being married was consistently related to less drinking. In the current study females were more likely to return to a family unit. This finding partly explains these results. The attitude towards drinking in the family can exert positive or negative effects (Gordon and Zrull 1991) and explains very little part in the variance of alcohol outcomes (Dobkin et al 2002).

Employment/Unemployment/Alcohol Consumption

Employment during the study was associated with less likelihood of relapse at 12 months and RAOR. It provided a protective effect with regard to alcohol consumption. Similar findings in the opposite direction were evident for those participants unemployed throughout the study period. Both sets of findings were significant after controlling for confounding factors. The link between unemployment and alcohol consumption is particularly noteworthy, because individuals who consume greater amounts of alcohol and are unemployed have significantly high ten year mortality rates (Finney and Moos 1992). Age was a confounding factor in the regression concerning both employment and unemployment. Unemployed individuals were likely to be older. Baseline alcohol consumption was a predictor of the level of study consumption, this is consistent with Eckardt et al (1982). All the findings concerning alcohol consumption and process variables have been previously described. The only other noteworthy finding in this sphere was that there was only one variable that significantly differentiated controlled drinkers from abstainers. This was the amount of alcohol consumed during the study.

Changes in Quality of Life Resulting from Relapse and Non-Relapse to Heavy Drinking

Before the "within group" results could be analysed it was necessary to establish that the non-relapsing and relapsing individuals came from different groups, i.e. there were statistically significant differences in twelve month scores between these two groups. With one exception there were statistically significant differences in all the QoL/QoL-related variables; this was in the number of cigarettes smoked daily.

"Within Group Results"

In order to investigate which variables contributed to the "within group" effects, a regression model was built based upon the results of the current study, the pilot study (See Study B in chapter three) and previous empirical findings.

Quality of Life Changes Resulting from Not Relapsing to Heavy Drinking

Sixty-five (27%) participants did not relapse to heavy drinking during the 12-month follow-up period.

There were significant univariate "within group" improvements in both RSCL physical and psychological sub-scores, GHQ-28 and LSS total scores. However in all four cases significance was lost on controlling for confounding factors. Two confounding variables contributed significantly to these effects, social class and social isolation (NHP). Firstly individuals from Social classes I/II (professional and managerial occupations) had larger improvements in RSCL physical sub-scores than non-relapsing participants from the other social classes. Secondly individuals who perceived themselves to be more socially isolated at baseline *and did not relapse* to heavy drinking had the largest improvements in life situation scores.

In the NHP the only sub-score that produced significant univariate differences was emotional reactions. However this difference too was lost on further statistical controls. The most plausible reason for the inability of the NHP to detect these differences relate to its psychometric properties. The main difficulty concerns the frequency of zero scores resulting from the application of the NHP (Kind and Carr-Hill 1987). Zero scores imply a non-problematic health state and are treated by the computer as missing data. When testing "within-group" changes in non-relapsing individuals this problem was compounded for improvements were likely to result in zero scores on a number of occasions. Thus the ability of the NHP to detect differences was lost.

The SF-36 is scored so that an improving health state is reflected in higher scores. Significant univariate changes in all the SF-36 sub-scores were seen (other than those specifically relating to physical health status), but these significant findings were not maintained after controlling for confounding effects. Once more membership of social classes I/II was linked to significant improvements in QoL scores (in two variables: general health, and social functioning). In this study impaired physical health has been shown to be associated with poor outcomes. Non-relapsing individuals had a better physical health status at baseline. In addition fewer baseline alcohol problems were associated with a greater improvement in social functioning scores and fewer previous residential alcohol treatments were similarly related to an improvement in reported health transition scores.

The most likely reason why the SF-36 "within group" changes relating to physical health status were not significant is what is termed the "ceiling effect" of questionnaires. This means that the baseline scores were too high to enable a statistically significant improvement without going above the maximum score! As the RSCL physical symptoms checklist showed significant improvements then the conclusion must be either that separate constructs were being measured or that the ceiling effect had less impact in the RSCL.

The longitudinal changes between baseline and three months, three to six months and six to twelve months were all tested separately to ascertain whether the improvement in QoL/QoL-related scores was linear. Each measure produced a significant improvement in scores between baseline and three months. Any changes thereafter were minimal. This provides clinicians with important information, for it suggests that the individual will experience improvements in QoL when not relapsing to heavy drinking in the *short-term* only. Thereafter the task is to come to terms with the *present* life situation and that a subsequent large improvement in QoL is *unlikely*. Creation of unrealistic expectations may induce a sense of failure increasing the likelihood of relapse.

In summary there were significant improvements in QoL resulting from not relapsing to heavy drinking however they can be explained by confounding factors, most notably the protective effects provided by membership of social classes I/II. However these significant improvements only occurred during the early stages of "recovery" in the current sample.

Changes in Quality of Life Resulting from Relapsing to Heavy Drinking

There were significant univariate "within-group" changes in both RSCL categories, LSS and GHQ-28 scores. Significance was lost on controlling for confounding factors. The trend for better outcomes in those ADI from Social Classes I/II continued. There were no increases in RSCL psychological symptom scores in relapsing participants from Social Class I/II, whereas participants from Social Classes, III and IV/V all had a significant deterioration in similar scores.

Once again living alone at baseline contributed significantly to a worsening of RSCL physical symptom scores. In addition the SF-36 reported health transition sub-score (RHT) contributed to the worsening of GHQ-28 scores. There were two plausible explanations for this relationship. The RHT asks the individual to compare their health now to 12 months previously on a likert scale. Higher scores indicated a perception of worsening health status. The first possibility is that the RHT reflected a predominantly psychological construct in this sample. Further investigations are required to ascertain what is being measured. The second relates to a "ceiling effect". The sample was divided into those with the "same or better health status" and those with a "worsening health status" at baseline. There was a significant difference between the two groups and the "same or better health status" group had a larger deterioration in scores than the other grouping. This was because the baseline scores for the "worsening health status" group were skewed towards the top end of scale. It is unlikely that the worsening health group had a better QoL, the most likely explanation is that the design of the scale meant this could not be detected.

All the NHP sub-scores produced univariate significant "within group" changes and significance was lost following statistical controls. One confounding variable was a significant contributor to the emotional reactions sub-scores this was LSS scores. Those ADI with higher LSS scores (i.e. better QoL) had a smaller decline in emotional reaction scores as a result of relapse. There is little evidence of the ceiling effect operating in relation to LSS scores.

All but two of the SF-36 sub-scores had significant "within group" changes. Consistent with previous trends, this significance was lost on controlling for confounding factors. The two sub-scores which were not significant in the univariate analyses were role functioning and emotional role. The most likely explanation for these two findings once more lies with zero scores. Zero scores for the SF-36 equate to an extremely poor health state and the tendency was to endorse all items indicating physical impairment. If this were the case then a zero score would result. The consequences of this are that the computer treats zero scores as missing data, statistical comparison is impossible and statistical power to detect significant differences is reduced.

There were three significant confounding relationships, (SF-36 sub-scores first) physical functioning and vitamins, general health and living alone and RHT and GHQ-28 scores. Even individuals who relapsed had an overall improvement in physical health status. Those individuals who were prescribed vitamins in the 12 months prior to baseline assessment had a greater improvement in physical health scores than those who did not. The reduction in the prophylactic use of intra-muscular vitamin preparations has already been touched upon, even the prescription of oral vitamins may have important benefits. These benefits might be enhanced if all individuals were given intra-muscular B vitamins at baseline. The question to establish is whether it would be cost effective to do so?

ADI who lived alone at baseline assessment had poorer "within group" SF-36 general health scores. Living alone was a significant predictor of a poor six-month outcome. Finally in order to investigate the link between SF-36 and GHQ-28 scores, the "within group" changes in the latter were analysed. Participants were divided into a good and poor GHQ-28 status at a cut –off point of 14 (i.e. halfway on the scale). Scores equal to or below 14 were considered to be "Good" and above 14 "Poor". Once again individuals who had a poorer baseline status produced scores skewed towards the end of the range so that a statistically significant change was impossible. Indeed the median "within group" changes were minimal. Those who had a better baseline assessment had a worsening of scores. This is yet another example of the "ceiling effect" in operation. The "ceiling effect" is clearly of great importance when measuring QoL in ADI. However there remains the possibility that this could be impossible to circumvent because of the tendency for ADI to skew their answers at the extreme end of any scale. This is a conundrum for future research.

The relationships between the time taken to relapse/re-admission following relapse and QoL/QoL-related variables were investigated. There were no significant interactions in either case. Thus QoL/QoL-related measures were unable to estimate time to relapse/re-admission following relapse with any degree of accuracy.

This study has shown that there were many significant changes in QoL/QoL-related scores when univariate analyses were used. None of the findings remained significant after controlling for confounding factors. Living alone at baseline played an important role in poor outcomes particularly related to physical health. The other significant associations revealed a difficulty when assessing the QoL of this group; namely the tendency to produce skewed (extremely skewed) baseline scores. This makes the detection of significant interactions hard and leads to the somewhat paradoxical finding that those individuals with a better baseline status who relapse fare worse than those with an even more impaired status.

Sometimes a problem that was not anticipated at the inception of a study becomes apparent, this was the case in the present study. Whereas in the pilot study the follow-up period was sufficiently short that none of the subjects required re-admission, this was not the case when the follow-up period was extended to twelve months. One hundred and twelve (47%) of the sample were re-admitted following relapse (RAOR); how was this data to be handled? To have followed these individuals up at 6 months or 12 months and not take the RAOR into account would make comparison with the non-relapse group meaningless. Such individuals could be in rehabilitation, having a period of brief abstinence and their enhanced QoL status would fail to take into account the fact they had received another detoxification. After consultation with a statistician the following methodology was devised. Individuals were seen on re-admission and asked to complete the questionnaires retrospectively focusing on the period immediately prior to re-admission. They were shown their last answers so they had a benchmark to decide whether there had been any changes. These results were then used for the rest of the study i.e. if they represented six-months figures then they were also used as twelve-months figures.

We decided this was the best possible methodology in the circumstances. It is not perfect and its main deficiency is whether there is a sufficiently accurate re-call. The study has involved a rigorous testing of numerous effects and interactions. The author concludes that where there have been significant changes, they can largely be explained by confounding factors. Longitudinal QoL studies in ADI are an important endeavour-that to date have been attempted rarely. Future studies should tackle the problem of RAOR in a systematic manner.

Strengths or Limitations of the Study?

The limitations of the findings relating to AA attendance on leaving treatment and the relapse group have already been discussed and will not be discussed further. The gold-standard by which research findings are traditionally judged is the randomised controlled trial (RCT), the main aim of which is to eliminate selection bias. Moncrieff and Drummond (1998) outline a quality rating system for the design and reporting of alcohol treatment research. Whilst the drive towards high standards is to be encouraged, some form of pragmatism is also necessary. Realistically randomisation is only possible if outcomes are being tracked in one or two study centres or if there is an enormous research budget (Project MATCH is a case in point here!). In the current study one researcher attempted to follow-up 240 individuals across six study centres! The scientific puritanism of the RCT does not cut any ice in certain treatment settings that regard randomisation as unethical. It is viewed as withholding treatment from a group who specifically approached their service for treatment. In our study this belief was especially prevalent in the voluntary sector and non-randomisation of participants was a condition of their co-operation.

Despite being the main body offering alcohol treatment services in the United Kingdom the voluntary sector has been under-researched, Foster et al (1998a) was the first study to investigate a residential voluntary sector unit in the United Kingdom. Carrying out an RCT usually requires biochemical validation, in consequence it is very difficult to perform an RCT outside a clinical setting. Drawing conclusions merely from clinical settings *may* produce unrepresentative findings. Some comments need to be made about the selection procedures employed especially those in the medical ward sample. By using as our selection criteria "individuals identified as having an alcohol problem by general hospital nurses and doctors" there was a strong possibility that only those with a particularly poor prognosis were selected. Canning et al (1999) found that there were many more "at risk" individuals who were identified by a screening questionnaire in comparison to identification by general hospital doctors. However our intention was to replicate "real situations" and in reality those individuals identified by general hospital staff are at the severe end of the dependency continuum. Furthermore this is the likely avenue of treatment for those individuals who have been drinking at harmful level for many years, have minimal social supports and remained outside the ambit of treatment services.

The current study is "naturalistic" and well designed. There is now support for naturalistic studies in alcohol treatment from eminent sources (Finney et al 1996) on the grounds that pre-selection and random assignment of patients does not "mirror treatment selection processes in non-research situations".–Two British naturalistic studies has been published (Long et al 1998; Foster et al 2000c). The possibility that the samples in the current study were self-selecting and biased cannot be discounted and these findings could be used as the basis for a RCT (ensuring that the interviewer remains blind to the original allocation) with a cost benefit analysis.

One of the chief strengths of the current study is the number of safeguards built into the analysis before statistical significance could be concluded. An attempt was made to take account of multiple testing by setting the cut-off point for assessing the significant probability level at one per cent. In addition the impact of a series of confounders have been thoroughly tested for, and significance was not inferred, unless present after rigorous statistical controls. This means that the chances of a Type I error is minimal. However, the flip side of such rigour is that there may be Type II errors which have not been detected. The intention was to replicate the methodology employed in the pilot study, thus within-group changes were investigated rather changes in scores for the total sample at 12 months. This can be criticised, as by adopting this approach little insight can be provided as to the question of causation. In hindsight analysis of the changes in scores would have been a better option to have followed.

Finney et al (1996) concluded that treatment settings had a minimal impact on outcomes, the key variable was maintenance of "treatment intensity". The present analysis can add little to this debate as treatment intensity was not assessed. To find a way of standardising this over six diverse treatment settings and carry out the follow-up visits would have required far greater research resources.

The last sentence points to one of the greatest strengths of the study and this is the excellent follow-up rate (95%). The methodology employed to achieve this is described in Foster (2004). However despite the excellent follow-up, the study was enhanced by analysing those lost to follow-up by means of an intention to treat analysis (Chick 1995).

There are two other limitations of note. Due to resource constraints the interviewer could not be blinded to the original treatment allocation and the possibility that subconscious bias was inadvertently introduced is always possible. Secondly the study was dependent upon self-report data for the validation of relapse status. Traditionally there are two ways of validation, by biochemical measurement or corroborative report. The voluntary sector projects both operated non-medical philosophies and felt collecting blood samples ran contrary to this ethos. In addition, many of the follow-up visits took place in the evenings often miles from the hospital, thus precluding biochemical investigations.

Corroboration would also have presented difficulties, for many of the participants lived alone and had no contact with significant others to corroborate their drinking status. Often the only participants who could do this were fellow drinkers and little reliability could be placed on such reports! A number of studies reviewed by Sobell and Sobell (1986) have shown that self-report data need not detract from any findings. For self-report data from alcoholics in treatment agreed closely with official records, biochemical measures and family reports. Further confirmation of these comments has come from Project MATCH (Babor et al 2000). These researchers concluded that resources were better spent attempting to enhance the validity of self-report data rather than looking for alternative corroborative sources. The need to concentrate resources aimed at enhancing the validity of self-report points to one of the possible criticisms of the study. This relates to the gap between 6-12 month follow-up and the difficulty of accurate recall over such a period. Ideally more follow-up points should have been built into the study, however the resources were not available to facilitate this. One other point is noteworthy, namely that the 12-month relapse rate in the range of 70% is consistent with previous research. Thus we have no reason to suspect under or over reporting of relapse status.

Chapter 18

THE FUTURE

INTRODUCTION

The previous chapters have discussed the results of the study. The final section will provide a synthesis of the findings and considers the following areas;

a. Implications of these findings for clinicians, commissioners of services and policy makers.
b. Future research questions arising from the study
c. Concluding Remarks.

IMPLICATIONS OF THESE FINDINGS FOR CLINICIANS, COMMISSIONERS OF SERVICES AND ALCOHOL POLICY MAKERS

Holder and Blose (1992) in a now classic study tracked the outcomes of 2516 individuals who received alcohol treatment compared to 661 participants who had a chronic medical alcohol-related problem which was untreated. The methodology they employed was to collect data over 14 years from insurance company records. There were two main conclusions. Firstly the costs incurred by participants who abstained from alcohol decreased over time. Secondly the health care costs for the treated group were 24% lower than those who were untreated. However this was a study conducted in the United States and there are major differences between the US and alcohol services in the United Kingdom. Most notably there are greater outpatient and community treatments in the United Kingdom and there is a tendency for ADI from the United Kingdom to be of lower social status (Godfrey 1994). The Godfrey paper provides some guidelines for designing studies with the aim of assessing the cost-effectiveness of alcohol services. Health services in the United Kingdom are competing for scarce resources and therefore it is imperative that clinicians and researchers demonstrate services provide cost benefits. There is now some optimism in this sphere as result of the UKATT study (UKATT Research Team 2005 b). This paper reports a fivefold benefit in terms health, social and criminal justice costs as a result of alcohol treatments.

The issue of "treatment matching" has become particularly prevalent in alcohol research recently. The rationale behind the "matching hypothesis" is that if individuals are matched to appropriate treatments then their outcomes should be enhanced (Institute of Medicine 1990). The "matching hypothesis" has not been fully supported in alcohol research. PROJECT MATCH concluded that aside from "psychiatric severity" there were no robust matching effects (PROJECT MATCH RESEARCH GROUP 1997). Outpatients without psychiatric severity were well-matched to a Twelve-Step philosophy (i.e. Alcoholics Anonymous). The present analysis can add little to the treatment-matching debate.

The author submits that the most important finding for policy makers is the impact of Jarman (living in an underprivileged area) scores upon negative outcomes. This suggests that clinicians should be lobbying policy makers to concentrate on community-wide interventions. These should include funding of investigations into what are the characteristics of areas marked by social deprivation that are particularly linked to the increased likelihood of relapse to heavy drinking. As previously mentioned the real price of alcohol has fallen continuously for thirty plus years. Harrison and Gardiner (1999) put forward the theory that this is largely responsible for the finding that the mortality rate in young males from social classes IV/V was 10-20 times higher than equivalent subjects from social classes I/II. Cartwright et al (1978) found that when the real price of alcohol was reduced the increase consumption was far larger in social classes IV/V than the other social classes. In fact, in social classes I/II, it declined. One other factor that may be related to this is the easier availability of alcohol in supermarkets and off-licences during the past thirty years.

The major task of researchers and clinicians is twofold

a) to continue demonstrating to policy makers that treatment of ADI has significant cost-benefits to society.
b) to continue lobbying for a change in policy re-pricing and availability of alcohol and producing empirical evidence of the wider benefits from doing so.

Recommendations for Future Quality of Life Studies with Alcohol Dependent Individuals

This study has provided further evidence that QoL studies in alcohol dependent individuals are a worthwhile endeavour. Amongst other findings it has confirmed that the QoL scores are markedly poorer than the general population in a group recruited from different treatment settings. It has also demonstrated that there are significant improvements in QoL scores in consequence of not relapsing and an equally significant deterioration in QoL scores in the event of relapsing to heavy drinking. However both of these are mediated by confounding factors. The findings point to need for further longitudinal QoL studies.

Papers which report QoL scores but little besides are difficult to interpret and run the risk of lacking any meaningful context. Thus it is recommended that when reporting QoL findings the following are included; detailed sociodemographic variables; dependency and psychological/psychiatric disturbance scores, alcohol consumption patterns prior to the study, length of time alcohol free and comparisons with other populations. All these other than the last listed item can then be controlled for and their effects teased out.

Each of the longitudinal measures used in the current study will now be considered in turn. It is questionable whether the Rotterdam Symptoms Checklist (RSCL) meets the criteria of a QoL measure as outlined by Shumaker and Berzon (1995) and Testa and Simonson (1996). These authors felt that a QoL index should measure physical, psychological and social constructs. It has no problems meeting the first two criteria, but at best only measures social factors indirectly The RSCL can provide data that is of clinical utility (see Foster et al 1999b) but whether it should be considered to be a QoL measure is doubtful.

The General Health Questionnaire-28 (GHQ-28) has somatic symptom, anxiety and insomnia, social dysfunction and severe depression sub-scores. It was designed as a screening tool for "psychiatric caseness". Thus although its primary aim is not to measure QoL, it meets the criteria of a QoL measure. Significant changes in GHQ-28 scores resulting from relapse and non-relapse were detected prior to statistical adjustment. There was one problem relating to the GHQ-28 revealed by this study; this was the "ceiling" effect. GHQ-28 scores contributed significantly to the increase in Short-Form-36 (SF-36) reported health transition scores. Individuals who were less impaired at baseline had larger changes in GHQ-28 scores in consequence of relapse. The explanation for this is that there was a tendency for GHQ-28 scores to be skewed towards the top of the scale at baseline. Thus it is impossible to detect a statistically significant change in those individuals with a poorer baseline status. The tendency for many ADI to score poorly on mood/affect measures seems to be a feature of the group. However psychological disturbance is an important factor in the QoL of ADI and QoL studies should always include a specifically designed measure of mood/affect. Sub-scores measuring this as part of generic questionnaires are not sufficient. Despite the "ceiling effect" which may be impossible to circumvent the author feels that the GHQ-28 has utility in QoL studies.

The Life Situation Survey (LSS) has no difficulty in fulfilling the criteria of a QoL measure. There were significant changes in LSS scores prior to statistical controls in both the relapse and non-relapse groups. It has a scale that quantifies both improvements and deterioration in QoL scores. The LSS can provide useful contextual information such as environmental variables that the two main generic measures used in the current study lack. The author endorses its use in future QoL studies.

The Short-Form-36 is becoming the generic measure of choice in QoL studies and is being used increasingly in alcohol related studies. It too was able to detect significant changes in scores in both individuals who relapsed and those who did not. It should be the generic measure of choice in future QoL studies with ADI.

The NHP has been criticised on the ground that it produces too many zero scores making meaningful statistical comparison difficult. It is likely that this is the reason it could only detect one significant change in the non-relapsing individuals. The question is, can the NHP be consigned to the dustbin of history? The answer is not as yet. Foster et al (2004) have shown that the four NHP sub-scores; (emotional reactions, pain, energy and physical mobility) had correlations of $r > 0.8$ to their equivalent SF-36 sub-scores. These findings provide evidence that the bracketed NHP variables may be redundant. This leave two other NHP sub-scores; social isolation and sleep. The correlation of the social isolation sub-score and its SF-36 equivalent was $r < 0.5$, which suggests they are measuring different constructs. The NHP social isolation sub-score was a significant contributor to the improvement in LSS scores resulting from non-relapse. The SF-36 social functioning sub-score did not contribute significantly to any findings. Thus it is possible to enter the proposition that that the NHP social isolation variables have greater relevance to ADI. It should now be the task of researchers to design and validate an adequate measure of social isolation/functioning using the NHP social isolation variables as a basis.

The SF-36 has no sleep sub-score; eighty-five percent of the individuals endorsed at least one sleep item in the NHP sleep sub-score at baseline. Although sleep did not contribute significantly to any of the outcomes in the current study the above finding stresses its importance in the QoL of ADI. The LSS has one item pertaining to sleep "My sleep is restful and refreshing" scored on a Likert scale. Correlation co-efficients were computed to ascertain the level of agreement between this variable and the NHP sleep sub-score to see if the NHP sleep score could be discarded from future studies. The statistics that resulted following the calculation of partial correlation co-efficients were as follows ($r = 0.63$, $p < 0.001$). A judgement has to made as to whether this is an acceptable trade-off:-probably not. There are a number of sleep specific questionnaires such as Pittsburgh Sleep Quality Index (PSQI) (Buysee et al 1989). It takes approximately ten minutes to complete and provides information relating to subjective sleep quality, latency, duration, habitual sleep efficiency, sleep disturbance, use of sleep medication and daytime dysfunction. Whether this constitutes and overload of information is a subject for clinical judgement. Though clinicians should bear in mind that one of the recommendations for a good follow-up rate (Desmond et al 1995) is to keep the follow-up interview *short!*

There is a perhaps a compromise position and this is to use the NHP sleep sub-scale as a stand-alone measure. Hunt et al (1986) (designers of the NHP) state that "It would be meaningless to simply add up the number of affirmative responses out of the 38 possible". The implication from this statement is that there is no meaningful total score for the NHP and each sub-score stands alone. Kind and Carr Hill (1987) criticise the methodology employed to derive the weights for each NHP item. They were divided into their sub-sections *a priori*, but in reality there is a substantial overlap between the items. For example "I sleep badly at night" (sleep), "I'm tired all the time" (energy), "Things are getting me down" (emotional rections) *may* have been measuring parts of the same construct. However if there is an NHP item which can stand alone it is the sleep sub-score. Kind and Carr Hill (1987) found that of the five most endorsed NHP items in 1700 individuals, three came from the NHP sleep sub-scale. One of the previously cited authors Kind (1982) tested the weightings against a simplified scoring method in the NHP sleep sub-score only. He recommended that each response be scored either 0 or 1 according to whether they were positive or negative. Thus the possible range of scores would then be 0-5.

There is one issue that needs to be considered. In the current study QoL was measured by a battery of generic questionnaires; could the same task be achieved by an alcohol-specific measure? Once more we are in the area of a trade-offs. Two global factors would have to be considered. Firstly could the research endeavour be justified in terms of cost and ultimate clinical benefit i.e. would it be used sufficiently? Secondly would there be significant benefits when compared to the existing generic measures. In considering these factors there are a number of issues which would have to be considered.

a. Could the variables that have been measured in this study be encapsulated satisfactorily into 20-30 variables? Alcohol dependency can result in a gradual physical, psychological and social disintegration with an accompanying stigma. It is this stigma that sets it apart from for example cancer, and makes it questionable whether 20-30 items could adequately encapsulate QoL in ADI.

b. Should such a measure if designed be alcohol-dependent specific? If so research costs would be cheaper but arguably such a measure would have a narrow clinical utility.
c. Who should be involved in the judgement of what constitutes QoL in this sample? Clearly patients and clinicians and carers would be consulted, however not solely. QoL measures although focusing upon the subjective views are intrinsically linked to cost and subsequently resource allocation. Thus arguably to develop an adequate QoL measure the views of health economists, policy makers and possibly the wider general public should be canvassed. This would not be a cheap measure to design!!!
d. Can the "ceiling effects" evident in the SF-36 be circumvented? One possible way of doing this would be to design a scoring scale based upon the methodology employed in the LSS. This in effect has two Likert scales that can measure deterioration and improvement in health status. If there were ceiling effects in the LSS, they were not of note.
e. Would there be significant improvements in terms of sensitivity and specificity over the generic measures? This cannot be answered without a specially designed study. However the current study does give some pointers. With the exception of the NHP (its psychometric deficiencies have already been described i.e the tendency to produce many zero scores) all the generic measures used were able to detect significant changes in consequence of both relapse and non-relapse. When establishing the psychometric validity of a measure one of the requirements to be satisfied is that it is "responsive to change" (Leidy et al 1999). The generic measures of QoL have already shown this and a great deal of expense has already been employed in their development and validation. It is unlikely that further expense could be justified.
f. Does a QoL measure in alcohol dependent individuals already exist? Arguably yes; the APQ would provide the information specifically aimed at ADI which the generic measures lack. With hindsight the APQ should have been used as a longitudinal measure in the current study.

This is the first time that the author has considered whether the development of an alcohol dependent-specific questionnaire is justified, to date he has taken the view that it is. Though quite clearly from the comments and by examining the data from this study his conclusion is that this is no longer the case. However the author wholeheartedly endorses QoL studies, in particular longitudinal ones. The following measures are recommended in future QoL studies, APQ, LSS, GHQ-28, SF-36, the NHP sleep and social isolation sub-scores as stand-alone measures scored as suggested in Kind (1982). The SADQ should be used at baseline only. Whether the RSCL should be used is dependent upon the research question being asked. It is not however a QoL measure *per se*. Finally rather than designing an alcohol-specific QoL index, research efforts should be put into designing an instrument which adequately encapsulates the social situation of ADI.

RECOMMENDATIONS FOR FUTURE RESEARCH

As each of these has been discussed elsewhere they will be presented in the form of a summary table (table 18.1).

Table 18.1. Recommendations for Future Research Arising from the Study

- Repetition of the study with sufficient resources to conduct a randomised controlled trial with a cost benefit analysis.
- The design and subsequent validation of a measure to assess the social functioning/isolation of ADI.
- Design and subsequent evaluation of intervention packages aimed at two patient groups. Firstly young polydrug users who live alone. Secondly older individuals who also live alone and have a particularly compromised physical health status.
- A randomised-controlled trial into the impact of the prophylactic use of parenteral vitamin supplements.
- More systemised investigations into the possibility of alcohol being used as a self-medication for physical pain
- Research into what are the variables present in underprivileged areas that make ADI prone to relapse. Thereafter the design and evaluation of appropriate interventions.
- Greater work into the link between cigarettes and outcomes. The findings from the current study (suggesting there is no link to outcome) run contrary to most research to date
- The design and evaluation of packages aimed at enhancing the up-take of Alcoholics Anonymous. Running alongside this should be studies investigating the level of ambivalence felt towards AA in both patients and staff.
- A randomised controlled trial to investigate whether there are cost benefits and significant outcomes resulting from interventions designed to enhance the up-take of community support services prior to leaving treatment (e.g. nurse accompanying patient on first or second visit to a day centre.)
- A study to establish whether there is a sub-group of patients for which long-term rehabilitation (longer than six months) can be justified in terms of cost-benefits?
- Methodologies to address whether the tendency of mood/mood-related questionnaires to produce "ceiling effects" can be satisfactorily addressed?
- An up-dated study investigating the impact of a drop in the real price of alcohol during the past thirty years upon the alcohol health burden across social class.

Concluding Remarks

By examining the baseline QoL scores of individuals recruited from six sociodemographically diverse study centres this study has shown that the QoL of ADI is uniformly poor when compared to general population norms.

A number of significant predictors of outcome emerged, the most consistent being Jarman Index scores, this predicted relapse at 3, 6 and 12 months and RAOR (re-admission on relapse). Prescription of vitamins in the 12 months prior to the study resulted in poor three-month outcomes. Bodily pain as measured by the Short-Form-36 (SF-36) also predicted outcome at both three and six months. Living alone resulted in a negative prognosis at six months only. The other significant predictors of a negative 12-month outcome were alcohol consumption and number of previous alcohol-related residential treatments. In addition to the Jarman Index score, the number of previous alcohol-related residential treatments, and reported health transition sub-scores (SF-36) predicted an increase in the likelihood of RAOR. None of the QoL/QOL-related variables were significantly associated with time to relapse or time to RAOR.

All significant "within group" changes in individuals who relapsed and did not relapse to heavy drinking by 12 months were explained by confounding factors. There were two other longitudinal findings of note, both associated with positive outcomes, being in employment and attending Alcoholics Anonymous after leaving the original treatment unit.

References

Agence Nationale d'Accreditation et d'Evaluation en Sante (ANAES) (2002) Consensus conference. Treatment of Hepatitis C. *Gastroenterologie Clinique et Biologique 26 Spec No,* B303-320

Akerlind I and Hornquist J. (1990) Loneliness and alcohol abuse: a review of evidences of an interplay. *Social Science and Medicine,* 28, 405-413.

Akerlind I, Hornquist J and Bjurulf P. (1988) Prognosis in alcohol rehabilitation. The relative significance of social psychological and medical factors. *International Journal of The Addictions,* 23, 1171-1178.

Akerlind I, Hornquist J and Hansson B. (1987) Loneliness correlates in advanced alcohol abusers. I Social factors and needs. *Scandinavian Journal of Social Medicine,* 15, 175-183.

Alcohol Concern. (2000) *Proposals for a national alcohol strategy for England.* Alcohol Concern, London.

Allan C. (1995) Alcohol problems and anxiety disorders- a critical review. *Alcohol and Alcoholism,* 30, 145-151.

American Psychiatric Association. (1994) *Diagnostic and Statistical Manual of Mental Disorders, Third Edition,* American Psychiatric Association Publications, Washington DC.

American Psychiatric Association. (1987) *Diagnostic and Statistical Manual of Mental Disorders, Fourth Edition revised 1987,* American Psychiatric Association Publications, Washington DC.

Amodeo M, Kurtz N and Cutter H. (1992) Abstinence, reasons for not drinking and life satisfaction. *International Journal of the Addictions,* 27, 707-716.

Anonymous. (1995) The burnout syndrome increases during the recession. Burnout a taboo topic like alcoholism (German). *Krankenpflege-Soins Infirmiers.* 88, 9-13.

Ansoms C, Deckers F, Lehert P, Pelc I and Potgeiter A. (2000) An open study with acamprosate in Belgium and Luxemburg: results on sociodemographics, supportive treatment and outcome. *European Addiction Research,* 6, 132-140

Armor D, Polich J and Stambul H. (1978) *Alcoholism and Treatment*, Wiley Publications, New York.

Ashton T and Casswell S. (1984) Estimated cost of alcohol to the New Zealand public hospital system. *New Zealand Medical Journal,* 97, 683-686.

Averina M, Nilssen O, Brenn T, Brox J, Arkhipovsky V and Kalinin A. (2005) Social and life style determinants of depression, anxiety, sleeping disorders, and self evaluated quality of life in Russia—a population based study in Arkhangelsk. *Social Psychiatry and Psychiatric Epidemiology,* 40, 511-518

Babor T. (2004) Admirable Ends, Ineffective Means: Comments on the Alcohol Harm Reduction Strategy for England. *Drugs: Education Prevention and Policy,* 11, 361- 365

Babor T, Caetano R, Casswell S, Edwards G, Giesbrecht N, Graham K, Grube J, Gruenewald P, Hill L, Holder H, Homel R, Osterberg E, Rehm J, Room R and Rossow I. (2003) *Alcohol; No Ordinary Commodity- Research and Public Policy.* Oxford, Oxford University Press.

Babor T, Steinberg K, Anton R, and Del Boca F. (2000) Talk is cheap: Measuring drinking outcomes in clinical trials. *Journal of Studies on Alcohol,* 61, 55-63.

Baier Manwell L, Mindock S and Mundt M. (2005) Pateint reaction to traumatic injury and inpatient AODA consult: six month follow-up. *Journal of Substance Abuse Treatment,* 28, 41-47.

Banks M. (1983) Validation of the General Health Questionnaire in a young community sample. *Psychological Medicine,* 37, 340-353.

Barber J and Gilbertson R. (1997) Coping with a partner who drinks too much: does anything work? *Substance Use and Misuse,* 32, 485-494.

Beattie M. (2001) Meta-Analysis of social relationships and posttreatment drinking outcomes: comparison of relationship structure, function and quality. *Journal of Studies of Alcohol,* 62, 518-527.

Beattie M, Longabaugh R, Elliot G, Stout R, Fava J and Noel N. (1993) Effect of social environment on alcohol involvement and subjective well-being prior to alcoholism treatment. *Journal of Studies of Alcohol,* 54, 283-296.

Beck A, Mendelson M, and Mock J. (1961) Inventory for measuring depression. *Archives of General Psychiatry,* 4, 561-571.

Bell D (1956) Alcohol and loneliness. *Journal of Social Therapy,* 2, 171-178.

Berglund K, Berggren U, Bokstrom K, Eriksson M, Fahlke C, Karlsson M and Balldin J. (2004) Changes in mental well-being during Minnesota treatment. *Nordic Journal of Psychiatry,* 58, 383-388.

Berk J. (1998) Trauma and resilience during war: a look at the children and humanitarian aid workers of Bosnia. *Psychoanalytic Review,* 85, 640-658.

Berzon R. (1998) Understanding and using HRQL instruments within clinical research studies. In Staquet M, Hays R and Fayers P (eds). *Quality of Life Assessment in Clinical Trials.* Oxford, Oxford University Press.

Biefang S and Potthoff P. (1995) Assessment methods for rehabilitation (review). *International Journal of Rehabilitation Research,* 18, 201-213.

Bobo J, McIlvian H, Lando H, Walker D and Leed-Kelly A. (1998) Effect of smoking cessation on recovery from alcoholism: findings from a randomized community intervention trial. *Addiction,* 93, 877-887.

Bond J, Kaskutas L and Weisner C. (2003) The persistent influence of social networks and alcoholics anonymous on abstinence. *Journal of Studies on Alcohol,* 64, 579-588.

Boning J. (2004) Risk behaviour in association with addictive drugs-data and insights on treatment (German). *Gesundheitswesen,* 66, Suppl 1 S71-79.

Bourquin-Tieche D, Besson J, Lambert H and Yersin B. (2001) Involuntary treatment of alcohol-dependent patients: a study of 17 consecutive cases of civil commitment. *European Addiction Research,* 7, 48-55

Bowling A. (1995) Measuring Disease: *A review of disease-specific quality of life measurement scales* Second Edition. Open University Press, Buckingham, England.

Bowling A. (1991) Measuring Health:-*A review of quality of life measurement scales.* Open University Press, Milton Keynes, England.

Bradburn N. (1969) The structure of psychological well-being. Chicago, Aldine Press.

Braucht G, Reichardt C, Geissler L, Kwiatowski C and Kirby Jnr M. (1995) Effective services for homeless substance abusers. *Journal of Addictive Diseases,* 14, 87-109.

Brazier J, Harper R, Jones N, O'Caithan A, Thomas K, Usherwood T and Westlake L. (1992) Validating the SF-36 health survey questionnaire: a new outcome measure for primary care. *British Medical Journal,* 305, 160-164.

Brewer C. (1993) Invited Review. Recent developments in Disulfiram treatment. *Alcohol and Alcoholism,* 28, 383-395.

Bronisch T and Hecht H. (1987) Comparison of depressed patients with and without suicide attempts in their past history. *Acta Psychiatrica Scandinavica*, 76, 438-449.

Brooks R with the EuroQoL Group. (1996) EuroQoL: the state of play. *Health Policy,* 37, 53-72.

Brunette M, Noordsly D, Xie H and Drake R. (2003) Benzodiazepine use and abuse among patients with servere mental illness and co-occuring substance use disorders. *Psychiatric Services,* 54, 1395-1401.

Brymer C and Rusnell I. (2000) Reducing substance dependence in elderly people: the side effects program. *Canadian Journal of Clinical Pharmacology,* 7, 161-166.

Bullenkamp J and Voges B. (1994) Alcohol consumption and its significance in therapeutic residences for psychiatric patients. (German) *Psychiatische Praxis,* 21, 179-183.

Bullock J, Warwar R, Bienenfeld D, Marcinisyn S and Markert R. (2001) Psychosocial implications of blepharoptosis and dermatochalasis. *Transactions of the American Ophthalmological Society,* 99, 65-71

Burke W and Wengel S. (2003) Late-life mood disorders. (Review) *Cliniics in Geriatric Medicine,* 19, 777-797.

Bustamante Schneider J and Fernadez Ramos JR.. (2001) Hepatic transplant in alcoholic hepatopathy (Review) *Gastroenterologia y Hepatologia*, 24 (Suppl) 1, 64-69

Buysse D, Reynolds C, Monk T, Berman S, and Kupfer D. (1989) The Pittsburgh Sleep Quality Index: A new instrument for psychiatry practice and research. *Psychiatry Research,* 28, 193-210.

Caetano R and Tam T. (1995) Prevalence and correlates of DSM-IV and ICD-10 alcohol dependence: 1990 US National Alcohol Survey. *Alcohol and Alcoholism,* 30, 177-186.

Calsyn D, Saxon A, Bush K, Howell D, Baer J, Sloan K, Malte C and Kivlahan D. (2004) The Addiction Severity Index medical and psychiatric composite scores measure similar domains as the SF-36 in substance dependent veterans: concurrent and discriminant validity. *Drug and Alcohol Dependence,* 76, 165-171.

Canning U, Kennell-Webb S, Marshall EJ, Wessely SC and Peters TJ. (1999) Substance misuse in acute general medical admissions. *Quarterly Journal of Medicine,* 92, 319-326.

Carman R, Fitzgerald B and Holmgren C. (1983) Alienation and drinking motivations among adolescent females. *Journal of Personality and Social Psychology*, 15, 1021-1029.

Carstairs V and Morris R. (1989a) Deprivation, explaining differences in mortality between Scotland, England and Wales. *British Medical Journal,* 299, 886-889.

Carrington P, Tarter R, Switala J and Van Theil D. (1996) Comparison of quality of life between alcoholic and nonalcoholic patients after liver transplantation. *American Journal on Addictions,* 5, 18-22.

Carter B. (1997) Women's experiences of lymphedema. *Oncology Nursing Forum,* 24, 875-882.

Cartwright A, Shaw S and Spratley T. (1978) The relationship between per capita alcohol consumption, drinking patterns, and alcohol related problems in a population sample 1965-1974. Part I: Increased consumption and changes in drinking patterns. *British Journal of Addiction,* 73, 237-246.

Casswell S, Pledger M and Hooper R. (2003) Socioeconomic status and drinking patterns in young adults. *Addiction,* 98, 601-610.

Chaturvedi S, Kirthana R, and Desai M. (1997) Quality of Life and alcoholism: What aspects are perceived as important. *Quality of Life Research,* 6, 632 (published abstract).

Chaturvedi S. (1987) Family morbidity in chronic pain patients. *Pain,* 30, 159-168.

Chick J. (1997) Alcohol and the brain. *Current Opinion in Psychiatry,* 10, 205-210.

Chick J. (1997) Evidence suggesting increasing health damage in Scotland related to alcohol. *Health Bulletin,* 55, 134-139.

Chick J. (1995) Alcoholism treatment evaluation: the drop out dilemma. *Alcoholism,*_31, 79-86.

Chick J and Erickson C. (1996) Conference summary: Consensus Conference on Alcohol Dependence and the Role of Pharmacotherapy in its Treatment. *Alcoholism Clinical and Experimental Research,* 20, 391-402.

Chick J, Ritson B, Connaughton J and Stewart A. (1988) Advice versus extended treatment for alcoholism: a controlled study. *British Journal of Addiction,* 83, 159-170.

Chick J, Rund D and Gilbert M. (1991) Orthopaedic trauma in men; the relative risk among drinkers and the prevalence of problem drinking in male orthopaedic admissions. *Annals of the Royal College of Surgeons of England,* 73, 311-315.

Christo G, Spurrell S and Alcorn R. (2000) Validation of the Christo Inventory for Substance-misuse services (CISS): a simple outcome evaluation tool. *Drug and Alcohol Dependence,* 59, 189-197.

Chubon R. (1995) *Manual for the Life Situation Survey.* Columbia USA, University of South Carolina Press.

Chubon R. (1987) Development of a Quality of Life rating scale for use in health care evaluation. *Evaluation and Health Professions,* 10, 1034-1038.

Cisler R and Zweben A (1999) Development of a composite measuring for assessing alcohol treatment outcome: Operationalization and validation. *Alcoholism Clinical and Experimental Research,* 23, 263-271.

Clark D, Gibbons R, Haviland M and Hendryx M. (1993) Assessing the severity of depressive states in a recently detoxified alcoholic. *Journal of Studies on Alcohol,* 54, 107-114.

Clark D, and Kirisci L. (1996) Posttraumatic stress disorder, depression, alcohol use disorders and quality of life of adolescents. *Anxiety,* 2, 226-233.

Claus R, Mannen K and Schicht W. (1999) Treatment career snapshots: Profiles of first treatment and previous treatment clients. *Addictive Behaviours,* 24, 471-479.

Coffmann H, Hoffman A, Sher L, Rojter S, Vierling J and Makowka L. (1997) Treatment of postoperative alcoholic liver transplant recipient with other addictions. *Liver Transplantation and Surgery,* 3, 322-327.

Cohen C, Onserud H and Monaco C. (1993) Outcomes for the mentally ill in a program for older homeless persons. *Hospital and Community Psychiatry,* 44, 650-656.

Cohen J. (1992) A power primer. *Psychological Bulletin,* 112, 155-159.

Cohn T, Foster JH and Peters TJ. (2003) Sequential studies of sleep disturbance and quality of life in abstaining alcoholics. *Addiction Biology,* 8, 455-462.

Committee on Safety of Medicines. (1989) Parentrovite and allergic reactions. *Current Problems,* 24, 1.

Conigliaro J, Maisto S, McNeil M, Kraemer K, Kelley M, Conigliaro R and O'Connor M. (2000) Does race make a difference among primary care patients with alcohol problems who agree to enroll in a study of brief interventions? *American Journal on Addictions,* 9, 321-330.

Cook C. (1988) The Minnesota Model in the management of Drug and Alcohol Dependency: miracle, method or myth? Part I. The Philosophy and programme. *British Journal of Addiction,* 83, 625-634.

Cooke S. (1979) Assessing nutrition services in an alcohol rehabilitation unit: the role of the registered dietitian. *Qrb Quality Review Bulletin,* 5, 17-19.

Coryell W, Turvey C, Endicott J, Leon A, Mueller T, Solomon D and Keller M. (1998) Bipolar affective disorder: predictors of outcome after 15 years. *Journal of Affective Disorders,* 50, 109-116.

Cosden M, Ellens J, Schnell J and Yamini-Diouf Y. (2005) Efficacy of a Mental Health Treatment Court with assertive community treatment. *Behavioural Sciences and the Law,* 23, 199-214.

Costa J, Silvera M, Gaxalle F, Oliveira S, Hallal P, Menezes A, Gigante D, Olinto M and Macedo S. (2004) Heavy alcohol consumption and associated factors: a population-based study. (Portuguese) *Revista de Saude Publica,* 38, 284-291.

Cotton N. (1979) The familial incidence of alcoholism: A review. *Journal of Studies on Alcohol,* 40, 89-116.

Counillet C. (1997) An 18 day withdrawal treatment. The nurse's role (French). *Soins,* 617, 22-25.

Crawford M, Patton R, Touquet R, Drummond C, Byford S, Barrett B, Reece B, Brown A and Henry J. (2004) Screening and referral brief intervention of alcohol-misusing patients in an emergency department: a pragmatic randomised controlled trial. *Lancet,* 364, 1334-1339.

Crumbaugh J and Maholick L. (1964) An experimental study in existentialism: The psychometric approach to Frankl's concept of nogenic neurosis. *Journal of Clinical Psychology,* 20, 200-207.

Crumbaugh J, Raphael M (Snr), and Shraeder R. (1970) Frankls' will to meaning in a religious order. *Journal of Clinical Psychology,* 26, 206-297.

Cueto-Manzano A, Cortes-Sanabria L, Martinez-Ramirez H, Rojas-Campos E, Barragan G, Alfaro G, Flores J, Anaya M and Canales-Munoz J. (2005) Detection of early nephropathy in Mexican patients with type 2 diabetes mellitus. *Kidney International-Supplement,* 97, S40-45

Cunningham J and Breslin F. (2004) Only one in three people with alcohol abuse or dependence ever seek treatment. *Addictive Behaviours,* 29, 221-223.

Daeppen J, Krieg M, Burnand B and Yersin B. (1998) MOS-SF-36 in evaluating health-related quality of life in alcohol dependent patients. *American Journal of Alcohol and Drug Abuse,* 24, 685-694.

Dammer R, Neiderdellmann H, Friesenecker J, Fleischmann H, Herrmann J and Kreft M. (1998) Withdrawal therapy of patients with alcoholism and nicotine dependence with carcinoma's in the area of the head and neck. Luxury or necessity? (German) *Mund-,Keifer-und Gesichtschirurgie,* 2, 78-84.

Da Silva Lima A, Fleck M, Pechansky F, de Boni R and Sukop P. (2005) Psychometric properties of the World Health Organisation quality of life instrument (WHOQoL-BREF) in alcoholic males- a pilot study. *Quality of Life Research,* 14, 473-478.

Davidson K. (1995) Diagnosis of depression in alcohol dependence: Changes in prevalence with drinking status. *British Journal of Psychiatry,* 166, 199-204.

Davidson R and Raistrick D. (1986) The validity of the Short Alcohol Dependence Data (SADD) Questionnaire: a short-report questionnaire for the assessment of alcohol dependence. *British Journal of Addiction,* 81, 217-222.

Dawson D. (2000) Alcohol consumption, alcohol dependence and all-cause mortality. *Alcoholism Clinical and Experimental Research,* 24, 72-81.

Dawson D. (1996) Correlates of past-year status among treated and untreated persons with former alcohol dependence: United States 1992. *Alcoholism Clinical and Experimental Research,* 20, 771-779.

Dedobbeleer N and Desjardins S. (2001) Outcomes of an ecological and participatory approach to prevent alcohol and other drug "abuse" among multi-ethnic adolescents. *Substance Use and Misuse*, 36, 1959-1991.

deHaes J, Olschewski M, Fayers P, Visser M, Cull A, Hopwood P, and Sanderman R. (1996) Measuring the quality of life of cancer patients with the Rotterdam Symptoms Checklist (RSCL)- A manual. Northern Centre for Health Care Research (NCH), University of Groningen, The Netherlands.

de Haes J, van Knippenburg F, and Neijt J. (1990) Measuring psychological and physical distress in cancer patients: structure and application of the Rotterdam Symptoms Checklist. *British Journal of Cancer.* 62, 1034-1038.

Demers A and Bourgault C. (1996) Changing society, changing drinking: solitary drinking as a non-pathological behaviour. *Addiction,* 91, 1505-1516.

Derogatis LR, Rickels K and Rock A. (1976) The SCL-90 and the MMPI: a step in the validation of a new self-report scale. *British Journal of Psychiatry,* 128, 280-289.

Desmond D, Maddux J, Johnson T and Confer B. (1995) Obtaining follow-up interviews for treatment evaluation. *Journal of Substance Abuse,* 12, 95-102.

Devinsky O. (2003) Psychiatric comorbidity in patients with epilepsy: implications for diagnosis and treatment. *Epilepsy and Behaviour,* 4 Suppl S2-10.

Di Michele V and Bolino F. (2004) The natural course of schizophrenia and psychopathological predictors of outcome. A community-based cohort study. *Psychopathology,* 37, 98-104.

Diener E, Emmons R, Larsen R and Griffin S. (1985) The Satisfaction with Life Scale. *Journal of Personality Assessment,* 49, 71-75

Dixon L, McNary S and Lehman A. (1998) Remission of substance use disorder among psychiatric inpatients with mental illness. *American Journal of Psychiatry,* 155, 239-243.

Dixon L, Postrado L, Delahunty J, Fischer P and Lehman T. (1999) The association of medical comorbidity in schizophrenia with poor physical and mental health. *Journal of Nervous and Mental Disease,* 187, 4986-502.

Dobkin P, De C, Paraherakis A and Gill K. (2002) The role of functional social support in treatment retention and outcomes among outpatient substance abusers. *Addiction,* 97, 347-356.

Donovan D, Mattson M, Cisler R, Longabaugh R and Zweben A. (2005) Quality of life as an outcome measurement in alcoholism treatment research. *Journal of Studies on Alcohol,* Supplement (July) 15. 119-139, discussion 92-93,

Donovan D, and Mattson M. (1994) Alcoholism treatment matching research: methodological and clinical issues, In Donovan D, and Mattson M (Eds) Alcoholism Treatment Matching Research: methodological and clinical approaches. *Journal of Studies in Alcohol* (Supplement), 12, 138-148.

Dooley D and Prause J. (1998) Underemployment and alcohol misuse in the National Longitudinal Survey of Youth. *Journal of Studies on Alcohol,* 59, 669-680.

Droomers M, Schrijvers C and Mackenbach J. (2004) Educational differences in starting excessive alcohol consumption: explanations from the longitudinal GLOBE study. *Social Science and Medicine,* 58, 2023-2033.

Droomers M, Schrijvers C, Stronks K, van de Mheen D and Mackenbach J. (1999) Educational differences in excessive alcohol consumption: the role of psychosocial and material tressors. *Preventive Medicine,* 29, 1-10.

Drummond C. (2004) An alcohol strategy for England: The good, the bad and the ugly. *Alcohol and Alcoholism,* 39, 377-379.

Drummond, C. (2000). UK government announces first major relaxation in alcohol licensing laws for nearly a century, drinking in the UK goes 24/7. *Addiction*, 95, 997-998.

Drummond C. (1990). The relationship between alcohol dependence and alcohol related problems in a clinical population. *British Journal of Addiction,* 85, 357-366.

Duckert F. (1993) Predictive factors for outcome of treatment for alcohol problems. *Journal of Substance Abuse,* 5, 31-44.

Dunbar B, Argenbright S and Griffiths C. (1998) It takes a village and time...a collaborative case study. *Journal of Psychosocial Nursing and Mental Health Services,* 36, 43-45.

DuPont R and McGovern J. (1992) Suffering in addiction:alcoholism and drug dependence. Nln Publications, 15-2461, 155-201.

Duvoux C. (2001) Liver transplantation which indications? which results? *Presse Medicale,* 30, 711-716.

Eckardt M, Graubard B, Ryback R and Gottschalk L. (1982) Pretreatment consumption as a predictor of posttreatment consumption in male alcoholics. *Psychiatry Research,* 7, 337-344.

Edwards G and Gross M. (1976) Alcohol dependence: provisional description of a clinical syndrome. *British Medical Journal,* 1, 1058-1061.

Edwards G, Kyle E, Nicholls P and Taylor C. (1978) Alcoholism and mortality: implications for epidemiology. *Journal of Studies on Alcohol,* 39, 1607-1617.

Elias C and Inui T. (1993) When a house is not a home; exploring the meaning of shelter among chronically homeless older men. *Gerontologist,* 33, 396-402.

Elton M and Hornquist J. (1983a) Grounds for disability pension. The younger abuser as compared with older abusers of alcohol. *Scandinavian Journal of Social Medicine,* 11, 53-58.

Elton M and Hornquist J. (1983b) Abusers of alcohol immediately prior to pension. *Acta Psychiatrica Scandinavica,* 68, 44-52.

Endicott J, Nee J, Harrison W and Blumenthal R. (1993) Quality of Life Enjoyment and Satisfaction Questionnaire: a new measure. *Psychopharmacological Bulletin,* 29, 321-326.

Eronen M. (1995) Mental disorders and homicidal behaviour in female subjects. *American Journal of Psychiatry,* 152, 1216-1218.

Fabsitz R, Sholinsky P and Goldberg J. (1997) Correlates of sleep problems among men: the Vietnam Era Twin Registry. *Journal of Sleep Research,* 6, 50-56.

Fakhoury W, Priebe W and Quarashi M. (2005) Goals of new long stay patients in supported housing: a UK study. *International Journal of Social Psychiatry,* 51, 45-54.

Feeney G, Connor J Young R, Tucker J, and McPherson A. (2004) Alcohol dependence: the impact of cognitive behaviour therapy with or without naltrexone on subjective health status. *Australian and New Zealand Journal of Psychiatry* 38, 842-848

Fergusson D, Horwood L and Lynskey M. (1997) The effects of unemployment on psychiatric illness during young adulthood. *Psychological Medicine,* 27, 371-381.

Finn P. (1985) Decriminalization of public drunkeness: response of the health care system. *Journal of Studies on Alcohol* 46, 7-23.

Finney, J. and Monaghan, S. (1996) The cost-effectiveness of treatment for alcoholism: A second approximation. *Journal of Studies on Alcohol* 57, 229-243.

Finney, J. Hahn, A. and Moos, R. (1996) The effectiveness of inpatient and outpatient treatment for alcohol abuse: The need to focus on mediators and moderators of setting effects. *Addiction* 91, 1773-1796.

FinneyJ and Moos R. (1992) The long-term course of treated alcoholism: II Predictors and correlates of 10-year functioning and mortality. *Journal of Studies on Alcohol* 53, 142-153.

Firth-Cozens J. (2001) Interventions to improve physicians' well-being and patient care: a commentary. *Social Science and Medicine,* 52, 223-225.

Foster JH, Marshall EJ and Peters TJ. (2004) Comparison of two quality of life measures in a sample of 240 alcohol dependent research participants. (Conference Abstract) *Alcoholism Clinical and Experimental Research, 28,* (8) 46A.

Foster JH. (2004) Conducting Research in Different Alcohol Centres: achieving a follow-up rate of ninety three percent. *Drugs: Education Prevention and Policy.* 11, 263-274.

Foster JH. (2003) Extended Licensing Hours in England and Wales: There will be a large price to pay. Viewpoint Drugs: Education Prevention and Policy *10, 285-287.*

Foster JH, Marshall EJ and Peters TJ. (2003) Non NHS Residential Alcohol Resources are allocated in an inconsistent manner: Some Preliminary Data. Drugs: Education Prevention and Policy, *10, 271-28.*

Foster JH, Peters TJ and Kind P. (2002) Quality of life, sleep, mood and alcohol consumption: a complex interaction. *Addiction Biology 7,* 55-65.

Foster JH, Marshall EJ and Peters TJ. (2000a) Quality of Life measures and outcome in alcohol dependent men and women. *Alcohol, 20,* 45-52.

Foster JH, Marshall EJ and Peters TJ. (2000b) Application of a Quality of Life measure, the Life Situation Survey (LSS) to alcohol dependent subjects in relapse and remission. *Alcoholism Clinical and Experimental Research*, 24, 1687-1692.

Foster JH, Marshall EJ and Peters TJ. (2000 c) Inpatient detoxification service for the treatment of alcohol abuse: Comparison of 7 and 21 days inpatient stay. *Alcohol and Alcoholism, 35,* 480-485.

Foster J, Powell JE, Marshall EJ and Peters TJ. (1999a) Quality of Life in alcohol dependent subjects: a review. *Quality of Life Research* 8, 255-261.

Foster JH, Marshall EJ, Hooper RL and Peters TJ. (1999b) Comparison of Quality of Life in Dependent Alcoholics and Cancer Patients. *Alcohol 20,* 105-110.

Foster JH, Marshall EJ, and Peters TJ. (1999c) Sleep as a Quality of Life Indicator and predictor of relapse in Alcohol Dependents. *Alcoholism Clinical and Experimental Research*, 23, 1044-1051.

Foster JH, Marshall EJ, Hooper R and Peters TJ. (1998a) Quality of life measures in alcohol dependent subjects and changes with abstinence and continued heavy drinking. *Addiction Biology,* 3, 321-332.

Foster JH, Marshall EJ and Peters TJ. (1998b) Predictors of relapse to heavy drinking in alcohol dependent subjects following alcohol detoxification-the role of quality of life measures, ethnicity, social class, cigarettes and drug use. *Addiction Biology,* 3, 333-343.

Frankish C, Hwang S and Quantz D. (2005) Homelessness and health in Canada: research lessons and priorities. *Canadian Journal of Public Health,* 96, Suppl 2 S23-29.

Friend K, and Pagano M. (2004) Smoking initiation among nonsmokers during and following treatment for alcohol use disorders. *Journal of Substance Abuse Treatment,* 26, 219-244.

Fuchs W and Riebenfeld D. (2002) Acamprosate and psychosocial intervention. An integrative treatment approach for prevention of alcohol dependendent patients in Switzerland (German) *Schweizerische Rundschau fur Medizin Praxis,* 91, 735-742.

Gaa'l C, and Freebairn C. (1979) Ear-acupuncture relaxation therapy in alcoholics. Report on a follow-up survey. *Medical Journal of Australia,* 2, 179-180.

Gaev D. (1976) *The Psychology of Loneliness,* Adams Press, Chicago.

George A and Tucker J. (1996) Help-seeking for alcohol-related problems: social contexts surrounding entry into alcoholism treatment for alcoholics. *Journal of Studies on Alcohol* 57, 449-457.

George F. (1994) Pharmacotherapy in alcoholism treatment: integrating and understanding the use of serotonin reuptake inhibitors (Review). *Alcohol and Alcoholism,* Supplement, 2, 537-543.

Gerrirty M. (2001) Interventions to improve physicians' well-being and patient care:. *Social Science and Medicine,* 52, 215-222.

Gillet C, Paille F, Wahl D, Aubin H, Pirollet P, and Prime T. (1991) Outcome of treatment in alcoholic women. *Drug and Alcohol Dependence,* 29, 189-194.

Glickman R. (1995) A 35 year old man with epigastric pain (clinical conference). *Journal of the American Medical Association,* 274, 495-500.

Godrey C. (1994) Assessing the cost-effectiveness of alcohol services. *Journal of Mental Health,* 3, 3-21.

Goldberg D. (1972) The detection of psychiatric illness by questionnaire (Maudsley Monograph No 2).London, Oxford University Press.

Goldberg D and Hillier V. (1979) A scaled version of the General Health Questionnaire. *Psychological Medicine,* 9, 139-145.

Goldberg D and Williams P. (1988) A users guide to the General Health Questionnaire. Windsor, NFER-Nelson.

Goldstein R, Leskovjan A, Hoff A, Hitxemann R, Bashan F, Khalsa S, Wang G, Fowler J and Volkow N. (2004) Severity of neuropsychological impairment in cocaine and alcohl addiction: association with metabolism in the prefrontal cortex. *Neuropsychologia,* 42, 1447-1458.

Gomberg E. (1993) Women and Alcohol: Use and Abuse. *Journal of Nervous Mental Disease,* 181, 211-219.

Gordon A and Zrull M. (1991) Social networks and recovery: one year after inpatient treatment. *Journal of Substance Abuse Treatment,* 8, 143-152.

Gorman D, Potamianios G, Williams K, Frank A, Duffy S and Peters T. (1987) Relationship between alcohol abuse and low back pain. *Alcohol and Alcoholism,* 22, 61-63.

Gossop M, Harris J, Best D, Man L, Manning V, Marshall J and Strang J. (2003) Is attendance at Alcoholics Anonymous meetings after inpatient treatment related to improved outcomes? A 6-month follow-up study. *Alcohol and Alcoholism,* 38, 421-426.

Gould L and Luckoff I. (1977) Selecting a study design. in Johnson L, Nurco D and Robbins L. (Eds) *Conducting follow-up research on drug treatment programs (DHEW Publications NO ADM 77-487),* Rockville MD, US Department of Health and Human Services 29-46.

Grant B. (1996) Toward an alcohol treatment model: a comparison of treated and untreated respondents with DSM-IV alcohol use disorders in the general population. *Alcoholism Clinical and Experimental Research,* 20, 372-378.

Gray G. (1989) Nutrition and dementia (see comments) (review) *Journal of the American Dietetic Association,* 89, 1795-1802.

Grichting W and Barber J. (1989) The impact of quality of family life on drug consumption. *International Journal of the Addictions,* 24, 963-971.

Gual A, Lligona A and Colom J. (1999) Five-year outcome in alcohol dependence. A naturalistic study of 850 patients in Catalonia. *Alcohol and Alcoholism*, 34, 183-192.

Guethmundsson O and Tomasson K. (2002) Quality of life of parents of children with mental health problems. *Nordic Journal of Psychiatry,* 56, 413-417.

Gupta M and Gupta A. (1997) Psoriasis and sex: a study of moderately to severely affected patients. *International Jouranl of Dermatology*, 36, 259-262.

Gupta P and al Kawas F. (1995) Acute pancreatitis: diagnosis and management. *American Family Physician,* 52, 435-443.

Gutierrez E, Zanetta D, Saldiva P and Capelozzi V. (2002) Autopsy-proven determinants in HIV-infected patients treated for pulmonary tuberculosis in Sao Paulo, Brazil. *Pathology, Research and Practice,* 198, 339-346.

Hamilton J. (1979) Evaluation of a detoxification service of habitual drunken offenders. *British Journal of Psychiatry,* 135, 28-34.

Hamilton M. (1967) Development of a rating scale for primary depressive illness. *British Journal of Social and Clinical Psychology*, 6, 278-296.

Harris J, Best D, Gossop M, Marshall J, Man H, Manning V and Strang J. (2003) Prior Alcoholics Anonymous (AA) affiliation and the acceptability of the Twelve Steps to patients entering UK statutory addiction treatment. *Journal of Studies on Alcohol,* 64, 257-261.

Harrison L and Gardiner E. (1999) Do the rich really die young? Alcohol-related mortality and social class in Great Britain, 1988-94. *Addiction,* 94, 1871-1880.

Harter M, Reuter K, Weisser B, Schretzmann B, Aschenbrenner A and Bengel J. (2002) A descriptive study of psychiatric disorders and psychosocial burden in rehabilitation patients with musculoskeletal diseases. *Archives of Physical Medicine and Rehabilitation,* 83, 461-481

Health Education Authority. (1995) *The Big List, the ultimate guide to alcohol units.* The Astley Street Project, Dukinfield, Cheshire, England.

Heather N, Rollnick S and Bell A. (1993) Predictive validity of the Readiness to Change Questionnaire. *Addiction,* 88, 1667-1677.

Hemmingsson T, Lundberg I, Romelsjo A and Alfredsson L (1997) Alcoholism in social classes and occupations in Sweden. *International Journal of Epidemiology,* 26, 584-591.

Hertling I, Ramskogler K, Riegler A, Walter H and Lesch O. (2001) Craving for alcohol and prevention of relapse. *Wiener Klinische Wochenschrift,* 113, 717-726.

Hilton M, Maisto S, Conigliaro J, McNeil M, Kraemer K, Kelley M, Conigilaro R, Samet J, Larson M, Savetsky J, Winter M, Sullivan L, Saitz R, Weisner C, Mertens J, Parthasarathy S, Moore C, Hunkeler E, Hu T, Selby J, Stout R, Zywiak W, Rubin A, Zwick W and Shepard D. (2001) Improving alcoholism treatment across the spectrum of services. *Alcoholism Clinical and Experimental Research,* 25, 128-135.

Hoffmann N and Miller N. (1993) Perspectives of effective treatment for alcohol and drug disorders. *Psychiatric Clinics of America,* 16, 127-140.

Hoffman N, Olofsson O, Salen B and Wickstrom L. (1995) Prevalence of alcohol abuse dependency in chronic pain patients. *International Journal of the Addictions,* 30, 919-927.

Holder H and Blose J. (1992) The reduction of health care costs associated with alcoholism treatment: a 14 year longitudinal study. *Journal of Studies on Alcohol* 53, 293-302.

Holroyd S, Currie L, Thompson-Heisterman A and Abraham I. (1997) A descriptive study of elderly community-dwelling alcoholic patients in the rural south. *American Journal of Geriatric Psychiatry,* 5, 221-228.

Hornquist J. (1982) Abusers of alcohol and disability pension. The effect of liberalization in Sweden in 1977. *Scandinavian Journal of Social Medicine,* 10, 113-118.

Hornquist J, and Akerlind I. (1987) Loneliness correlates in advanced alcohol abusers. II. Clinical and psychological factors. *Scandinavian Journal of Social Medicine,* 15, 225-232.

Hornquist J and Elton M. (1983) A prospective longitudinal study of abusers of alcohol granted disability pension. *Scandinavian Journal of Social Medicine,* 11, 91-96.

Hornquist J, Elton M and Ostlund R. (1983) Predictors of outcome of disability pension for alcohol abusers. *Acta Psychiatrica Scandinavica,* 68, 426-436.

Hoyumpa A. (1983) Alcohol and thiamine metabolism. *Alcoholism Clinical and Experimental Research,* 7, 11-14.

Hubschmid T, Pfister F and Spalinger J. (1988) Reintegration in residential facilities-a catamnestic study (German) *Psychiatrische Praxis,* 15, 78-83.

Humphreys K, Moos R and Cohen C. (1997) Social and community resources and long-term recovery from treated and untreated alcoholism. *Journal of Studies on Alcohol,* 58, 231-238.

Hunt S, McKenna S, and McEwen J. (1994) The Nottingham Health Profile User's Manual. Galen Research Publications, Manchester, England.

Hunt S, McEwen J and McKenna S. (1986) *Measuring Health Status*, Croon Helm, London.

Hunt S, Sonja M, McEwen J, and McKenna S. (1985) Perceived health and social inequalities. *Effective Health Care,* 2, 151-160.

Hunt S, Sonja M, McKenna S, McEwen J, Backett E and Papp E. (1980) A quantitative approach to perceived health status: a validation study. *Journal of Epidemiology and Community Health,* 34, 281-286.

Hunt W, Barnett W and Branch L. (1971) Relapse rates in addiction studies. *Journal of Consulting Clinical Psychology,* 27, 455-456.

Institute of Medicine. (1990) *Broadening the base of treatment for alcohol problems.* Washington D.C. National Academy Press.

Itzen M, Sheldon J, Meyers C, Green D, Long C and Buckley B. (2002) Neuropsychological and emotional challenges in a 38-year-old man with a brain tumour. *Cancer Practice,* 10, 266-268.

Iyengar G and Nair P. (2000) Global outlook on nutrition and the environment: meeting the challenges of the next millenium. *Science of the Total Environment,* 249, 331-346

Jarman B. (1983) Identification of underprivileged areas. *British Medical Journal,* 286, 1705-1709.

Jarvinen H, Kallio H and Lempinen M. (1981) Interposition mesocaval shunt for bleeding oesophageal varices in moderate and poor risk cirrhosis. *Annales Chirurgiae Gynaecologiae,* 70, 45-49.

Jenkinson C, Coulter A, and Wright L. (1993) Short form 36 (SF-36) health survey questionnaire: normative data for adults of working age. *British Medical Journal,* 306, 1437-1444.

Johnson B, Ait-Daoud N Akhtar F and Ma J. (2004) Oral toprimate reduces the consequences of drinking and improves the quality of life of alcohol-dependent individuals: a randomized controlled trial. *Archives of General Psychiatry,* 61, 905-912.

Johnson D, Fontana A, Lubin H, Corn B and Rosenheck R. (2004) Long-term course of treatment-seeking Vietnam veterans with posttraumatic stress disorder: mortality, clinical condition and life satisfaction. *Journal of Nervous and Mental Disease,* 192, 35-41.

Johnson J, Spitzer R, Kroenke K, Williams J, Linzer M, Brody D, DeGruy F and Hahn S. (1995) Psychiatric comorbidity, health-status and functional impairment associated with alcohol abuse and dependence in primary–care patients- Findings of the PRIME–MD-1000 study. *Journal of Consulting and Clinical Psychology,* 63, 133-140.

Jones J, Boehmer U, Berlowitz D, Christiansen C, Pitman A and Kressin N. (2003) Tooth retention as an indicator of quality dental care: development of a risk adjustment model. *Medical Care,* 41, 937-949.

Jones W. (1985) The psychology of loneliness: some personality issues in the study of social support. In *Social Support: Theory,Research and Applications.* Sarason I (Ed), Matrinus Nijhoff, Dordrecht.

Jowsey S, Taylor M, Schneekloth T and Clark M. (2001) Psychosocial challenges in transplantation. *Journal of Psychiatric Practice,* 7, 404-414.

Kairouz S and Dube L. (2000) Abstinence and well-being among members of Alcoholics Anononymous: personal experience and social perceptions. *Journal of Social Psychology,* 140, 565-579

Kaplan R, Atkins C and Timms R. (1984) Validity of the quality of well-being scale as an outcome measure in chronic obstructive pulmonary disease. *Journal of Chronic Disease,* 37, 85-95.

Keefe E and Esquivel C. (1993) Controversies in patient selection for liver transplantation (Review). *Western Journal of Medicine,* 159, 586-593.

Keller M. (1994) Dysthymia in clinical practice: course, outcome and impact on the community. (Review). *Acta Psychiatrica Scandinavica,* Supplementum, 383, 24-34.

Kessler R. (2203) The impairments caused by social phobia in the general population:implications for intervention. *Acta Psychiatrica Scandinavica,* Supplementum, 417, 19-27.

Kessler R, Wittchen H-U, Abelson J, McGonagle K, Schwartz N and Kendler K, Knauper B and Zhao S. (1998) Methodological studies of the Composite International Diagnostic Interview CIDI in the US National Comorbidity Survey (NCS) *International Journal of Methods in Psychiatry Research,* 7, 33-55

Khan S, Murray R and Barnes G. (2002) A structural equation model of the effect of poverty and unemployment on alcohol abuse. *Addictive Behaviours,* 27, 405-423.

Kingree J and Thompson M. (2000) Mutual help groups, perceived status benefits, and well being: a test with adult children of alcoholics with personal substance abuse problems. *American Journal of Community Psychology,* 28, 325-342.

Kind P. (1996) The EuroQoL instrument: an index of health related quality of life In Spilker B (ed) *Quality of Life and Pharmacoecomomics in Clinical Trials* (2nd edition), New York, Raven-Lippincott Press.

Kind P. (1982) A comparison of two models for scaling health indicators. *International Journal of Epidemiology,* 11, 271-275.

Kind P and Carr-Hill R. (1987) The Nottingham Health Profile: A useful tool for epidemiologists? *Social Science and Medicine,* 25, 905-910.

Kiritze-Topor P, Huas D, Rosenzweig C, Comte S, Paille F and Lehert P. (2004) A pragmatic trial of acamprosate in the treatment of alcohol dependence in primary care. *Alcohol and Alcoholism* 39, 520-527.

Knutsen E. (1977) On the emotional well-being of psychiatrists: overview and rationale. *American Journal of Psychoanalysis,* 37, 123-129.

Korolenko C and Densin D. (2001) The quality world change as a cause of addiction development in conditions of the north. *Circumpolar Health,* 60, 294-299

Kraemer L, Bauer E, Funk G, Hofer H, Jessner W, Steindl-Munda P, Wrba F, Madl C, Gangl A, and Ferenci P. (2002) Subclinical impairment of brain function in chronic hepatitis C infection. *Journal of Hepatology,* 37, 349-359.

Krawczynski M, Wozniak Z, Sluzewski W, Krzyzaniak A and Wiewiorowska M. (1993) Home environment of children with alcoholic parents (Polish). *Polski Tygodnik Lekarski,* 48, 354-357.

Krom R. (1994) Liver transplantation and alcohol who should get transplants? (Review) *Hepatology,* 20, S28-S-32.

Kulikova N. (2004) Primary prevention of complicated involution-and-age deregulations in person above 40. (Russian) *Problemy Sotsianoi Gigieny I Istoriia Mediitsiny,* 5, 27-28.

Kusznir A, Cooke R, and Young L. (2000) The correlates of community functioning in patients with bipolar disorder. *Journal of Affective Disorders,* 61, 81-85

Lambert T, Velakoulis D and Pantelis C. (2003) Medical comorbidity in schizophrenia. *Medical Journal of Australia,* 178 Suppl, S67-70.

Lehman A. (1983) The well-being of chronic mental patients: Assessing their quality of life. *Archives of General Psychiatry,* 40, 369-373.

Lehman A. (1988) A quality of life interview for the chronically mentally ill. *Evaluation of Program Planning,* 11, 51-62.

Leidy N, Revicki D and Geneste B. (1999) Recommendations for evaluating the validity of quality of life claims for labelling and promotion. *Value in Health, 2,* 113-127.

Lepine J and Pelissolo A. (2000) Why take social anxiety seriously? *Depression and Anxiety 11, 87-92*

Levine E, Degutis L, Pruzinsky T, Shin J and Persing J. (2005) Quality of life and facial trauma: psychological and body image effects. *Annals of Plastic Surgery,* 54, 502-510.

Li G, Keyl P, Rothman R, Chanmugam A and Kelen G. (1998) Epidemiology of alcohol-related emergency department visits. *Academic Emergency Medicine,* 5, 788-795.

Lima A, Fleck M, Pechansky F and de Boni R. (2005) Association between psychiatric symptoms and severity of alcohol dependence. *Journal of Nervous and Mental Disease,* 193, 126-130.

Lindholm H. (1983) Sectorized psychiatry. A methodological study of the effects of re-organization on patients treated at a mental hospital. *Acta Psychiatrica Scandinavica, Supplementum,* 304, 1-127.

Linzer M, Spitzer R, Kroenke K, Williams J, Hahn S, Brody D and deGruy F. (1996) Gender quality of life and mental disorders in primary care: Results from the PRIME--MD study. *American Journal of Medicine,* 101, 526-533.

Little J. (1983) Chronic pancreatitis: the results of protocol management. *Australian and New Zealand Journal of Surgery,* 53, 403-409.

Long, C. Williams, M. and Hollin, C. (1998) Treating alcohol problems: a study of programme effectiveness and cost effectiveness according to length and delivery of treatment. *Addiction* 93, 561-571.

Longabaugh R, Mattson R, Connors G, and Cooney N. (1994) Quality of Life as an outcome variable in Alcoholism Treatment Research. *Journal of Studies on Alcohol, (Supplement),* 55, 119-129.

Longabaugh R, Wirtz P, Zweben A and Stout R. (1998) Network support for drinking, alcoholics anonymous and long-term matching effects. *Addiction* 93, 1313-1133.

Lubin B and Van Whitlock R. (2004) Psychometric properties of the Brief Life Satisfaction Scales. *Journal of Clinical Psychology,* 60, 11-27.

Lundberg J, and Passik S. (1997) Alcohol and cancer: a review for psycho-oncologists. *Psycho-oncology,* 6, 253-266.

Makela K. (1994) Rates of attrition among membership of Alcoholics Anonymous in Finland. *Journal of Studies on Alcohol,* 55, 91-95.

Malseed J, Sharma S, Mellor I and Faruqui S. (1990) *Alcohol in Asian and Afro-Caribbean communities.* Lancaster University.

Mann K, Morlock P, and Mezger A. (1997) Quality of Life and drinking status in alcoholics 6 years after treatment. *Quality of Life Research,* 6, 688 (published abstract).

Martin C, Clifford P, Maisto S, Earleywine M, Kirisci L and Longabaugh R. (1996) Polydrug use in an inpatient treatment sample of problem drinkers. *Alcoholism Clinical and Experimental Research,* 20, 413-417.

Martinez-Raga J, Marshall J, Keaney F, Ball D and Strang J. (2002). Unplanned versus planned discharges from inpatient alcohol detoxification: retrospective analysis of 470 first-episode admissions. *Alcohol and Alcoholism* 37, 277-278.

Mathurin P, Canva V, Dharancy S and Paris J. (2002) Treatment of chronic Hepatitis C and alcohol consumption. *Gastroenterologie Clinique et Biologique 26 Spec No,* B248-251

Maisto S, Sobell L and Sobell M. (1979) Comparisons of alcoholics self-reports of drinking behaviour with reports of collateral informants. *Journal of Consulting and Clinical Psychology,* 46, 106-112.

Massion A, Warshaw M and Keller M. (1993) Quality of life and psychiatric morbidity in panic disorder and generalised anxiety disorder. *American Journal of Psychiatry,* 150, 600-607.

McCrady B, Epstein E and Hirsch L. (1996) Issues in the implementation of a randomised clinical trial that includes Alcoholics Anonymous: studying AA-related behaviours during treatment. *Journal of Studies on Alcohol,* 57 604-612.

McDonnell R and Maynard A. (1985) Estimation of life years lost from alcohol-related premature death. *Alcohol and Alcoholism,* 20, 435-443.

McDowell I and Newell C. (1987) *Measuring Health: A guide to rating scales and questionnaires.* New York, Oxford University Press.

McGee H, O'Boyle C, Hickey A, O'Malley and Joyce C. (1991) Assessing the quality of life of the individual: the SEIQoL with a healthy and gastroenterology unit population. *Psychological Medicine,* 21, 749-759.

McLellan A, Luborsky L, O'Brien C and Woody G. (1980) An improved diagnostic instrument for substance abuse patients, The Addiction Severity Index. *Journal of Nervous and Mental Disorders,* 171, 26-33..

McKenna M, Chick J Buxton M, Howlett H, Patience D and Ritson B. (1996) The SECCAT Survey : 1. The costs and consequences of alcoholism. *Alcohol and Alcoholism,* 31, 565-576.

McKenna S, Hunt S and McEwen J. (1981) Weighting the seriousness of perceived health problems using Thurstone's method of paired comparisons. *International Journal of Epidemiology,* 10, 93-97.

Medora N and Woodward J. (1991) Factors associated with loneliness among alcoholics in rehabilitation centres. *Journal of Social Psychology,* 131, 769-779

Mejias D, Ramirez P, Rios A, Munitiz V, Hernadez Q, Bueno F, Robles R, Torregrosa N, Miras M, Ortiz M, Barcia D and Parrilla P. (1999) Recurrence of alcoholism and quality of life in patients with alcoholic cirrohosis following liver transplantation. *Transplantion Proceedings,* 31, 2472-2474.

Mijuskovic B. (1988) Loneliness and adolescent alcoholism. *Adolescence,* 23, 503-511.

Miller W. (1983) Motivational interviewing with problem drinkers. *Behavioural Psychotherapy,* 11, 147-172.

Miller W and Hester R. (1986) Inpatient alcoholism treatment: Who benefits? *American Psychologist* 41, 794-805.

Miller W, Tonigan J and Longabaugh R. (1995) The drinker inventory of consequences (DrInC): An instrument for assessing adverse cosequences of alcohol abuse in Mattson M (ed) *NIAAA Project MATCH Monograph Series, vol 4,* Bethsada, US Department of Health and Human Services.

Miyake H, Harada H, Kunicka K, Ochi I and Kimura I. (1987) Clinical course and prognosis of chronic pancreatitis. *Pancreas,* 2, 378-385.

Mohr C, Averna S, Kenny D and Del Boca F. (2001) "Getting by (or getting high) with a little help from my friends: an examination of adult alcoholics' friendships. *Journal of Studies on Alcohol,* 62, 637-645.

Moncrieff J and Drummond C. (1998) The quality of alcohol treatment research: an examination of influential controlled trials and development of a quality rating system. *Addiction,* 93, 811-823.

Moore S, Grunberg L and Greenberg E. (2000) The relationships between alcohol problems and well-being, work attitudes, and performance are they monotonic? *Journal of Substance Abuse,* 11, 183-204

Moos R and Moos B. (2004) The interplay between help-seeking and alcohol-related outcomes: divergent processes for professional treatment and self-help groups. *Drug and Alcohol Dependence,* 75, 155-164.

Morales M, Llopis A and Ballester M. (1994) Epidemiologic study of tuberculous disease in Hospital La Fe in Valencia (review) (Spanish). *Enfermedades Infecciosas y Microbiologia_Clinica,* 12, 71-78.

Morgan M, Landron F, Lehert P for the New European Alcoholism Treatment Study. (2004) Improvement in quality of life after treatment for alcohol dependence with acamprosate and psychosocial support. *Alcoholism Clinical and Experimental Research,* 28, 64-77.

Moser K, Sowell R and Phillips K. (2001) Issues of women dually diagnosed with HIV infection and substance use in the Carolinas. *Issues in Mental Health Nursing,* 22, 23-49.

Mouton C and Espino D. (1999) Health screening in older women. (Review) *American Family Physician,* 59, 1835-1842.

Murphy B, Herrman H, Hawthorne G, Pinzone T and Evert H. (2000) *Australian WHOQoL instruments: User's manual and interpretation guide.* Australian WHOQoL Field Study Centre, Melbourne, Australia.

Naidoo J and Wills J. (1994) *Health Promotion: foundations for practice.* Bailliere Tindall, London.

Nakahara T, Hirano M, Uchimura H, Shirali S, Martin C, Bonner A and Preedy V. (2002) Chronic alcohol feeding and its influence on c-Fos and heat shock protein-70 gene expression in different brain regions of male and female rats. *Metabolism: Clinical and Experimental,* 51, 1562-1568.

National Institute of Health. (1990) *Quality of Life Assessment. Practice, Problems, and Promise. Proceedings of a Workshop.* Bethsada Md.

O'Brien P. (1995) Parenteral vitamin therapy in alcoholism. *Psychiatric Bulletin,* 19, 789-796.

Office of National Statistics. (2001) *National Statistics Socio-economic Classification,* (NS-SEC) London HMSO.

Office of Population Censuses and Surveys. (1991) *Classification of occupations and coding index.* London, HMSO.

Olah A, Kelemen D, Horvath O and Belagyi T. (2004) Long-term follow-up results of surgery for chronic pancreatitis. *Hepato-Gastroenterology,* 51, 1179-1182.

Oleson M. (1990) Subjectively perceived quality of life. *Image,* 22, 187-190.

Olszynski W, Shawn Davison K, Adachi J, Brown J, Cummings S, Hanley D, Harris S, Kedler D, McClung M, Miller P and Yuen C. (2004) Osteoporosis in men: epidemiology, diagnosis, prevention and treatment (Review). *Clinical Therapeutics,* 26, 15-28.

Orford J and Edwards G. (1977) *Alcoholism: A comparison of Treatment and Advice with a study on the Influence of Marriage.* Maudsley Monographs No 26, Oxford University Press, New York.

Okoro C, Brewer R, Naimi T, Moriarty D, Giles W and Mokdad A. (2004) Binge drinking and health-related quality of life: do popular perceptions match reality? *American Journal of Preventative Medicine,* 26, 230-233

O M, Orloff M, Rambotti M and Girard B. (1992) Is portal-systemic shunt worthwhile in Child's class C cirrhosis? Long-term results of emergency shunt in 94 patients with bleeding varices. *Annals of Surgery,* 216, 256-268.

Orozco H, Mercado M, Takahashi T, Rojas G, Hernadez J and Tielve M. (1994) Survival and quality of life after portal blood flow preserving procedures in patients with portal hypertension and liver cirrhosis. *American Journal of Surgery,* 168, 10-14.

Oslin D, O'Brien and Katz I. (1999) The disabling nature of comorbid depression among older DUI recipients. *American Journal of Addictions,* 8, 128-135.

Oslin D, Thompson R, Kallan M, TenHave T, Blow F, Bastani R, Gould R, Maxwell A, Rosansky J, Van Stone W and Jarvik L. (2004) Treatment effects from UPBEAT: a randomised trial of care management for behavioural health problems in hospitalised elderly patients. *Journal of Geriatric Psychiatry and Neurology,* 17, 99-106.

Parker H, Newcombe R and Bakx K. (1987) The new heroin users: prevalence and characteristics in Wirral, Merseyside. *British Journal of Addiction,* 82, 147-157.

Pastore G, Krengli M, Gambaro G, Turri L and Pisani P. (1990) Post-radiotherapy complications in malignant tumors of the nasopharynx. Analysis of 141 cases (Italian). *Radiologia Medica,* 80, 510-513.

Patience D, Buxton D, Chick J, Howlett H, McKenna M, and Ritson B. (1997) THE SECCAT SURVEY: II. The alcohol related problems questionnaire as a proxy for resource costs and quality of life in alcoholism treatment. *Alcohol and Alcoholism,* 32, 79-84.

Paton A. (1996) Thoughts on "Alcohol problems into the next century". *Alcohol and Alcoholism,* 31, 231-234.

Patrick D and Deyo R. (1989) Generic and disease-specific measures in assessing health status and quality of life. *Medical Care,* 27, (Supplement) S217-232.

Pearlman, R and Uhlmann, R. (1988) Patient and physician perceptions of patient quality of life across chronic diseases. *Journal of Gerontology,* 43, 25-30.

Pearlman S, Zweben A, and Li S. (1989) The comparability of solicited versus clinic subjects in alcohol treatment research. *British Journal of Addiction,* 84, 522-532.

Peters TJ. (2004) Commentary on the Alcohol, Harm Reduction Strategy for England. *Drugs: Education Prevention and Policy,* 11, 359-360.

Peters TJ, Millward L and Foster JH. (2003) Quality of life in alcohol misuse: comparison of men and women. *Archives of Womens Mental Health,* 6, 239-243.

Polak K. (2001) The evaluation of the quality of life among professional soldiers with diagnosed alcohol addiction syndrome. (Polish) *Psychiatria Polska,* 35, 1057-1070.

Poldrugo F. (2003) Homogenizing alcoholism treatment across Europe. *Journal of Neural Transmission, Supplementum.* 66, 97-111.

Popovic V, Popovic I, Lilic V, Tosic S, Zlatanovic L, and Vukic D. (1997) Some aspects of Quality of Life of alcoholics. *Quality of Life Research*, 6, 700 (published abstract).

Potamianos G, Gorman D, Duffy S and Peters T. (1984). The use of the severity of alcohol dependence questionnaire (SADQ) on a sample of problem drinkers presenting at a district general hospital. *Alcohol,* 1, 441-445.

Powell J and Crome I. (1999) Quality of Life (QoL) treatment outcome instruments in alcohol misusers demonstrating the effects of treatment? *Addiction Biology,* 4, 240-241 (published abstract).

Power C and Estaugh V. (1990) Employment and drinking in early adulthood: a longitudinal perspective. *British Journal of Addiction,* 85, 487-494.

Priebe S, Kaiser W, Huxley P, Roder-Wanner U and Rudolf H. (1998) Do different subjective evaluation criteria reflect distinct constructs? *Journal of Nervous and Mental Disease,* 186, 385-392.

Prochaska J and DiClemente C. (1986) Towards a comprehensive model of change. In *Treating Addictive Behaviours; Processes of Change* (Miller W and Heather N Eds). New York, Plenum.

PROJECT MATCH RESEARCH GROUP. (1997) Matching alcoholism treatments to client heterogeneity: Project MATCH posttreatment drinking outcomes. *Journal of Studies on Alcohol,* 58, 7-29.

PROJECT MATCH RESEARCH GROUP. (1993) Project MATCH: Rationale and methods for a multi site clinical research trial matching patients to alcoholism treatment.*Alcoholism Clinical and Experimental Research,* 17, 1130-1145.

Ramaya A and Jauhar P. (1997) Increasing incidence of Korsakoff's psychosis in the East End of Glasgow. *Alcohol and Alcoholism,* 32, 281-285.

Rather B and Sherman M. (1989) Relationship between alcohol expectancies and length of abstinence among alcoholics anonymous members. *Addictive Behaviours,* 14, 531-536.

Reeck U, Egerer G, Otto G, Hoffmann W, Arnold J, Theilman L, Conradt C, Herfarth C and Seitz H. (1997) Rehabilitation of patients with alcoholic liver cirrhosis after orthotopic liver transplantation: a 7-year follow-up. (German) *Rehabilitation,* 36, 116-120.

Regier D, Farmer M, Rae D, Locke B, Keith S, Judd L and Goodwin F. (1990) Comorbidity of mental disorders with alcohol and other drug abuse: results from the Epidemiologic Catchment Study. *Journal of the American Medical Association,* 264, 2511-2518.

Rehm J, Room R and Anderson P. (1996) WHO working group on population levels of alcohol consumption: Oslo 14-16 December 1994 (published erratum appears in Addiction 1996 Jun 91 (6) 896). *Addiction,* 91, 275-283.

Reilly M, Preedy V and Peters T. (1995) Investigations into the toxic effects of alcohol on the skeletal muscle. *Adverse Drug Reactions and Toxicological Reviews,* 14, 117-150.

Reuler J, Girard D and Cooney T. (1985) Current concepts, Wernicke's encephalopathy. *New England Journal of Medicine,* 312, 1035-1039.

Richter D, Venzke A, Settelmayer J, Reker T. (2002) High rates of inpatient readmissions of alcohol addicted patients-heavy users or chronically ill patients? *Psychiatrische Praxis,* 29, 364-368.

Rios G and Adams D. (2001) Does intraoperative electrohydraulic lithotripsy improve outcome in the surgical management of chronic pancreatitis? *American Surgeon,* 67, 533-537.

Rogers J, Stewart P, Stapleton J, Hribar D, Adams P and Gale A. (2000) An interdisciplinary approach to the management of complex medical and dental conditions. *Americsan Dental Journal, 45,* 270-276.

Rollnick S, Heather N and Bell A. (1992) Negotiating behaviour change in medical settings: The development of brief motivational interviewing. *Journal of Mental Health,* 1, 25-37.

Romeis J, Waterman B, Scherrer J, Goldberg J, Eisen S, Heath A, Bucholz K, Slutske W, Lyons M, Tsuang M and True W. (1999) The impact of sociodemographics,comorbidity and symptom recency on health-related Quality of Life in alcoholism. *Journal of Studies on Alcohol* 60, 653-662.

Room R. (2004) Disabling the public interest: alcohol strategies and policies for England. *Addiction,* 99, 1083-1089.

Rossow I and Amundsen A. (1996) The disadvantage of being advantaged? On a social gradient in excess mortality among alcohol abusers. *Addiction,* 91, 1821-1829.

Royal College of Psychiatrists. (1986) *Alcohol, Our Favourite Drug, a new report of a special committee.* London, Tavistock Publications.

Rubenstein C and Shaver P. (1982) The experience of loneliness. In *Loneliness: A Sourcebook of Current Theory, Research and Therapy.* Peplau L (Ed) Wiley Publications, New York.

Rudolf H and Priebe S. (2002) Subjective quality of life and depressive symptoms in women with alcoholism during detoxification treatment. *Drug and Alcohol Dependence,* 66, 71-76.

Rudolf H and Priebe S. (1999) Similarities and differences in subjective quality of life of alcoholic women (German). *Psychiatrische Praxis,* 26, 116-121.

Russell D and Hardman G. (1980) Juvenile delinquency and the quality of life: the 17-year depression. *Journal of Forensic Sciences,* 25, 908-911.

Ryan J, Verado L, Kidd J, Horbatuk E, Bonnanno R, Fahrenwald R, Kirsch S and Stretch G. (1997) Health outcomes of women exposed to household alcohol abuse: a Family Practice Training Site Research Network (FPTSRN) study. *Journal of Family Practice,* 45, 410-417.

Ryle P and Thompson A. (1984) Nutrition and vitamins in alcoholism. *Contemporary Issues in Clinical Biochemistry,* 1, 188-224.

The Prime Ministers Strategy Unit. (2004) Alcohol Harm Reduction Strategy for England. London, HMSO.

Thompson A and Cook C. (1997) Parenteral thiamine and Wernicke's encephalopathy: The balance of risks and perception of concern. *Alcohol and Alcoholism,* 32 207-209.

Samet J, Larson M, Horton N, Doyle K, Winter M and Saitz R. (2003) Linking alcohol and drug dependent adults to primary medical care: a randomised controlled trial of a multi disciplinary health intervention in a detoxification unit. *Addiction,* 98, 509-516.

Sareen J, Stein M, Campbell D, Hassard T and Menec V. (2005) The relation between perceived need for mental health treatment, DSM diagnosis and quality of life: a Canadian population-based survey. *Canadian Journal of Psychiatry,* 50, 87-94.

Saunders P. (1998) The good practice of the police: an alternative approach in dealing with offenders who abuse/misuse alcohol. *Alcohol and Alcoholism,* 33 73-77.

Saunders J, Aasland O, Babor T, de la Fuente J and Grant M. (1993) Development of the Alcohol Use Disorders Identification Test (AUDIT): WHO Collaborative Project on

Early Detection of Persons with Harmful Alcohol Consumption-II. *Addiction,* 88, 791-804.

Scherrer J, Xian H, Shah K Volberg R, Slutske W and Eisen S. (2005) Effect of genes, environment and life time co-occurring disorders on health-related quality of life in problem and pathological gamblers. *Archives of General Psychiatry,* 62, 677-683

Schneider K, Kviz F, Isola M and Filstead W. (1995) Evaluating multiple outcomes and gender differences in alcoholism treatment. *Addictive Behaviours,* 20, 1-21.

Schonfeld L. (1993) Behavioural treatment of addictions (letter;comment). *Addictive Behaviours,* 18, 105-106.

Schuckit M. (1999) New findings in the genetics of alcoholism. *Journal of the American Medical Association,* 281, 1875-1876.

Schuckit M and Tipp J. (1994) Are daughters of alcoholics more likely to marry alcoholics? *American Journal of Drug and Alcohol Abuse,* 20, 237-245.

Shakil A, Pinna A, Demetris J, Lee R, Fung J and Rakela J. (1997) Survival and quality of life after liver transplantation for acute alcoholic hepatitis. *Liver Transplantation and Surgery,* 3, 240-244.

Shumaker S and Berzon R (eds). (1995) *The International Assessment of HRQoL, Theory, Transalation, Measurement and Analysis.* Oxford, Rapid Communications.

Single E, Brewster J, MacNeil P, Hatcher J and Trainor C. (1995) The 1993 General Social Survey II: alcohol problems in clinic. *Canadian Journal of Public Health. Revue Canadienne de Sante Publique.* 86, 402-407.

Slevin, M. Plant, H. Lynch, D. Drinkwater, J. Gregory, W. (1988) Who should measure quality of life the doctor or the patient? *British Journal of Cancer,* 57, 109-112.

Smith M Huang M and Manber R. (2005) Cognitive behavioural therapy for chronic insomnia occurring within the context of medical and psychiatric disorders. *Clinical Psychology Review,* 25, 550-592.

Snow V, Weiss K, LeFevre M, McNamara R, Bass E, Green L, Micchi K, Owens K, Susman J, Allen D, Mottur-Pilson C- AAFP Panel on Atrial Fibrilation. ACP Panel on Atrial Fibrillation. (2004) Management of newly detected atrial fibrillation: a clinical practice guideline from the American Academy of Family Physicians and American College of Physicians. *Annals of Internal Medicine.* 139, 1009-1017.

Sobell L and Sobell M. (1986) Can we do without alcohol abusers self-reports? *Behaviour Therapy,* 7, 141-146.

Sobell L, Sobell M, Leo G, and Cancilla A. (1988) Reliability of the Timeline method: assessing normal drinkers' reports of recent drinking and comparative evaluation across several populations. *British Journal of Addiction,* 83, 393-402.

Sohn T, Campbell K, Pitt H, Sauter P, Coleman J, Lillemo K, Yeo, C and Cameron J. (2000) Qualiity of life and long-term survival after surgery for chronic pancreatitis. *Journal of Gastrointestinal Surgery, 4, 355-364.*

Soran A, Chelluri L, Lee K and Tisherman S. (2000) Outcome and quality of life of patients with acute pancreatitis requiring intensive care. *Journal of Surgical Research,* 91, 89-94.

Spalding A and Metzs G. (1997) Spirituality and Quality of Life in Alcoholics Anonymous. *Alcoholism Treatment Quarterly,* 15, 1-14.

Spitzer R, Kroenke K, Linzer M, Hahn S, Williams J, deGruy F, Brody D and Davies M. (1995) Health-related quality of life in primary care patients with mental disorders.

Results from the PRIME-MD study. *Journal of the American Medical Association,* 274, 1511-1517.

Srisurapanont M and Jarusuraisin N. (2005) Opioid antagonists for alcohol dependence. [update of Cocrane Database Systematrc Review 2002] *Cochrane database of Systematic Reviews* (1) CD001867.

Srisurapanont M and Jarusuraisin N. (2002) Opioid antagonists for alcohol dependence. [update of Cocrane Database Systematrc Review 2000] *Cochrane database of Systematic Reviews* (2) CD001867.

Srisurapanont M and Jarusuraisin N. (2000) Opioid antagonists for alcohol dependence. [update in Cocrane Database Systematrc Review 2002 CD001867; PMID: 12076425] *Cochrane database of Systematic Reviews* (2) CD001867.

Stein M, Mulvey K, Plough A and Samet J. (1998) The functioning and well being of persons who seek treatment for drug and alcohol use. *Journal of Substance Abuse*, 10, 75-84.

Stockwell T, Murphy D, and Hodgson R. (1983) The Severity of Alcohol Dependence Questionnaire: Its use reliability and validity. *British Journal of Addiction,* 78, 145-155.

Stockwell T, Hodgson R, Edwards G, Taylor C,and Rankin H. (1979) The development of a questionnaire to measure the severity of alcohol dependence. *British Journal of Addiction,* 74, 79-87.

Stein M, Mulvey K, Plough A and Samet J. (1998) The functioning and well being of persons who seek treatment for drug and alcohol use. *Journal of Substance Abuse,* 10, 75-84.

Sternbach R. (1978) Clinical aspects of pain. In *The psychology of pain* Sternbach R (Ed), Raven Press, New York.

Stewart A, Hays R, and Ware J. (1988) The MOS Short-Form General Health Survey: reliability and validity in a patient population. *Medical Care,* 26, 724-732.

Stewart S, Finn P and Pihl R. (1995) A dose response study of the effects of alcohol on the perceptions of pain and discomfort due to electric shock in men at high familial genetic risk for alcoholism. *Psychopharmacology,* 119, 261-267.

Streissguth A, Bookstein F, Barr H, Sampson P, O'Malley K and Young J. (2004) Risk factors for adverse life outcomes in fetal alcohol syndrome and fetal alcohol effects. *Journal of Developmental and Behavioural Pediatrics,* 25, 228-238.

Stuyt E. (1997) Recovery rates after treatment for alcohol/drug dependence. Tobacco users vs. non-tobacco users. *American Journal on Addictions,* 6, 159-167.

Sullivan G, Wells K, Morgenstern H and Leake B. (1995) Identifying modifiable risk factors for rehospitalization: a case-control study of seriously mentally ill persons in Mississippi. *American Journal of Psychiatry,* 152, 1749-1756.

Sullivan J, Sykora K, Schneiderman J, Naranjo C and Sellers E. (1989) Assessment of Alcohol Withdrawal: The revised Clinical Institute Withdrawal Assessment for alcohol Scale (CIWA Ar) *British Journal of Addiction,* 84, 1353-1357.

Sundquist J, Bajekal M, Jarman B, Johansson S. (1996) Underprivileged area score, ethnicity, social factors and general mortality in district health authorities in England and Wales. *Scandinavian Journal of Primary Health Care,* 14, 79-85.

The Prime Ministers Strategy Unit. (2004) *Alcohol Harm Reduction Strategy for England.* London, HMSO.

Talley J. (1990) But what if the patient gets hooked? Fallacies about long-term use of benzodiazepines (see comments) (review). *Postgraduate Medicine,* 87, 187-203.

Tarter R, Hegedus A and Van Theil D. (1984) Neuropsychiatric sequelae of portal-systemic encephalopathy: a review. *International Journal of Neuroscience*, 24, 203-216.

Testa M and Simonson D. (1996) Assessment of Quality of Life outcomes. *New England Journal of Medicine,* 334, 835-840.

Timko C, Finney J, Moos R, Moos B and Steinbaum D. (1993) The process of treatment selection among previously untreated help-seeking drinkers. *Journal of Substance Abuse,* 5, 203-220.

Tollefson G. (1990) Recognition and treatment of major depression (review). *American Family Physician*, 42 (Supplement), S59-S69.

Torchalla I Albrecht F, Buchkremer G and Langle G. (2004) Homeless women with psychiatric disorders- a field study. (German) *Psychiatrische Praxis,* 31, 228-235.

Townsend P and Davidson N. (1982) *Inequalities in Health: The Black Report,* London , Penguin.

Townsend P, Phillmore P and Beattie A. (1986) *Inequalities in health in the northern region,* Newcastle Upon Tyne, Northern Regional Health Authority and University of Bristol.

Trent L. (1998) Evaluation of a four versus six week length of stay in the navy's alcohol treatment programme. *Journal of Studies on Alcohol* 59, 270-279.

True R, Romeis B, Waterman J, Scherrer J, Goldberg J, Eisen S, Heath A, Bucholz K, Slutske W, Lyons M and Tsuang M. (1997) Alcoholism and health related quality of life. *Alcoholism Clinical and Experimental Research,* 21 Supplement, 116A (published abstract).

Tucker J and Gladsjo J. (1993) Help-seeking and recovery by problem drinkers: characteristics of drinkers who attended Alcoholics Anonymous or formal treatment or who recovered without assistance. *Addictive Behaviours,* 18, 529-542.

Tucker J, Gavornik M, Vuchinich R, Rudd E and Harris C. (1989) Predicting the drinking behaviour of older adults from questionnaire measures of alcohol consumption. *Addictive Behaviours,* 14, 655-658.

Tucker J, Vuchinich R and Rippens P. (2004) A factor analytic study of influences on patterns of help-seeking among treated and untreated alcohol dependent persons. *Journal of Substance Abuse Treatment* 237-242.

UKATT RESEARCH TEAM. (2001). United Kingdom Alcohol Treatment Trial: hypotheses, design and methods. *Alcohol and Alcoholism,* 36, 11-21.

UKATT Research Team. (2005a) Effectiveness of treatment for alcohol problems: findings of the randomised UK alcohol treatment trial (UKATT) *British Medical Journal,* 331, 527-528.

UKATT Research Team. (2005b) Cost effectiveness of treatment for alcohol problems: findings of the randomised UK alcohol treatment trial (UKATT) *British Medical Journal,* 331, 544.

Vaillant G. (2003) A 60-year follow-up of alcoholic men. (see comment) *Addiction,* 98, 1043-1051.

Valliant G and Milofsky E. (1982) Natural history of male alcoholism IV. Paths to recovery. *Archives of General Psychiatry,* 39, 127-133.

van Oers J, Bongers I, van de Goor L and Garretsen H. (1999) Alcohol consumption, alcohol-related problems, problem drinking and socioeconomic status. *Alcohol and Alcoholism,* 34, 78-88.

Van Theil D, Kumar S, Gavaler J and Tarter R. (1990) Effect of liver transplantation on the hypothalamic-pituitary-gonadal axis of schronic alcoholic men with advanced liver disease. *Alcoholism Clinical and Experimental Research*, 14, 478-481.

Ventegodt S, Clausen B, Langhorn M, Kromann M, Andersen N and Merrick J. (2004a) Quality of life as medicine III. A qualitative analysis of a five day intervention with existential holistic group therapy or a quality of life course as a modern rite of passage. *The scientificworldjournal,* 4, 124-133

Ventegodt S, Morad M, Kandel I and Merrick J. (2004b) Clinical holistic medicine: a psychological theory of dependency to improve quality of life. *The scientificworldjournal,* 4, 638-648

Ventegodt S, Merrick J and Andersen N. (2003) Quality of life as medicine. II. A pilot of a study of a five-day "quality of life and health" cure for patients with alcoholism. *The scientificworldjournal,* 3, 842-852.

Vial M, Alvear J and Artaza C. (1991) Social environment in marasmic malnutrition (Spanish) *Revista Chilena de Pediatria,* 62, 268-272.

Vitiello M. (1997) Sleep, Alcohol and Alcohol Abuse. *Addiction Biology,* 2, 151-159.

Volk R, Cantor S, Steinbauer J, and Cass A. (1997) Alcohol use disorders, consumption patterns, and health-related quality of life of primary care patients. *Alcoholism Clinical and Experimental Research,* 21, 899-905.

Vorma H, Naukkarinen H and Sarna S. (2005) Predictors of benzodiazepine discontinuation in subjects manifesting complicated dependence. *Substance Use and Misuse,* 40, 499-510.

Waddington A, Zeltner L, Robin M, Mauriac F, Ampelas J, Bronchard M and Mallat V. (2004) Posttraumatic stress state: a therapeutic lever. (French) *Encephale,* 30, 323-330.

Wahlstrom J and Dobs A. (2000) Acute and long-term effects of AIDS and injection drug use on gonadal function. *Journal of Acquired Immune Deficiency Syndromes: JAIDS. Suppl1, S27-36.*

Ware J, Snow K, Kosinski M and Gandek B. (1993) *SF-36 health-survey: a manual and interpretation guide.* The Health Institute New England, Medical Centre, Boston.

Ware J and Sherbourne C. (1992) The MOS 36-item short-form health survey (SF-36). I Conceptual framework and item selection. *Medical Care,* 30, 473-483.

Warshaw M, Fierman E, Pratt L, Hunt M, Yonkers K, Massion A and Keller M. (1993) Quality of life and dissociation in anxiety disorder patients with histories of trauma or PTSD. *American Journal of Psychiatry*, 150, 1512-1516.

Watson C, Hancock M, Malovrh P, Gearhart L, and Raden M. (1997) A comparative outcome study of frequent, moderate, occasional, and nonattenders of Alcoholics Anonymous. *Journal of Clinical Psychology,* 53, 209-214.

Watson C, Hancock M, Malovrh P, Gearhart L, and Raden M. (1996) A 48-week natural history follow-up of alcoholics who do and do not engage in limited drinking after treatment. *Journal of Nervous and Mental Disease,* 184, 623-627.

Weise J, Shilpak M and Browner W. (2000) The alcohol hangover. *Annals of Internal Medicine,* 132, 897-902

Weissman M. (1991) Panic Disoder: impact on quality of life. *Journal of Clinical Psychiatry,* (Supplement), 52, 6-8.

Welsh J, Buchsbaum D, and Kaplan C. (1993) Quality of Life of alcoholics and non alcoholics: does excessive drinking make a difference in an urban setting. *Quality of Life Research,* 2, 335-340.

Willenbring M and Olson D. (1999) A randomized trial of integrated outpatient treatment for medically ill alcoholic men. *Archives of Internal Medicine,* 159, 1946-1952.

Williams A. (1985) Economics of coronary artery bypass grafting. *British Medical Journal,* 291, 326-329.

Williams B and Drummond C. (1994) Alcohol Problems Questionnaire: Reliability and validity. *Drug and Alcohol Dependence,* 35, 239-243.

Wilsnack R, Wilsnack S and Klassen A. (1984) Women's drinking and drinking problems: Patterns from a 1981 national survey. *American Journal of Public Health,* 74, 1231-1238.

Wilson A, Blanchard R, Davidson W, McRae L and Maini K. (1984) Disulfiram implantation: a dose response trial. *Journal of Clinical Psychiatry,* 45, 242-247.

Wittchen H. (1994) Reliability and validity studies of the WHO-Composite International Diagnostic Interview (CIDI): a critical review. *Journal of Psychiatric Research* 28, 57-84.

Wolber C, Carne W and Alexander R. (1990) The validity of self-reported abstinence and quality of sobriety following chemical dependency treatment. *International Journal of the Addictions,* 25, 495-513.

World Health Organisation. (1948) *Constitution of the World Health Organisation.* Geneva, World Health Organisation Basic Documents.

Wurst F, Seidl S, Alt A and Metzger J. (2001) Direct ethanol metabolite ethyl glucuronide. Its value as alcohol intake and recurrence marker, methods of detection and prospects. *Psychiatrische Praxis,* 27, 367-371.

Wustrow T and Mahnke C. (1996) Causes of immunosuppression in squamous cell carcinoma of the head and neck (review). *Anticancer Research,* 16 (4C), 2433-2468.

Yersin A, Rochat S, Wietlisbach V and Burnand B. (1999) Health-related quality of life as a sensitive outcome measure in the follow-up of alcohol dependent patients. *Quality of Life Research* 8, 564. (published abstract).

Zatzick D, Jurkovich G, Gentilello L, Wisner D and Rivara F. Posttraumatic stress, problem drinking, and functional outcomes after injury. *Archives of Surgery,* 137, 200-205

Zemore S and Kaskutas L. (2004) Helping, spirituality and Alcoholics Anonymous in recovery. *Journal of Studies on Alcohol,* 65, 383-391.

Zigmond A and Snaith R. (1983) "The Hospital Anxiety and Depression Scale" *Acta Psychiatrica Scandinavica,* 67, 361-370.

Zweben A and Cisler R. (2003) Clinical and methodological utility of a composite outcome measure for alcohol treatment research. *Alcoholism Clinical and Experimental Research,* 27, 1680-1685

INDEX

B

C

D

E

F

G

H

I

J

K

L

M

N

O

P

Q

R

S

T

U

V

W

Y